SUMMER

The Vegetable Plate of Summer

Macaroni and Cheese

Fried Eggplant

scalloped or fresh tomatoes

Pole Beans Simmered in Pork Stock

or

Fresh Crowder Peas

Roasted Beets in Ginger Syrup

Okra Pancakes

Chowchow

Blackberry Cobbler

Also by Edna Lewis

The Edna Lewis Cookbook
The Taste of Country Cooking
In Pursuit of Flavor

The Gift of
Southern Cooking

The Gift of Southern Cooking

RECIPES AND REVELATIONS FROM TWO GREAT SOUTHERN COOKS

Edna Lewis
and Scott Peacock
with David Nussbaum

Photographs by Christopher Hirsheimer

ALFRED A. KNOPF   NEW YORK   2006

THIS IS A BORZOI BOOK
PUBLISHED BY ALFRED A. KNOPF

www.aaknopf.com

Library of Congress Cataloging-in-Publication Data
Lewis, Edna.
The gift of Southern cooking : recipes and revelations from two great Southern cooks / by Edna Lewis and Scott Peacock. —1st ed.
p. cm.
Includes index.
ISBN 0-375-40035-4
1. Cookery, American—Southern style. I. Peacock, Scott. II. Title.
TX715.2.S68 L45 2003
641.5973—dc21 2002073153

Manufactured in Singapore
Published April 23, 2003
Reprinted Two Times
Fourth Printing, August 2006

PHOTOGRAPHIC CREDITS
The photographs reproduced in this book were provided with the permission and courtesy of the following:
Marion Cunningham: 127
John T. Hill: 55, 63, 81, 189, 206, 246, 259, 262
Judith Jones: 111
Doug Snelgrove: 131
Personal collections of the authors: 17, 57, 94
All other photographs are by Christopher Hirsheimer.

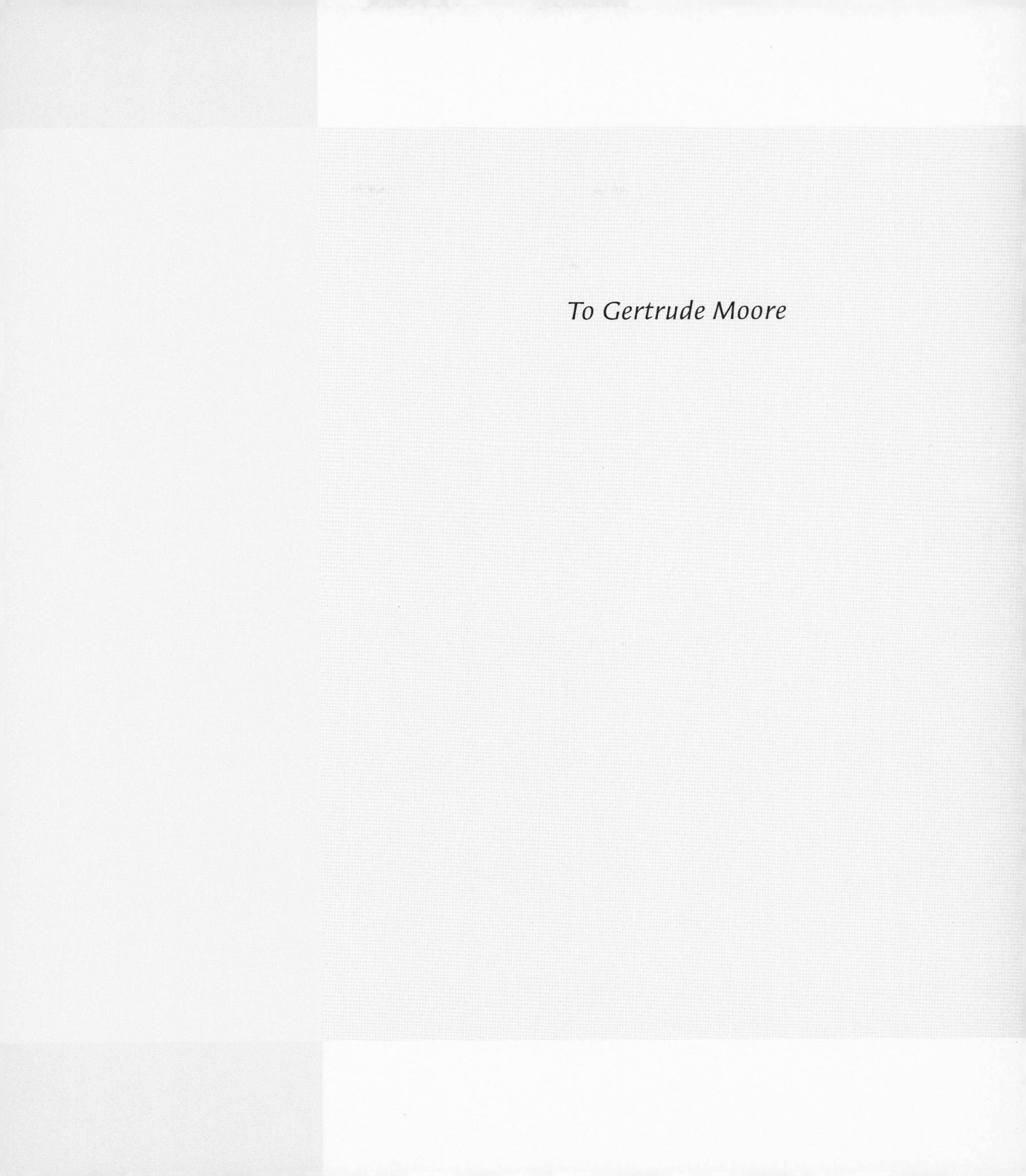

To Gertrude Moore

"As God is my witness, I'll never be hungry again."

—Scarlett O'Hara in *Gone with the Wind*

Contents

Introduction

During the years that Edna Lewis and I have been friends and colleagues, we have cooked together and done a lot of research on the foods of the South. We weren't surprised to discover how many different cooking styles and traditions, and how much diversity of ingredients, flavors, and cooking techniques there are throughout the southeastern states. In other words, Southern cooking is not a single cuisine.

In the South we are blessed with a long growing season and have always depended on fresh produce, both cultivated and wild. There's an old saying that what grows together goes together, and the dishes we put on our tables have that natural seasonal affinity. We also tend to enjoy life at a leisurely pace. Good cooks in the South see the preparation of food as satisfying, a natural part of the rhythm of daily life. It is all of these qualities that we have tried to translate into the pages of this book so that you can really taste what good Southern cooking can be.

It has certainly been a process of discovery for me. Even being a Southerner myself, I didn't have a sense of the breadth and depth of the food. I first met Miss Lewis (as I always call her) in 1988, when she was already well known as an authority on the flavorful country cooking of Virginia. The truth is that at the time I wasn't even sure that Virginia was really part of the South. As a child in the southern reaches of Alabama—as Deep as the South gets—all I knew of Virginia is that it lay far to the north and that Virginians (based on my mother's comments about a woman who lived in our little town) talked in a peculiar way. So I was surprised and delighted to find that Miss Lewis, whom I admired greatly as a writer and a chef, was as much a Southerner as I was—and she didn't talk funny at all.

What we further discovered as we came to know each other was that the foods that nurtured us reflected both the commonality and the diversity that makes Southern cooking so fascinating. For starters, it was quickly apparent that we came from Southern worlds as different as can be. It's nearly seven hundred miles from the now disappeared settlement of Freetown in north-central Virginia, where Miss Lewis was born and raised, to my hometown of Hartford, barely an hour from the Gulf of Mexico. As well, we were separated by generations and cultures. Miss Lewis, a grandchild of slaves, came of age in the 1920s in a nearly self-sufficient community that grew its own crops, raised and slaughtered its own animals, and preserved its own foods. My ancestors were also small subsistence farmers, but by the 1960s and '70s, when I grew up, our family had moved into town and ran a business that served the predominantly white farms around Hartford. We Peacocks enjoyed the convenient foods of the supermarket as well as the bounty of the land.

Miss Lewis and I found that our common food memories (like those of most Southerners) reflected this agricultural heritage, in particular the crops that built the South—corn, root vegetables, legumes, leafy greens, fruits and berries, wheat, and rice—along with the cows and hogs that we all raised. We shared a deep appreciation for the foods of our childhood, such as cornbread, biscuits, greens flavored with smoked pork, fried chicken, flaky pies, hand-churned ice cream. And despite our generational differences, we both came from homes where the seasonal harvest was a ritual in which the children participated, where vegetables straight from the garden were often the main feature of the supper table, where skilled home cooking was admired and expected daily. And we realized that we both brought the values of home cooking to our work as chefs.

At the same time, we were aware of the differences in our family foods, shaped by geography, climate, and the farming economy. In Alabama's peanut country, oil was cheap and plentiful, so we used it freely as cooking fat. For Miss Lewis, lard and butter from their own livestock were generally used. They used more cream than we did, too. During our hot summers, greens grew bitter and lettuce bolted, so the only lettuce I ate was iceberg from the store, while cooked turnip and mustard greens served us during the cool months. Up in Freetown, they grew tender leaf lettuces for salad, and rape, kale, and turnip and beet greens went into the cooking pot, to which they added wild cresses, lamb's quarters, and purslane. Asparagus also grew wild and Miss Lewis's mother cooked the slender spears in a skillet; not so my mom—at best she would occasionally open a can of asparagus onto a platter and serve it with mayonnaise (the only spears I ever saw, but I loved them).

Not that the Deep South isn't rich in other ways: we had fresh oysters and succulent fish from the Gulf in variety and abundance that Miss Lewis never imagined. And summertime in Hartford was filled with the delicious "field peas"—lady peas, pink-eyed peas, Crowder peas, and a score of others—that were cooked every day and frozen for the winter. Except for black-eyed peas, grown primarily as a cover crop, Miss Lewis never heard of these treasures.

There were cultural influences, too. At first, I was surprised that in humble

Freetown, Miss Lewis enjoyed blancmange, brandied peaches, cats' tongues, and beef à la mode—dishes that were as familiar to her as grits, but utterly foreign to me. Later, as we began to trace the roots of Southern cooking in old recipe books, plantation journals, and slave narratives, the direct influence of English and French cookery in Virginia was clear. But in Alabama, the cooking was flavored with "black Irish," Native American, Caribbean, and African influences.

Obviously this book is not a comprehensive compendium of Southern cooking. In our research we unearthed quite a few forgotten dishes that proved very appetizing, such as Caveach, or pickled fish, and Jefferson Davis Custard, which is particularly good with gooseberries. Many recipes come from regions that weren't familiar to us until our work took us there, in particular the seafood specialties of the Carolina Low Country. But mostly we have focused on the foods we grew up with, the ones we love the most and believe are the staples of the Southern table. Some of the recipes belong to Miss Lewis and her family; others are mine or my mother's or Grandmaw's. In several instances, you will find our quite different versions of related dishes—the Peacock cornbreads, for example, and the very different Virginia and Alabama fruit cobblers.

Most of the recipes here we have, in fact, created together. Some have evolved over years of collaborative cooking, perhaps when a technique or a dish that I learned from Miss Lewis inspired me to tinker with it, to use different ingredients or to add an Alabama spin. Her distinctive approach to soup making—slowly coaxing the essence of flavor from a vegetable or a stewing hen, for example—led to a number of the original soups and braised dishes that we've included here. And then there are those familiar dishes that exist in countless versions as many generations of cooks have left their own imprint on them—fried chicken, sourmilk cornbread, yeast rolls, shortcakes, pound cake, pie dough. For all of these we came up with our own preferred version, one that we developed together and that represented our shared taste. It's often the little tricks of technique that make the difference, and we have tried to convey that necessary attention to detail in writing the recipes. Sometimes we would go off on a "cooking retreat," where we would go through bags of flour or bushels of potatoes or tomatoes in search of the best way to prepare a dish.

Finally, there are recipes in this book that mark the course of our friendship and collaboration. The turtle soup recipe in the second chapter is perhaps the most personally significant: it was the dish that Miss Lewis prepared the first time I ever met her, at a gala celebration of great Southern cooks in Atlanta in 1988. I was chef at the Georgia governor's mansion at the time, attending the dinner as a guest. I was not particularly interested in Southern food then—I was just twenty-five years old and wanted to live and cook in Italy. But I was so struck by Miss Lewis's integrity and the ethereal, almost indescribable complexity and delicacy of her turtle soup that I knew I had to go to New York, where she was the executive chef at the historic Brooklyn restaurant Gage & Tollner, and to cook with her. Right away Miss Lewis had some strong words of advice for me. "Some good cooks have to stay in the South," she said, and she admonished me to stay where I was and learn about my own culinary heritage.

So I did, and I continued to learn from Miss Lewis. I visited her in New York and she shared with me stories from Freetown—as well as damson plum preserves and sugared raspberries. When she returned to Atlanta in 1989 for another dinner event, I helped her prepare pies and cobblers. And a few months later she visited Atlanta again; this time we had our first cooking "retreat"—an entire week of talking about food and cooking together, culminating in a great dinner for some lucky friends of mine. The star dish, at my insistence, was turtle soup. And it gave me a glimpse into a Southern world that's long gone: a vision of the spring rains that washed big turtles up on the riverbanks near Freetown, to be captured, put into an open wooden barrel and purged with cornmeal and milk before Miss Lewis's mother would slaughter and cook them slowly to bring out their extraordinary flavor. The week was a defining moment in my professional life and in our friendship. That turtle soup recipe as we refined it together several times since is now in our soup chapter.

In many ways this entire book embodies the personal and professional closeness that Miss Lewis and I have enjoyed. In the nineties we began to work more directly and steadily together. Together we founded the Society for the Revival and Preservation of Southern Food, an organization devoted to promoting Southern foodways; we taught together and ran workshops. We researched and traveled, always gathering material for the book. In 1992, Miss Lewis moved to Atlanta and four years later, she came to live with me. Today we cook and eat together regularly, so you will find among these recipes many that reflect our daily life—a love for pancakes for supper, for instance, some great sandwiches, and shrimp paste stirred into a bowl of creamy grits.

A word about why this book is written in my voice: Miss Lewis and I both felt that a first-person-plural voice speaking for both of us was awkward, not allowing us to differentiate between her tastes and experiences and memories and mine. So I took on the writing, and I trust that it reflects both her passion for exploring what it means to be Southern, what the Southern experience is, and how it is reflected in food. In fact, that is why we really started writing this book. Our hope now is that it will help readers who share that curiosity. But above all, we hope it will move you to make the dishes we describe. Real Southern cooking is home cooking and to understand it—to taste it—you have to make it yourself.

We invite you to begin . . .

Scott Peacock
Decatur, Georgia, 2002

BAIL HERE

Relishes, Condiments, and Drinks

Shrimp Paste
Pimento Cheese
A Note on Roasting and Peeling Peppers
Spicy Eggplant Relish
Candied Bacon
Red Pepper Catsup
Dried Fig Relish
A Note on About Ceylon Cinnamon
Cranberries with Orange Zest and Port
Green Tomato Preserves
Cucumber Pickles
Chowchow
Hot Pepper Vinegar
Candied Kumquats
Apple Chutney
Old-Fashioned Fig Preserves
Pear Relish
Strawberry Preserves
Sugared Raspberries
Hot Chocolate
Eggnog
Homemade Lemonade
Iced Tea
Mulberry Acid
Agua de Sandia (or Watermelon Punch)
Blackberry Cordial

In this chapter, we welcome you to the Southern table with an unusual assortment of recipes. They don't really fit into any one category, but they provide both a useful introduction to the flavors Southerners particularly like and to the ways in which relishes and condiments and drinks are served—usually everything is put on the table at once.

There's not a big tradition of hors d'oeuvre in the South, but our first two recipes happen to make very good appetizers. Shrimp Paste has long been enjoyed by Charlestonians as a savory accompaniment to whiskey and apéritifs. Pimento and Cheese was a favorite sandwich spread of my childhood in "dry" Geneva County in southeastern Alabama, where a drink before dinner—or any-time—was considered a scandal. But "pimenocheese" on a cracker or with celery sticks is a terrific cocktail nibble.

Most of the rest of the dishes in this section represent a sampling of the South's great heritage of preserves and pickles. In a region where barren winter cold and withering summer heat necessitated conserving the harvest, Southern cooks have for centuries put up every kind of vegetable and fruit they could fit in a canning jar. And their copious use of sugar, vinegar, salt, and peppers established the Southern taste for sweet, sour, salty, and hot.

The preserves we offer here are our favorites, ones we use to complement meats and vegetables—often in place of sauces—all year round. On holidays and special occasions, they go on the table in small dishes, sometimes laid out prettily on a relish tray, but often we just put the Mason jars right on the table.

We've included a few of our favorite and most distinctly Southern drinks as well. Like the relishes, they are part of the "preserving" tradition, turning fruits and flavorings into long-keeping beverages—alcoholic like Blackberry Cordial, and nonalcoholic like Mulberry Acid. A drink is an expression of Southern hospitality. When Miss Lewis was growing up in Virginia, a visitor to Freetown was offered a cordial or homemade wine, first thing. In hot (and dry) Alabama, anybody who came in the door was offered iced tea or lemonade immediately. We do the same these days in our home in Georgia.

Shrimp Paste

MAKES APPROXIMATELY 2½ CUPS—
ENOUGH TO FEED 8–10 IF MAKING GRITS WITH SHRIMP PASTE

- 1 cup (2 sticks) unsalted butter
- 1 pound fresh shrimp, peeled and deveined
- ½ teaspoon salt
- ½ teaspoon freshly ground black pepper
- ¼ cup sherry
- 2 tablespoons freshly squeezed lemon juice
- ¼ teaspoon cayenne pepper

A specialty of Charleston and the Carolina Low Country, this is a rich purée of sautéed shrimp, lots of sweet butter, sherry, and spice. It is ideal spread on Beni Wafers (page 227) as a cocktail nibble, or on white bread for tea sandwiches. Spoon a dollop on grilled or roasted fish as a garnish. A truly Southern way to enjoy shrimp paste is stirred into hot grits (pages 170–171), and served with buttered toast, as a breakfast or supper dish.

Heat 6 tablespoons of the butter in a large skillet until it is hot and foaming. Add the shrimp, salt, and pepper, and cook over high heat, stirring often, for 4–7 minutes, until the shrimp are pink and cooked through.

Remove the skillet from the stove, and use a slotted spoon to transfer the cooked shrimp to the bowl of a food processor fitted with a steel blade. Return the skillet to the stove, and add the sherry, lemon juice, and cayenne pepper. Cook over high heat until the liquid in the skillet is reduced to approximately 3 tablespoons and is quite syrupy. Immediately add this to the shrimp in the food processor and process until the shrimp are thoroughly puréed. With the motor running, add the remaining butter in pieces and process until thoroughly blended. Turn the food processor off, and carefully taste the shrimp paste for seasoning, adding more salt, black pepper, sherry, lemon juice, or cayenne pepper as needed. Transfer the shrimp paste to a ceramic crock and allow to cool completely.

If not using right away, cover the shrimp paste and refrigerate for up to 1 week. Refrigerated shrimp paste should be allowed to return to room temperature before serving.

Pimento Cheese

MAKES ABOUT 2 CUPS

- 2½ cups (10 ounces) grated extra-sharp cheddar cheese
- ⅛ teaspoon cayenne pepper, or to taste
- Salt to taste if needed
- 5 or 6 grinds of black pepper
- ¾ cup homemade Mayonnaise (page 60)
- 3 tablespoons finely chopped roasted red bell pepper (see box) or pimento

For many Southerners, pimento cheese—or "pimenocheese," as we tend to say it—is a touchstone of childhood, a favorite filling for lunchbox and picnic sandwiches. But this tangy blend of sharp cheese, mayonnaise, and roasted red peppers is great grown-up food too, spread on crackers or celery sticks to accompany cocktails.

My mother made this often, using pimentos from a little jar and a relatively mild orange cheddar that we called "mouse cheese," which the grocer cut from a big wheel. Today I use fresh roasted red peppers (see box) and a mixture of cheddars: sharp orange (for color) and extra-sharp white cheddar (for flavor).

Stir together all of the ingredients in a mixing bowl until they are well mixed and creamy. Taste carefully for seasoning and adjust as needed. Cover and store, refrigerated, until ready to use.

A NOTE ON ROASTING AND PEELING PEPPERS

There is more than one way to roast peppers, but the way we find easiest is this: Wash and dry the peppers you are going to roast, then rub the exterior of each pepper with a very small amount of vegetable or olive oil—less than a teaspoon per pepper. Put the oiled peppers into a baking dish, and bake in a preheated 425°F oven for 20 minutes. The peppers will look charred in patches and be blistered all over. Remove from the oven, and transfer the peppers into a bowl that can be tightly covered. Cover and let rest until the peppers are cool enough to handle. Once they are cooled, with a paring knife peel off the outer skin from the peppers, remove the stem, cut open, and remove the seeds as well. Resist the urge to rinse under water to clean the peppers perfectly. It is preferable to have an occasional seed or bit of charred pepper than to wash away the delicious pepper flavor. Roasted and peeled peppers can be kept refrigerated for 2 or 3 days before using.

Spicy Eggplant Relish

MAKES ENOUGH TO SERVE 8

- 2 large or 3 medium-sized eggplants (about 4½ pounds)
- ⅓ cup olive oil
- 1 large onion, cut into ½-inch pieces (about 1¼ cups)
- 2 small green bell peppers, seeded and cut into ½-inch pieces (about 2 cups)
- 1 teaspoon salt
- ½ teaspoon freshly ground black pepper
- 5 cloves garlic, finely chopped
- 2 teaspoons finely chopped fresh hot chili pepper (cayenne, fingerling, or jalapeño)
- 2 tomatoes, peeled and seeded and cut into ½-inch pieces (about 1¼ cups)
- ⅔ cup raisins, plumped in ½ cup cider vinegar for ½ hour or more
- ¼ cup honey

Spicy, sharp, and sweet, this blend of eggplant, onions, peppers, tomatoes, and raisins is as versatile as it is flavorful. Use it as a condiment on a cold plate or a sandwich of your leftover grilled meat (or poultry). Serve warm as a vegetable side dish with roasted or grilled meats or poultry—or spread it on buttered toast for a cocktail nibble; put it up in jars and give as a gift. Make the relish a day ahead of serving for best flavor.

Preheat the oven to 425°F.

Put the eggplants on a foil- or Silpat-lined baking sheet and bake in the preheated oven for 1 hour, or until the skins are shriveled and the eggplants are soft to the touch. Remove from the oven and allow to cool. When cool enough to handle, peel each eggplant and cut the flesh into ½-inch pieces and reserve.

Heat the olive oil in a large skillet, and add the chopped onion and bell peppers. Cook over medium heat, stirring often, just until the onion and peppers begin to soften, about 8 minutes. Add the salt and freshly ground pepper, the garlic, and chopped chili pepper. Stir well, and cook for 3–4 minutes longer. Add the chopped tomatoes, the raisins with their soaking liquid, the honey, and the eggplant. Gently simmer for 15 minutes, stirring often. Taste carefully for seasoning, and add more salt and freshly ground black pepper as needed. (Do not be alarmed if the eggplant tastes a bit hot from the chili pepper at this point; it will subside as the relish cools and mellows.)

Cool completely and refrigerate overnight before serving. May be served warm, at room temperature, or cold. Will keep refrigerated for 1 week.

Candied Bacon

MAKES ENOUGH TO SERVE 4

8 slices good-quality smoked bacon
1/3 cup light-brown sugar

Typically Southern in the combination of sweet and salt, these brown-sugar–coated bacon slices are great for a breakfast or brunch buffet. As the sugar caramelizes in the oven, the bacon strips become very, very crisp. And the baking sheet becomes very sticky too, so be sure to line it with foil (or a Silpat).

Preheat the oven to 400°F.

Line a rimmed baking sheet with foil, shiny side up. Dredge the bacon on both sides in the brown sugar, and arrange on the baking sheet. Bake in the preheated oven for 15–20 minutes, until brown. Remove from the oven, and use a pair of tongs to lift the bacon from the baking sheet, allowing all excess fat to drain from the bacon as you transfer it to a serving platter.

Red Pepper Catsup

MAKES ABOUT 3 PINTS

- 1/3 cup peanut or olive oil
- 5 or 6 red bell peppers (2 1/2 pounds) seeded and cut into 1/2-inch pieces (about 9 cups)
- 3 large onions, chopped (5 cups)
- 1/4 cup finely chopped fresh ginger
- 3 tablespoons finely chopped garlic
- 1 tablespoon plus 2 teaspoons salt
- 1/2 teaspoon freshly ground black pepper
- 1 1/4 teaspoons ground cloves
- 1/2 teaspoon ground cinnamon
- 1/2 teaspoon cayenne pepper
- 1 tablespoon paprika
- 1 teaspoon ground coriander
- 1 teaspoon ground cumin
- 1/2 teaspoon freshly grated nutmeg
- 1 bay leaf, finely crumbled
- 1/2 cup water
- 2 cups cider vinegar
- 2 cups light-brown sugar

In early Southern kitchens, catsups were made from a variety of ingredients, including mushrooms, walnuts, green tomatoes, and fruits, and used as a flavoring in cooking as well as a table condiment. This red-pepper catsup will enhance many dishes. You don't have to process the catsup if you don't want to; instead, you can store it in the refrigerator, where it will keep for months. We especially like it as a dipping sauce for Fried Oysters (page 91).

Heat the oil in a large, heavy pot, and add the chopped red peppers. Cook, stirring often, for about 3 minutes. Add the onions and cook for an additional 3 minutes. Add the ginger, garlic, salt and pepper, cloves, cinnamon, cayenne pepper, paprika, coriander, cumin, nutmeg, and crumbled bay leaf. Stir well to blend in the spices evenly, and continue cooking for 5 minutes. Pour in the water and simmer, covered, until the peppers and onions are tender, about 15–20 minutes, then remove from the stove.

Transfer everything to a blender or food processor and purée until smooth. Return the purée to the cooking pot, and stir in the cider vinegar and brown sugar. Simmer, uncovered, stirring often, until the catsup thickens and has the consistency of tomato catsup, about 30 minutes.

Transfer to sterilized preserving jars and refrigerate. Or process following the jar manufacturer's directions.

Dried Fig Relish

MAKES ABOUT 1 QUART

- 1 cup granulated sugar
- 1 cup cider vinegar
- 1 teaspoon salt
- ½ teaspoon coarsely cracked black pepper
- 1 stick Ceylon cinnamon
- ¼ teaspoon ground allspice
- ½ teaspoon ground cloves
- 2-inch piece fresh ginger, finely chopped (about 2 tablespoons)
- 3 cups dried figs, coarsely chopped

An excellent accompaniment to meats and poultry, especially pork or duck. A great treat is leftover Bay-Studded Pork Shoulder (pages 116–117) with fig relish, stuffed in a biscuit.

Put the sugar and vinegar into a nonreactive saucepan and bring to a simmer, stirring just until the sugar is dissolved. Add the salt, black pepper, cinnamon stick, allspice, cloves, and ginger, and simmer gently for 5 minutes. Stir in the chopped figs and simmer, stirring often, until the mixture thickens, about 20 minutes.

The fig relish may be put up in canning jars, following the manufacturer's directions, or stored, tightly covered, in the refrigerator for several weeks.

A NOTE ABOUT CEYLON CINNAMON

The quality of cinnamon can vary greatly, and most that you find on supermarket shelves is harsh and hot in flavor. Ceylon cinnamon is the exception and we use it a lot in our recipes. Ceylon cinnamon is best purchased in stick form, kept tightly covered away from sunlight, and ground in a spice mill or with a mortar and pestle for each recipe (we keep a small electric coffee grinder that we use only for sweet spices like cinnamon and clove). Unlike common cinnamon, which is thick, hard, and brittle, Ceylon cinnamon is paper thin and crumbles easily in the hand. It is complexly smooth and sweet, and very refined, both in aroma and flavor. We recommend seeking it out, as it makes all the difference in a dish. If, however, for some reason you simply cannot find Ceylon cinnamon, reduce the amount called for in our recipe by half if you are using an ordinary supermarket brand.

Cranberries with Orange Zest and Port

MAKES ABOUT 6 CUPS

This unusual method for cooking cranberries produces a not-too-sweet sauce with chunky whole berries. The flavorings are very English and complement the berries without mucking them up, the way many fancy recipes do. Serve cold or at room temperature.

- 24 ounces fresh cranberries (6 cups)
- 1 cup port wine
- 1½ cups granulated sugar
- ¼ teaspoon salt
- 2 tablespoons finely chopped orange zest

Wash and drain the cranberries, and pick them over carefully, removing any spoiled berries or foreign objects. Pour the port into a large nonreactive skillet, and bring to a boil over high heat. Add the cranberries, and cook, stirring constantly, until they begin to pop, about 5 minutes. When the cranberries are popping, pour the sugar, salt, and orange zest over them. Cook, stirring constantly, until the sugar melts and the mixture begins to simmer briskly, 3–5 minutes. Remove from heat and allow to cool before serving.

Green Tomato Preserves

MAKES ABOUT 5 PINTS

- 4 pounds green tomatoes, cored and cut into ½-inch pieces (about 8 cups)
- 2 lemons, sliced thinly
- 4 cups granulated sugar
- 1 teaspoon salt

In the autumn, Miss Lewis's family made a sweet preserve from the green tomatoes that wouldn't have time to ripen, and flavored it with the vine fruit citron. This is a simpler method, using lemons and less sugar, for a delicious condiment, packed in canning jars. We often eat it on toast or biscuits for breakfast or with tea. Be sure to use completely green tomatoes, with no trace of red or pink.

Put the tomatoes and lemon into a nonreactive Dutch oven or heavy pot. Pour the sugar and salt over, and let sit for 2 hours or overnight, until the sugar has begun to dissolve in the bottom of the pot and the tomatoes begin to give off their liquid.

Stir the ingredients well, and heat slowly until the sugar is dissolved. Simmer, uncovered, stirring often, until the tomatoes are soft and yielding and the mixture is somewhat thickened—about 20 minutes. Put the preserves into sterilized canning jars. Refrigerate, or process following the manufacturer's instructions.

Cucumber Pickles

MAKES 7 PINTS

6 pounds kirby cucumbers

THE BRINE

1 gallon water

1½ cups pickling salt

THE ALUM WATER

1 gallon water

1 tablespoon powdered alum

THE SYRUP

1 quart cider vinegar

4 cups granulated sugar

2 cups light-brown sugar

1 stick Ceylon cinnamon

About 3 inches fresh ginger, peeled and cut into ½-inch slices

2 tablespoons mixed pickling spices, tied in a double thickness of cheesecloth

The wonderful cucumber pickles that Miss Lewis's mother made took months. Starting in midsummer, she would drop freshly picked cucumbers into a barrel of brine, and they'd remain there, covered by grape leaves, until the harvest was over, in early October. Then she'd cook the cucumbers with seasonings in batches, and cool and can them.

Our method is somewhat shorter. Sliced kirby cucumbers (the pickling variety) stay in brine for 2 days, then overnight in a solution of alum and water, which makes them crisp. Cook with vinegar, sugar, and spices and set aside for another day before canning. These are absolutely delicious pickles; for the best flavor, you want to let them sit for 6 weeks before sampling.

Wash the cucumbers, trim off ends, and slice crosswise into ⅓-inch slices.

Make the brine by stirring the pickling salt into the water in a large crock or bowl until it is dissolved. Add the sliced cucumbers, and let them stand, covered, for 2 days in a cool place, stirring them twice a day. Drain the cucumbers by passing the contents of the crock through a colander, and rinse briefly under cold running water.

Dissolve the alum in the water in the crock. Add the cucumbers, and leave to soak overnight. Drain the cucumbers, and again rinse in cold water.

Make the syrup: Pour the vinegar into a large nonreactive pot and add the sugars, cinnamon, ginger, and bag of pickling spices. Bring to a boil, stirring until the sugars are dissolved, and cook briskly for 15 minutes. Add the cucumber slices, and simmer gently for 45 minutes. Remove from the heat, cover, and set aside for 1 day.

Drain the syrup from the pickles into a nonreactive saucepan, and boil for 15 minutes. Remove the spice bag from the cucumbers, and pour the boiling syrup over them. Bring the cucumbers to a boil, and cook for 3 minutes.

In the meantime, sterilize seven 1-pint canning jars. Use a slotted spoon to extract the cucumbers, and pack them into the jars. Pour the hot syrup over the cucumbers to cover, and fill to just below the rim of the jars. Wipe the rims with a damp towel, seal the jars, and process for 5 minutes in a simmering water bath, following the canning-jar manufacturer's directions. Store the pickles in a cool dark place for 6 weeks before using.

Chowchow

MAKES ABOUT 4 PINTS

- 12 large green tomatoes, cored
- 4 green bell peppers, seeded
- 1 red bell pepper, seeded
- 4 large yellow onions, peeled
- 1 tablespoon plus 2 teaspoons yellow mustard seeds
- 1 tablespoon celery seeds
- 2 cups cider vinegar
- 2 cups granulated sugar
- 1 tablespoon plus 2 teaspoons kosher salt

When I was a kid, there were some women in Hartford who had a cottage industry of relish-making. My mother and others would bring them their vegetables to be chopped and cooked into big batches of chowchow, piccalilli, or some other relish. Making your own relish at home is a memorable experience, though—whenever I serve this chowchow, Southern friends always wax nostalgic about preparing it with their mothers, aunts, and grandmothers.

We put up our chowchow in summer, when green tomatoes and fresh peppers are available—you can use hot chilis if you wish. And it's on the table throughout the fall and winter—delicious especially with cabbage and squash dishes and cold meats too.

Chop the tomatoes, peppers, and onions very finely—either by hand, or in small batches in a food processor. Or, if you have a meat grinder, put the vegetables through the holes of the grinder, which is the traditional way of doing it.

Put the chopped or ground vegetables into a large, heavy-bottomed nonreactive pot, and add the mustard seeds, celery seeds, vinegar, sugar, and salt. Stir well, and bring to a simmer over medium heat. Cook, stirring often and skimming as needed, until the chowchow cooks down and thickens into a relish, about 2 hours.

Turn into hot sterilized jars and seal.

Hot Pepper Vinegar

MAKES 1½ CUPS

This is the essential condiment of the Deep South, used to season greens, other vegetables, and meats. You'll find this vinegar on every table, often in old catsup or liquor bottles.

- 1 pound fresh hot peppers (such as fingerling or jalapeño) (about 2 cups)
- 1½ cups cider vinegar
- ½ teaspoon salt

Wash and drain the peppers. Leave them whole, and pack tightly into a pint jar or bottle. Heat the vinegar in a nonreactive saucepan until boiling. Stir in the salt, and allow to cool slightly. Pour the hot vinegar over the peppers, and seal tightly. Store in a cool area, away from sunlight. Allow to sit for 1 week before using; it improves with time.

Chowchow and hot pepper vinegar

Candied Kumquats

MAKES ABOUT 2 PINTS

- 1 pound kumquats, washed (about 2 cups)
- 1 cup granulated sugar
- Pinch of salt

There was a kumquat tree growing along the fencerow at our farm outside Hartford, and we'd stop occasionally to pick the tiny oranges and eat them out of hand. But I learned about candied kumquats years later from pastry chef Lindsey Shere, who sliced them onto her delicious Country-Style Rhubarb Tart (pages 248–249). Sweet and tart with a slightly bitter undertone, these are good on ice cream, or as a relish with rich savory dishes, like roast duck or holiday turkey.

Rinse and drain the kumquats, then slice them crosswise into ⅓-inch slices. Put them in a nonreactive saucepan, and pour the sugar over them, along with a pinch of salt. Bring to a boil, then reduce the heat and simmer, stirring often, until the kumquats become translucent, about 10–15 minutes. Transfer to sterilized jars and refrigerate; they will keep several weeks. For long-term storage, process according to manufacturer's instructions.

Apple Chutney

MAKES 2½ PINTS

- 2 cups apple-cider vinegar
- 2 cups granulated sugar
- 1½ pounds tart cooking apples (Winesap or Granny Smith), peeled and cut into ½-inch pieces
- 3 tablespoons freshly squeezed lemon juice
- 10 large cloves garlic, peeled
- About 3 inches fresh ginger, peeled and coarsely chopped
- 1½ tablespoons salt
- 6 dried red chili peppers
- 1½ cups raisins
- 2 tablespoons yellow mustard seeds

Miss Lewis made this chutney at Café Nicholson, where it was a favorite of India's ambassador to the United Nations, Madame Pandit—sister of the legendary Indian leader Jawaharlal Nehru. Serve this with Country Captain (pages 96–97) as well as roast pork and game dishes. You can substitute pears, peaches, or green tomatoes for the apples.

Put the vinegar and sugar in a large nonreactive saucepan or Dutch oven. Bring to a boil over high heat, stirring until the sugar is dissolved. Reduce the heat and simmer for 10 minutes. Toss the apples and lemon juice in a large bowl. Put the garlic, ginger, salt, and dried chilis in a food processor, and blend until finely chopped.

Add the apples, garlic mixture, raisins, and mustard seeds to the vinegar-sugar mixture, and simmer, stirring often, until the apples are tender and the chutney has thickened, about 45 minutes.

Spoon the hot chutney into sterilized canning jars, and seal following manufacturer's directions. Or simply put in jars and refrigerate.

Edna Lewis at Café Nicholson

Old-Fashioned Fig Preserves

MAKES ABOUT 3 PINTS

2 pounds firm, ripe figs
1/4 cup baking soda
Boiling water to cover the figs
2 cups granulated sugar
1/2 teaspoon salt

Whole fresh figs preserved in syrup are a simple and unusual treat. Serve these with toast or biscuits, or in a salad with a spicy vinaigrette and warm, pecan-crusted goat cheese, or as a relish with a roast, particularly duck. Choose heavy, ripe, yet firm figs for preserving, but not the black Mission variety, which can become tough and leathery when cooked this way.

Put the figs in a nonreactive saucepan or Dutch oven. Sprinkle the baking soda over them, and pour in enough boiling water to cover. Let stand for 5 minutes, then drain and rinse in two baths of clean, cold water.

Put the figs back in the pan, and cover with sugar and salt. Let stand at room temperature for 12–24 hours, until the sugar is mostly dissolved.

Heat gently until the syrup comes to a simmer, and cook the figs slowly for 10 minutes, shaking the pan occasionally to ensure that they are not sticking to the bottom of the pot. Remove from the heat and cool. Cover, and allow to sit at room temperature overnight.

Slowly heat and simmer the figs for 10 minutes, then cool and cover overnight for 2 more days. Repeat. On the third day, after the figs have simmered, use a slotted spoon to remove them from their syrup and pack into sterilized jars. Strain the syrup, and boil it until it reaches 220°F on a candy thermometer. Pour the hot syrup over the figs, and seal following canning-jar manufacturer's instructions. Allow to age for 1 month in a cool, dark place before using.

Pear Relish

MAKES ABOUT 5 PINTS

- 3 large green bell peppers, sliced into strips, seeds removed
- 5 large red bell peppers, sliced into strips, seeds removed
- 3 hot peppers (fingerling, jalapeño, or serrano), sliced lengthwise, seeds removed
- 10 firm but ripe pears, peeled, cored, and quartered
- 1 quart white or cider vinegar
- 3 cups granulated sugar
- 1 tablespoon salt

This is another gem from the South's treasure of relishes, pickles, and preserves. Serve with vegetables or meats, and spread it on sandwiches. A great gift. The relish may be served the day after it is made, but it improves greatly in flavor after a week.

Chop the peppers and pears by hand or in a food processor until they are coarsely chopped—about ¼-inch dice. Put the vinegar, sugar, and salt in a non-reactive Dutch oven or heavy pot, and bring to a boil, stirring until the sugar is dissolved.

Stir in the chopped vegetables and pears, and bring back to a boil. Cook, uncovered, at a full simmer for about 20 minutes, stirring often and skimming the scum off the surface as needed. When ready, the relish should be syrupy but not floating in liquid.

Ladle the relish into hot sterilized jars, and process using canning-jar manufacturer's instructions.

Strawberry Preserves

MAKES SIX TO EIGHT ½-PINT JARS

2 pounds fresh strawberries (about 4 cups)
1 pound granulated sugar
½ teaspoon salt

This method yields colorful jars of tender, fresh-tasting berries in a crystal-clear syrup. Handle the strawberries carefully each step of the recipe, especially when cooking them: you want to skim the syrup and simmer only until the berries are tender.

Put the berries in a large sieve, and gently run cold water over them. Take special care not to bruise the fruit. Drain well, then carefully turn the berries out onto a clean towel and let them drain for 15 minutes longer. Remove the caps and cut the berries into quarters. Put the berries into a large nonreactive pot or Dutch oven or preserving kettle. Pour the sugar and salt over them, and let the berries sit for 2 hours or longer (overnight is okay as long as the berries are covered and the room is cool), until they release some of their juice.

Set the pot over medium heat, and watch carefully, gently shaking the pot as needed rather than stirring, until the berries come to a simmer. Cook at a lively simmer, skimming carefully any scum that is released to the surface, for 12–15 minutes, just until the fruit is tender and the syrup clear. Be sure not to overcook or you will lose the flavor of the fresh fruit. Remove the berries from the stove, and set them aside to rest overnight. Do not cover the berries until they are completely cooled.

The following day, return the preserves to the stove and carefully bring to a full simmer without scorching. Spoon the hot preserves into sterilized ½-pint preserving jars up to ¼ inch beneath the rim of the jars. Seal the jars with sterilized tops and rings, following the jar manufacturer's directions. Store the preserves in a cool, dark place.

Sugared Raspberries

MAKES 2 CUPS

- 2 cups fresh, unblemished raspberries (about 1 pound)
- 2 cups granulated sugar

Here's an old method for preserving fruit with a very fresh taste, without cooking. The juicy crushed berries make a nice spread with bread, and a delicious filling for cake. But this kind of sweet preserve also has a place on the dinner table. Miss Lewis gave me a jar of sugared raspberries—the first I'd ever seen—when I visited her one springtime soon after we met. The following December, at my birthday dinner, I served them as an accompaniment to roast chicken and yeast rolls—very Southern and very delicious.

Sugared berries will keep for a year or longer under refrigeration. You can prepare strawberries or blackberries the same way but raspberries seem to do and taste best.

Carefully pick over the berries, removing any leaves, foreign objects, or spoiled berries. Put the berries in a mixing bowl, and pour the sugar over them. Use two large forks or a potato masher to mash the sugar into the raspberries until they are liquefied and there is no trace of whole berries left. (A blender is not good for this, because it will pulverize some of the raspberry seeds, which should remain intact.)

Transfer to jars and refrigerate for 2 days before using. Sugared raspberries will keep for 1 year or longer under refrigeration.

Hot Chocolate

MAKES ENOUGH TO SERVE 6

- 1/2 cup cocoa powder
- 3/4 cup granulated sugar
- 1/4 teaspoon salt
- 1/2 cup boiling water
- 1/2 cup heavy cream
- 2 ounces semisweet chocolate, finely chopped
- 1/2 teaspoon vanilla extract
- 1 teaspoon cognac (optional)
- 4 1/2 cups milk, heated

Here is a wonderfully rich, satisfying hot chocolate to enjoy before a fireplace, in bed, or poured from a thermos on a winter outing. With homemade Marshmallows it is even better.

For convenience, the recipe can be followed up to the point of adding the milk to make a base syrup that can be stored for a month. To make a cup of hot chocolate in a jiffy, simply whisk 1/4 cup of the syrup into 1 cup of heated milk. The addition of cognac is a refinement that comes from a very old Tennessee cookbook. It adds a depth of flavor but doesn't leave a taste of alcohol.

Put the cocoa, sugar, and salt in a heavy nonreactive saucepan. Slowly whisk in the boiling water, and cook at a simmer for 3 minutes. Whisk in the heavy cream, bring back to a simmer, and remove from heat. Add the chopped chocolate, and whisk until melted and smooth. Add the vanilla and optional cognac, and slowly stir in the heated milk. Cover tightly and let rest for 5 minutes before serving, so that the flavors can marry and develop. If the hot chocolate cools, gently heat to just below a simmer. Serve with homemade Marshmallows (page 286) floating on top.

Eggnog

MAKES ABOUT 2½ QUARTS (10 CUPS), TO SERVE 20

- 12 egg yolks (see Note)
- 1½ cups granulated sugar
- ½ cup brandy or cognac
- ¾ cup bourbon whiskey
- 1 teaspoon freshly grated nutmeg, plus more as garnish
- ¼ teaspoon salt
- 2 cups milk
- 3 cups heavy cream

This authentic eggnog is far superior to any processed mix sold in cartons at Christmastime. Our recipe makes a large batch and can be cut in half. It also makes a heady nog, but the spirits can be reduced to suit your personal taste. This eggnog improves in flavor if made an hour or two ahead of serving, and should be thoroughly chilled. You can even make it a day ahead if you like (store in the refrigerator, of course). I like to make this nog and deliver it to friends, packed in old-fashioned Mason jars, along with a tin of Christmas cookies.

Put the egg yolks into the bowl of an electric mixer. With the mixer running, slowly add the sugar, and continue mixing moderately fast for 5 minutes or longer, until the egg yolks have increased in volume several times over, are quite thick, and are light yellow in color. Reduce the mixer speed to low, and slowly pour in the brandy and bourbon. Add the grated nutmeg and salt, and slowly blend in the milk and heavy cream. Transfer to a chilled punch bowl, and grate fresh nutmeg over the top. Be sure to stir the eggnog well before ladling into cups, and grate additional nutmeg over each serving.

NOTE Raw egg yolks are essential to traditional eggnog, but this inevitably presents a risk, because of the micro-organisms that may be present in raw eggs. Free range or organic eggs are preferred. Eggs should always be purchased from a reliable source and kept refrigerated at all times. Soiled or broken eggs should never be used.

Homemade Lemonade

MAKES ENOUGH TO SERVE 8–12

- 2 cups granulated sugar
- 1½ cups freshly squeezed lemon juice
- ¼ teaspoon salt
- 2 quarts bottled spring water, chilled
- 2 lemons, washed and thinly sliced
- Fresh mint sprigs for garnish (optional)

A refreshing summer treat like no other—and certainly better than any powder or mix you can buy. We recommend organic lemons, but in any case rinse the lemons well under hot water and wipe vigorously to remove the wax coating and the dye label. For party serving, we like to make a big block of ice to float in the lemonade—it looks lovely and keeps the drink cold.

Put the granulated sugar, freshly squeezed lemon juice, salt, and the water into a large crockery or punch bowl. Stir well until the sugar is dissolved, then add the lemon slices. Refrigerate until ready to use. Serve garnished with the optional mint.

NOTE To make a block of frozen ice, put 1 quart of spring water into a 4-cup stainless-steel mixing bowl or a plastic container of the same size, and freeze several hours or overnight.

Iced Tea

MAKES ALMOST 1 QUART

- 3½ cups water
- 3 tablespoons loose black tea, or 4 standard-size tea bags
- 6 tablespoons granulated sugar
- 1 large sprig of mint (about 1 dozen mint leaves)

Iced tea—sometimes so sweet you can barely taste the tea—is a staple beverage in the South. In our house, it was as elemental as water—we drank 2 gallons every day during the hot summer months, and at dinner and supper a big tea pitcher and a huge glass tumbler were always set at my father's place. No one was else was allowed to use that glass.

The iced tea of my childhood was made exclusively with tea bags. In Hartford, you were partial to either Lipton or Luzianne brand, and arguments were frequent about which was better. We were loyal Lipton folks. Today, though, I prefer loose tea, such as a good orange pekoe or Darjeeling, though Lipton tea bags are fine too. I put fresh mint in my iced tea now, something my mother never did. I don't take lemon in my tea, but for those who do, I serve wedges on the side and let them squeeze it into their own glasses.

Bring 2½ cups of the water to a rolling boil. Put the tea or tea bags in a small, 2½–3-cup teapot, and pour the boiling water over. Cover, and let steep 10 minutes. Strain the tea into a large pitcher, add the remaining cup cold water, and stir in the sugar and the mint. Fill the pitcher with ice cubes and serve.

Mulberry Acid

MAKES ABOUT 8 CUPS

- 6 cups fresh mulberries, rinsed gently under cool water and drained
- 6 cups filtered or bottled water
- 2 tablespoons tartaric acid (see Note)
- Granulated sugar

An "acid" is a syrup used as the base for a refreshing cold drink. Fresh berries are steeped in hot water with a small amount of tartaric acid, and their strained juices are later sweetened into a thick syrup with a wonderful tang. We had a mulberry tree when I was growing up, and we called the concentrate from the berries "mulberry nectar." A similar process using vinegar instead of tartaric acid makes a syrup called, naturally, a "vinegar."

Mulberries yield an especially delicious acid, but blackberries or raspberries are also excellent. Store the concentrate in the refrigerator—you'll have enough to turn ice water, white wine, or cocktails into special beverages all summer long.

Put the mulberries into a stone crock or other heat-resistant, nonreactive container. Bring the water to a boil. Remove from the heat, and stir in the tartaric acid. Pour the water over the berries, then cover and let rest for 6 hours or overnight.

Without pressing on the berries, strain them through a cloth jelly bag or a fine sieve lined with a clean linen tea towel that has been rinsed in cool water and squeezed out. Once it is strained, measure the juice and pour into a nonreactive saucepan. Add the juice's volume in sugar, and stir over low heat until the sugar is dissolved.

Cool and store, tightly covered, in the refrigerator for 2 weeks before using.

To use, pour a tablespoon or two over a glass of ice, and fill with water. You could also add a little of it to white wine or use it in mixed drinks.

NOTE You can get tartaric acid at a health-food store or a pharmacy. For mail order, see page 317.

Agua de Sandia (or Watermelon Punch)

MAKES ABOUT 10 CUPS

- 1 large watermelon (about 10 pounds)
- Granulated sugar to taste
- 1/8 teaspoon kosher salt
- 2 cups crushed ice
- 1–2 cups white rum or vodka (optional)

Though few things feel more Southern than watermelon, this punch originates from a locale far more Southern than either Virginia or Alabama. As the name implies, it is a recipe from Mexico, and was prepared for us by a friend of ours from Acapulco. *Sandia* is the Spanish word for "watermelon," though our friend also calls this punch by the simple name *agua fresca.*

Watermelons vary in juiciness, but on average, a 10-pound melon will produce about 8 cups of strained juice. When selecting a watermelon, be sure to look for a smooth, unblemished rind, and choose a melon that feels heavy and sounds slightly hollow when tapped on its side.

This is the most refreshing summer drink I know of, especially when it is icy cold. So be sure it is completely chilled before serving. If serving from the table or at a party, we recommend putting it into a big, large-mouthed jar or glass pitcher, and burying it halfway up in a big bowl of crushed ice.

Using a stout knife, cut the watermelon in half crosswise, and then cut each half lengthwise into quarters. Cut or scoop out the red meat from the melon and put in a large mixing bowl. Using clean hands, squish the melon between your fingers until it is broken down into pulp. (This would be a great job for children.)

When the watermelon meat is thoroughly broken down, transfer in batches to a large sieve placed over a bowl, and, using a rubber spatula, gently press against the pulp and extract the juice. Discard the pulp.

Once all of the juice is extracted, taste for sweetness and add just enough granulated sugar so the juice is refreshingly sweet but not syrupy-tasting. Stir in the salt, which will help bring up the flavor of the melon, and refrigerate until thoroughly chilled. (This can be done the day before serving.)

When ready to serve, grind the ice in batches in a blender with the watermelon juice. Taste for sweetness, and add a bit more sugar if needed. Stir in white rum or vodka to taste, if you are using it. Serve icy cold in frozen glasses.

As the punch sits it tends to settle, so be sure to stir well just before serving.

Blackberry Cordial

MAKES ABOUT 2½ PINTS

- 4 cups fresh blackberries
- 3 cups bottled or spring water
- 1 bay leaf
- 3 black peppercorns
- 4 whole cloves
- 3 cardamom pods, crushed
- 1 stick Ceylon cinnamon, broken into pieces
- 1 cup light-brown sugar
- 1¼ cups cognac or brandy

This is a nice treat to have on hand for both before and after dinner. Serve as an apéritif over ice with some sparkling water, or add a spoonful to chilled sparkling wine. After dinner, serve in port or cordial glasses. And it isn't bad in the afternoon with tea cakes, either.

Put the blackberries, water, bay leaf, peppercorns, cloves, cardamom pods, and cinnamon in a nonreactive saucepan. Bring to a gentle simmer and cook for 30 minutes, stirring often and using the back of a spoon to crush the berries lightly while cooking.

Remove from the heat and strain, without pressing, through a fine-meshed sieve, until the berries have released all of their juice. You should have about 4 cups of blackberry juice. Stir in the brown sugar until dissolved, and let the juice cool completely before stirring in the cognac or brandy. Transfer the fortified blackberry juice to a tightly sealed bottle, and store in a cool, dark place for 2 weeks before serving.

II A DEMITASSE OF SOUP—THE ESSENCE OF FLAVOR

Good Soups and Stocks

Here are a dozen or so of our favorite soups—the ones we most often serve to guests or make for ourselves. For the most part, they are rather simple vegetable purées that reflect how much our cooking is shaped by the South's year-round fresh-vegetable bounty. There are also recipes for two classic shellfish soups—Oyster Stew and She-Crab Soup—whose origins lie in different parts of the South, as well as Miss Lewis's famous Turtle Soup with Dumplings.

Though full-flavored, most of these soups are light-bodied, suitable for a warm climate. It's nice to begin meals with a light touch. (As a former music student, I tend to think of a meal as a gradual *crescendo* and *decrescendo,* with soup as the quiet opening note.) We want to awaken the palate, and when we entertain, we want our guests to have plenty of room for everything else we've prepared. So, while everyone's gathering around, we often serve soup as an hors d'oeuvre, in demitasse or antique teacups (which we both collect). Sometimes we pour lighter soups and broths from china teapots. With rich soups, such small portions are perfect—and anyone who wants more can sneak into the kitchen for seconds.

Usually puréed vegetable soups are made by boiling vegetables in stock and puréeing everything. But you can make soup with deeper and more focused flavor, from most any vegetable, using a technique I learned from Miss Lewis. I noticed how she would cook the aromatic vegetable gently for a long time in just a little butter before she added any stock. What she was doing was extracting and concentrating the essence of the vegetable. The Pumpkin, Chestnut, Rutabaga, and Crookneck Squash soups in this chapter all follow this principle.

For producing fine, smooth texture in puréed soups, Miss Lewis and I both prefer an electric blender to a food mill or food processor. Be careful, however, when puréeing hot foods in a blender: work in batches; don't overfill the blender jar; and hold down the top, using a kitchen towel to protect your hands.

WHAT'S A GOOD SOUP POT?

For soup-making, we always use a large heavy-duty pot—what is often called a "Dutch oven." The kind I recommend is enameled cast iron, 4 or 6 quarts in volume, with a heavy bottom and heavy snug-fitting lid, both essential for cooking vegetables very slowly without coloring. But any good heavy-bottomed pot is fine as long as it has a "nonreactive" interior—enameled cast-iron or stainless-steel. Old-fashioned aluminum pots and ones with badly scratched nonstick surfaces will discolor food and impart a metallic flavor, especially when you are cooking with acidic foods such as tomatoes.

THE FLAVOR OF NUTMEG

Freshly grated nutmeg is one of our favorite seasonings, especially for soups and vegetable dishes, where it helps enhance the earthy, nutty flavors. We use it like freshly ground pepper, adding it during cooking and often grating just a bit more over a dish when we're about to eat. But nutmeg must always be used judiciously, as a subtle taste, because it can easily overpower other flavors. The ground nutmeg you get in jars tastes like sawdust or worse: if a recipe calls for nutmeg and preground is all you have, omit it! We always keep whole nutmegs on hand and grind just what we need for a recipe, using a nutmeg grater or the fine holes of a box grater.

Scott's Chicken Stock

MAKES 3 QUARTS OF STOCK

- One $2\frac{1}{2}$–3-pound chicken
- 3 quarts water
- 1 teaspoon kosher salt
- 1 inner stalk of celery, preferably with tender leaves
- 1 small yellow onion, peeled

A good stock is meant to support—not overwhelm—the flavor of a soup's primary ingredient, especially a delicate one like English peas or summer squash. This is my basic stock for soup-making: rich yet light, salted only slightly, so that it can be reduced for stronger chicken flavor.

The secret to this stock is unattended steeping: I put a whole chicken in a pot with water, bring it to a boil, and then let it cook *off the heat,* tightly covered. It is a very gentle, simple method, yet remarkably quick: the stock is finished in just over an hour. In addition, you reap the bonus of a perfectly poached chicken—silky, tender, and flavorful.

Rinse the chicken well, inside and out. Put the chicken in a large pot and add the water, salt, celery, and onion. Bring to a full boil, uncovered, and remove from heat. Cover the pot with a tight-fitting lid, and let sit in a warm area for 1 hour. Inspect the chicken for doneness; the leg and thigh should separate easily from the joint. If this doesn't occur, cover the pot again and let sit for 30 minutes longer.

Carefully remove the chicken to a platter, and discard the celery and onion. Strain the resulting stock through a fine sieve, and carefully skim the fat from the surface. If you don't need the stock immediately, you can cool it at room temperature, then refrigerate overnight, and the fat will solidify and be easier to remove.

IF YOU DON'T HAVE HOMEMADE STOCK

If you need soup but don't have homemade stock, use the best-quality canned broth you can buy—low-fat, low-sodium, made with organic ingredients if possible. You will probably need to adjust the amount of salt called for in the recipes here, depending on the saltiness of the broth you are using. Careful tasting is your best guide.

Miss Lewis's Very Rich Chicken Broth

MAKES APPROXIMATELY 8 CUPS OF VERY RICH, INTENSELY FLAVORED BROTH

- One 2½–3-pound chicken
- 1 tablespoon kosher salt
- 4 tablespoons (½ stick) unsalted butter
- 1 small inner stalk of celery, preferably with leaves
- 6 cups water, preferably bottled

Miss Lewis makes this intensely flavorful broth by slowly cooking small pieces of cut-up chicken in butter over very low heat for several minutes to release the natural juices of the chicken. It's the same principle for extracting flavor that we use in vegetable cookery. You will be surprised to find that the chicken releases nearly 2 cups of its natural juices before water is added.

This broth is so rich it is ideally savored alone. I recommend using bottled water in this recipe, unless you are fortunate enough to have excellent spring or well water as your drinking water. And because you will have extracted all flavor from the chicken, you won't want to eat the meat (but your cat or dog might enjoy it).

Rinse the chicken well, inside and out, and dry well with paper towel. Cut the chicken into two legs, two thighs, two breast halves, two wings, plus the backbone and neck if included. With a cleaver or a stout knife, carefully whack each of the pieces into smaller pieces, of about 2 inches. Rub a little of the kosher salt into the cut surfaces of the chicken pieces, and set aside.

In a wide, heavy-bottomed Dutch oven or saucepan, melt the butter over medium heat until hot and foaming. Add the chicken pieces, and stir well to coat with the butter. Cook, stirring often, until the skin of the chicken is golden, but don't let it brown. Reduce the heat to very low, add the celery, and cover with a tight-fitting lid. Check every 5 minutes, and stir well. Within 20 minutes, the chicken should have released its essence, so that liquid comes up almost even with the top of the chicken pieces. Add the water and bring to a gentle simmer. Cook slowly for 20 minutes, skimming often. Strain the broth, and discard the chicken pieces and celery (the chicken will have given up all of its flavor).

If not using immediately, cool the broth and refrigerate. Once chilled, the solidified fat can be easily removed.

Chicken and Seduced Vegetable Soup

MAKES ENOUGH TO SERVE 6–8

- 1 large leek
- 2 tablespoons unsalted butter
- 1 small yellow onion (1/4 cup finely chopped)
- 1/2 teaspoon kosher salt
- 2 ounces mushrooms, thinly sliced (1/2 cup) (see Note)
- 1 small carrot, finely diced
- 1 stalk of celery, finely diced
- 1 small clove garlic, mashed to a paste with a bit of kosher salt
- 1/2 teaspoon dried thyme
- 6 cups Scott's Chicken Stock (page 33), heated
- 1–2 cups poached chicken, from Scott's Chicken Stock, cut or torn into bite-sized pieces
- Freshly ground black pepper

The vegetables in this beautiful soup are "seduced" by careful, slow cooking in butter; you want them to soften gently, without browning. You could vary any leftover soup by adding cooked rice or noodles. This is a good soup to pack in a thermos for a picnic, to take to the office, or to tuck into a child's lunchbox.

Trim the leek by removing the root tip and all but 2 inches of the green top. Slice the leek in half lengthwise, and cut each half into 1/4-inch slices crosswise. Put the sliced leek into a bowl of cool water and swirl the pieces about with your hands to dislodge any dirt. Allow to sit for 2 minutes, so that all dirt and sediment settle to the bottom of the bowl. Use a slotted spoon or flat sieve to retrieve the leeks from the water (leaving the grit behind). Drain well and blot dry on paper towel.

Heat the butter in a large saucepan over medium heat until hot and foaming. Add the chopped onion, leek, and salt, and stir well to coat the vegetables with the butter and salt. Reduce heat to low, and cook gently, stirring often, for 5 minutes, taking care that the vegetables do not begin to brown. Add the mushrooms, carrot, celery, garlic, and thyme. Cook gently, stirring often to ensure even cooking without browning, for approximately 10 minutes. Pour in the heated chicken stock, and simmer gently for 10–15 minutes, to finish cooking the vegetables and develop the flavor of the soup. Add the poached chicken and cook 5 minutes longer. Taste very carefully for seasoning, adding salt as needed and a sparing amount of freshly ground black pepper.

NOTE We like shiitake and oyster mushrooms, but you can use any fresh mushroom except portobellos (which could turn the soup black).

She-Crab Soup

MAKES ENOUGH TO SERVE 6–8 AS A SUBSTANTIAL FIRST COURSE OR ENTRÉE, 16–20 IF SERVED IN DEMITASSE CUPS AS THE BEGINNING TO AN ELABORATE MEAL OR AT A COCKTAIL PARTY

- ½ cup (1 stick) unsalted butter
- 7 tablespoons all-purpose flour
- 3 cups milk, heated almost to boiling
- 2 teaspoons salt
- 4 cups heavy cream
- 1 pound lump crabmeat, carefully picked free of all shell and cartilage, preferably female crabs
- ¼ cup Harvey's Bristol Cream Sherry
- ⅛ teaspoon cayenne pepper, or more to taste
- Finely chopped parsley for garnish

She-crab soup has long been a traditional specialty of the Low Country in South Carolina. It is a Southern classic, and a tourist attraction in Charleston. Honestly, though, I never heard of she-crab soup while I was growing up in Alabama—nor did Miss Lewis in Virginia—which illustrates the wisdom of writer Wyatt Cooper's observation that the South is not one place, but many little worlds unto themselves.

When Miss Lewis lived and cooked near Charleston during the early 1980s, she came to know several versions of the soup, including this one—a simple but luxurious concoction of lump crabmeat, heavy cream, and Harvey's Bristol Cream sherry. Traditionally, the soup called for female blue crab—a "she-crab"—whose orange roe imparts a distinctive taste and characteristic orange speckles, but good lump crabmeat usually contains enough roe for proper flavor. This soup is *rich:* a demitasse cupful makes a lavish hors d'oeuvre, and a whole bowl is a satisfying supper, with only a simple salad alongside.

Melt the butter over low heat in a large nonreactive saucepan, and stir in the flour. Cook, stirring constantly, for 2 minutes, then slowly whisk in the hot milk, and continue whisking until perfectly smooth. Add the salt, and cook, stirring often, until the mixture comes to a boil. Stir in the heavy cream, and cook at a low simmer for 3–5 minutes, until the milk and cream no longer taste of raw flour. Add the crabmeat, and cook gently for 5 minutes longer. Cover the saucepan, remove it from the stove, and allow it to rest in a warm place for 30 minutes to develop the flavor of the crab.

Once the soup has rested and you are ready to serve, return it to the stove and gently bring to a simmer. Add the sherry and cayenne pepper. Simmer briefly, and taste carefully for seasoning, adding more salt, cayenne, or sherry as needed.

Serve in heated bowls or demitasse cups. Garnish with a little bit of finely chopped parsley.

Turtle Soup with Dumplings

MAKES ENOUGH TO SERVE 6, MORE IF SERVED IN DEMITASSE CUPS

This soup, as you may read in the introduction to this book, is what Miss Lewis made when I first met her. It is one of the most subtle, complex, beautiful soups you will ever taste.

Though exotic-sounding, turtle soup is actually very simple to make. The secret is long, gentle cooking, during which the turtle meat slowly surrenders its delicate flavor. And though Miss Lewis learned to make this soup in Freetown with wild turtles, they are now farm-raised in the Everglades, and fresh meat is completely dressed and ready for cooking. Ask your fishmonger if he can get it for you.

The poached, cloudlike turtle-meat dumplings make a wonderful garnish, but you can also enjoy the rich, clear turtle broth all by itself. To accompany the soup, it is customary to serve the fortified wine (Madeira or cream sherry) that you have used to flavor the broth.

THE SOUP

- 2 pounds fresh turtle meat with bones, cut into 1-inch pieces
- 1 medium-sized onion, peeled
- 1 clove, stuck into the onion
- 2 peppercorns
- ½ leek, split lengthwise, carefully washed and trimmed so that 3 inches of green top remain
- 1 stalk of celery, preferably with leaves
- 3 parsley stems, without leaves
- 1 small bay leaf
- ¼ teaspoon dried thyme
- ½ teaspoon salt
- 1 cup dry white wine
- 8 cups filtered or bottled water
- ½ to ¾ cup Madeira or sherry

THE DUMPLINGS

- 1½ cups all-purpose flour
- 1 teaspoon Homemade Baking Powder (page 230)
- ½ teaspoon salt

Put the turtle meat and all of the remaining soup ingredients except the Madeira or sherry into a nonreactive pot. Slowly, without stirring, bring the soup to a simmer over moderate heat. *Never stir or allow the soup to boil.* Reduce the heat until the soup, partially covered, slowly percolates below a simmer. Cook undisturbed for 3 or 4 hours, until the broth develops a delicate but rich flavor.

Remove from the stove, and very slowly and carefully strain the broth through a fine-meshed sieve. Take care to disturb the soup solids as little as possible, and do not press against them during straining. (If the strained soup contains a large amount of sediment, allow it to rest for 10 minutes and then carefully strain again. The turtle broth is not a consommé, but it should be naturally quite clear.) Reserve enough of the turtle meat to make ½ cup when chopped, and discard the other solids.

Rinse and wipe out the pot used to make the broth, and return to it the strained soup. Bring to a simmer and taste for seasoning (salt is especially helpful in bringing up the complex flavors of the turtle). Stir in the Madeira or sherry, and simmer for 1 minute. Taste the soup again for seasoning, and adjust if needed. Cover and keep warm until ready to serve. Meanwhile, prepare the dumplings.

Turtle Soup (cont.)

- ½ teaspoon granulated sugar
- ½ teaspoon dried thyme
- 1 tablespoon unsalted butter, melted
- 1 egg plus 1 egg white, lightly beaten
- ¼ cup milk
- ½ cup finely chopped turtle meat (reserved from making the soup)

To make the dumplings: Sift the flour, baking powder, salt, and sugar into a small mixing bowl. Add the dried thyme and mix to blend. Blend in the melted butter and egg, followed by the milk. The batter should resemble a very wet biscuit dough. If it is too dry and stiff, blend in 1 or 2 tablespoons more milk, then fold in the chopped turtle meat.

Bring to a simmer in a small, covered skillet 1 cup of the finished turtle broth and 2 cups lightly salted water. Dip two metal teaspoons into the simmering liquid, and use one spoon to scoop out a rounded teaspoonful of the dumpling dough, and the other to slide the dough carefully into the simmering liquid. Continue until the pan is nearly full, leaving some room for swelling—you may have to do this in two batches. Reduce the heat slightly and cover the skillet. Cook the dumplings gently for about 5 minutes, until a cake tester or toothpick inserted into one comes out clean. Use a slotted spoon to transfer the dumplings carefully to the hot soup. Repeat with the remaining dough. Serve immediately.

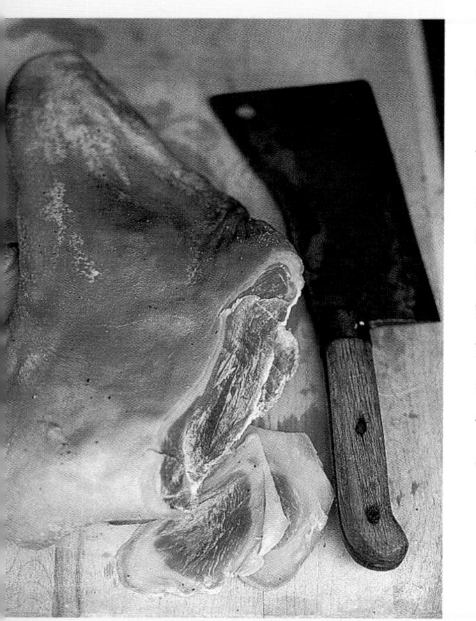

THE RIGHT PORK FOR SMOKED PORK STOCK

The pork you want is essentially traditional "country ham": dry-cured in salt, smoked, and aged (but not cooked). Cured smoked pork shoulder is a less available but more affordable alternative. It can sometimes be found in Chinese or Hispanic markets, or you can order it from the same sources as country hams (page 317). In the South, you can find packages of country-ham trimmings—bits of meat, fat, and skin that are perfect for making stock. *Do not* use supermarket ham hocks, which are usually processed with chemical "smoke." They are fake and taste fake. (If you can find a real hock from a real cured and smoked ham, that would be fine for stock.)

Smoked Pork Stock

MAKES ABOUT 1 GALLON

- 2 pounds cured and smoked pork shoulder, sliced or whole (see box)
- 1 gallon water

The authentic flavor of cured smoked pork is essential to Southern cooking. This rich stock is one of the best ways to bring that rich flavor—salt, smoke, and aged meat—to everyday cooking. We use the stock for cooking greens, peas, beans, and root vegetables, as a base for soups and stews, and as an essential part of many recipes throughout this book.

Traditionally, a Southern cook would often add a piece of cured pork as "seasoning" to a pot of water and vegetables—and cook them all together for a long time. However, while the cooking water is gradually extracting seasoning flavor from the pork, it is also leaching flavor and nutrients from the vegetables. But pork stock quickly imparts its rich flavor to whatever is cooked in it, and vegetables don't have to overcook to reach full flavor. And because pork stock can be defatted before you use it, foods never have the excessive greasiness that unfortunately is sometimes thought of as characteristic of Southern cooking.

Rinse the pork shoulder, and put it and the water into a large stockpot or Dutch oven. Cook, covered, at a full simmer for 2 hours, or until stock develops a strong smoked-pork flavor. Strain and discard the pork shoulder, because it will have rendered all of its flavor. Cool the stock completely, then refrigerate until needed. Pork stock may be kept refrigerated for up to 1 week, or frozen for 6 months.

NOTE Once stock is well chilled, any fat that is congealed on the surface may be removed and reserved for other uses.

A Simple Oyster Stew

MAKES ENOUGH TO SERVE 6

- 7 tablespoons unsalted butter
- 1 medium yellow onion, finely diced (about 1 cup)
- 1 teaspoon kosher salt
- 3 tablespoons all-purpose flour
- 5 cups milk, heated
- 2 cups heavy cream
- 3 dozen fresh oysters, shucked, with their liquor reserved
- Freshly ground black pepper
- Pinch of cayenne pepper

Miss Lewis remembers big barrels of fresh oysters arriving just before Christmas at the country store in Freetown. Oyster stew was often the highlight of her family's Christmas Eve supper (followed by pan-fried oysters for Christmas Day breakfast). Farther south, in Alabama, we feasted on oysters too, but since Hartford was only an hour's drive from the Gulf Coast, we'd get fresh Apalachicola oysters in the shell starting in October, all through the winter. Usually, my father would shuck them and we'd eat them raw, or my mother fried them (see page 91). I will never forget the first oyster stew I ever tasted made by a lawyer friend of my father's. It was just oysters, he said, a bit of onion, butter, and milk—and I was struck that something so simple could be so good.

This recipe is *really* easy if you have your fishmonger shuck the oysters (see box). The soup is light and rather delicate, only ever so slightly thickened with flour, and not too rich. It needs no garnish, for pools of butter float temptingly on the surface. Serve with a good green salad and Crispy Thin Biscuits (page 228) or Beni Wafers (page 227) for a satisfying winter or early-spring lunch or supper.

Melt 4 tablespoons of the butter over medium heat in a large nonreactive saucepan or Dutch oven. When the butter has melted and is bubbling, add the diced onion and salt and stir well to coat in the butter. Cook, slowly stirring often, until the onion is tender and translucent, about 10 minutes. Sprinkle the flour over, and cook for 2 minutes longer, stirring well to blend in the flour. Slowly whisk in the hot milk and heavy cream, along with the reserved oyster liquor. Gently bring just to a light simmer, stirring often to prevent scorching.

Heat the remaining 3 tablespoons of butter in a large nonstick skillet until hot and bubbling. Add the drained oysters in a single layer. Sprinkle on a little kosher salt and a few grindings of black pepper, and sauté the oysters just until they begin to curl around the edges and their gills are slightly exposed.

Transfer the entire contents of the pan to the Dutch oven. Add the cayenne, cover, and remove from the heat to mellow for 10 minutes. Heat again to just below a simmer. Taste carefully for seasoning, primarily salt, which brings out the flavor and sweetness of the oysters. Serve hot.

THE RIGHT OYSTERS FOR A SIMPLE STEW

For this stew you want oysters that are briny, not too big, and absolutely fresh. They should smell salty and sweet like the ocean, not at all fishy. Various Atlantic varieties would be suitable, such as Long Island Blue Points or Malpeques (originally from Prince Edward Island), which are farm-raised and widely available. Apalachicolas would be fine if you can get them, but you don't want to use Belons or other flat (and expensive) European types. You should depend on the advice of your fishmonger as to what's freshest. Unless you are an expert shucker, you should also ask him to shuck the oysters for you—saving all the juices, of course.

Tomato-Basil Soup

MAKES APPROXIMATELY 2 QUARTS OF SOUP, ENOUGH TO SERVE 6–8

- 5 tablespoons unsalted butter
- 2 medium-size yellow onions, sliced (about 1½ cups)
- 2 teaspoons kosher salt
- ½ teaspoon freshly ground black pepper
- 29 ounces San Marzano canned tomatoes, drained
- 3 tablespoons granulated sugar
- 4 cups water
- ½ cup loosely packed basil leaves

Canned tomatoes are rarely a substitute for fresh, vine-ripened tomatoes, but here they work very well. I use imported San Marzano tomatoes (the finest canned tomatoes available) in this recipe, which was inspired by a superb cold tomato soup that Miss Lewis makes in the summer from very ripe tomatoes. With San Marzanos, you can make soup year-round (it's delicious hot or cold), and you won't have to spend a lot of time carefully peeling soft, juicy tomatoes.

Careful seasoning is important here. Add the basil only after you've cooked the soup, to preserve the herb's fresh, bright flavor. And be sure to adjust salt, pepper, and sugar before serving, especially if the soup is cold. It might have been perfectly seasoned when warm, but can taste bland when chilled.

It's a very Southern touch to add a little sugar here—not enough to taste sweet, but just enough to balance the acid in the tomatoes.

Heat the butter in a nonreactive saucepan until foaming but not browned. Add the sliced onion, salt, and black pepper, stirring well to coat the onions with the butter and seasonings. Cook gently over medium heat, stirring often, for approximately 5 minutes, or until the onion is softened, before the pieces begin to brown. Add the tomatoes and sugar and stir well. Continue cooking approximately 5 minutes before adding the water. Then bring to a simmer and cook, stirring often, for 15 minutes.

Remove from heat and stir in the fresh basil leaves. Allow the soup to sit for 10 minutes before puréeing finely in a blender. Return the soup to the saucepan and taste for seasoning, adding more salt and pepper if needed, or even sugar if the tomatoes are especially acidic. Serve hot or cold.

Minted Soup of English Peas

MAKES 6–8 SERVINGS

- 4 tablespoons unsalted butter
- 1 large Vidalia onion, diced (about 1½ cups)
- ½ teaspoon dried thyme
- ½ teaspoon kosher salt
- 4 pounds fresh English peas in the shell (about 3 cups shelled)
- 3 cups Smoked Pork Stock (page 39)
- 3 cups Chicken Stock (page 33)
- 1 sprig of mint (about 12 young fresh leaves)
- 1 cup heavy cream
- Freshly ground black pepper
- 1–4 tablespoons unsalted butter, cold (optional)

Many Southerners—Miss Lewis and I among them—use the name "English peas" for sweet green peas of springtime, to distinguish them from "field peas," the starchy but delicious family of peas picked in the summer (box, page 68).

Where we live now in Georgia, English peas are one of the first spring vegetables from the garden. One year, blessed with a bushel of young, very sweet organic peas in mid-April, I made this soup for Miss Lewis's birthday. It shows off the peas' delicate flavor.

The flavor of the peas is by far the most important element of this soup, so be sure to sample a few before buying—they should be very fresh and truly sweet peas; bland and starchy ones won't improve with cooking. Similarly, try to find mild, young mint leaves (such as English mint or julep mint, rather than spearmint or peppermint) that will refresh and not overwhelm the pea flavor.

A combination of homemade Chicken and Pork Stock (both recipes in this chapter) makes the best base for this soup. If you don't have pork stock, however, you can add a light, smoky pork flavor by cooking a strip of good bacon along with the onions in the first step of the recipe. Remove the bacon after it has rendered its fat, and use all chicken stock in the recipe.

Melt the 4 tablespoons butter in a large nonreactive saucepan or Dutch oven over medium heat until bubbling but not colored. Add the diced onion, thyme, and salt. Cook, stirring often, until the onion is tender and translucent, about 5–8 minutes. Toss in the peas, and stir well to coat with the butter and seasonings. Cook for 5 minutes, stirring often. Add the pork and chicken stocks, and simmer until the peas are tender, about 15–20 minutes. Skim the soup as it simmers to remove any impurities. Sprinkle in the mint leaves and stir well.

Purée in batches in a blender until perfectly smooth. Return to the pot, and bring to a simmer before stirring in the heavy cream. Taste carefully for seasoning, and add a few grinds of black pepper. If the soup feels starchy on the tongue, whisk in the optional butter by tablespoons until the soup is velvety smooth.

Serve hot in preheated cups or bowls.

Purée of Yellow Crookneck Squash Soup

MAKES APPROXIMATELY 2½ QUARTS, ENOUGH TO SERVE 6–8

- 1½ pounds yellow crookneck squash
- 1 medium yellow onion
- 4 tablespoons (½ stick) unsalted butter
- Kosher salt and freshly ground black pepper
- ½ teaspoon dried thyme
- 4–6 cups Chicken Stock (page 33)
- 1 cup heavy cream
- Freshly grated nutmeg to taste

Like English peas and cucumbers, yellow crookneck squash appears very early in Southern gardens. In my part of the Deep South, one crookneck vine can produce so prodigiously all summer that many gardeners might toss half the fruit over the fence or onto the compost pile. Still, crooknecks are delicious, most often simply stewed as a side dish (see our version, page 139). They are also my favorite summer squash for soup, with a sweet and slightly nutty flavor that can be savored hot or cold. (You could use green or yellow zucchini or cymling here instead.)

This recipe follows the same principles as the soups with fall and winter vegetables, but as a summer dish, the soup should not be thick or heavy—you want the consistency of a light custard sauce. To concentrate the flavor, get rid of the seeds before cooking the vegetable flesh, but leave the skin on, because it gives a beautiful butter-yellow color to the purée. Also, don't be afraid to salt generously—especially if you are serving the soup cold—since the squash, onions, and cream have a sweetness that demands lots of seasoning. (We are generous with nutmeg in this soup, too.)

Wash the squash well in cold water. Do this carefully: they can sometimes be very sandy and gritty. Trim the squash at both ends, and quarter lengthwise. Use a paring knife or spoon to cut or scoop out the large section of seeds from each quarter. Discard the seeds, and slice the quartered squash into ⅓-inch slices. You should have approximately 7 cups of sliced squash.

Peel and finely chop the onion. Heat the butter in a heavy nonreactive Dutch oven or large saucepan over moderate heat until it is melted and foaming. Add the finely chopped onion and stir to coat well with the butter. Add the sliced squash and stir. Season with 2 teaspoons of kosher or sea salt, 3 or 4 grinds of the pepper mill, and the dried thyme. Stir again, reduce the heat to low, and cover the pot tightly. Cook for approximately 20 minutes, stirring often to ensure even cooking and no coloring or burning of the squash and onion. You only want to cook the squash until it becomes tender and releases its juices.

Meanwhile, in another pot, bring the chicken stock to a rolling boil, then remove from heat.

When the squash is tender, add the heated chicken stock, stir well, and simmer, partially covered, for 15–20 minutes.

Remove from heat and purée in a blender or food processor in batches until perfectly smooth. Strain through a fine sieve into another pot, and return to the stove. Heat the soup, uncovered, until it is at a low simmer. Stir in the heavy cream and 3 or 4 gratings of fresh nutmeg. Season with additional salt and grindings of black pepper if needed.

Serve hot or cold.

NOTE Do not be surprised by the seemingly large amount of salt that may be needed at the final seasoning to bring the soup to its full flavor. The onions, squash, and heavy cream are all sweet and may require heavier seasoning than you would expect. Taste and season carefully.

PURÉEING SOUPS

I think that a blender is the best tool for puréeing soup. But you have to be careful, because hot liquid expands and creates pressure, forcing the top off the blender and splattering hot soup all over the kitchen and you. So purée only in small batches (about a half-containerful at a time), and be sure to start at the lowest setting. It's better to remove the center portion of the lid, too, and use instead a clean thick towel to cover the opening.

Purée of Pumpkin Soup

MAKES ENOUGH TO SERVE 6–8

- 1 small pumpkin (about 4 pounds)
- 6 slices bacon, cut into ½-inch pieces
- 1 large onion, diced
- 2 small shallots, finely diced
- 1 small leek, thinly sliced
- 1 small clove garlic, crushed
- 1 teaspoon dried thyme
- 1 bay leaf
- 2 teaspoons salt
- ½ teaspoon freshly ground black pepper
- ½ teaspoon freshly grated nutmeg
- 6 cups Chicken Stock (page 33)
- ¼ cup cream sherry
- 1½ cups heavy cream or semi-ripened cheese as garnish (optional) (see box)

When I was a child, the big orange pumpkins sold around Hartford were just for carving jack-o'-lanterns at Halloween. I knew pumpkin was used for pie, too, but that came from a can. Miss Lewis, however, says that when she was growing up pumpkin was used as an autumn vegetable for savory and sweet cooking.

I began to view pumpkins differently after reading her recipe for pumpkin with sautéed onions (from *In Pursuit of Flavor*). And over the years we've prepared together pumpkin as a side or supper dish (like Pumpkin Roasted with Rosemary and Walnuts, page 180). In this recipe, pumpkin makes a fine soup. Roasting it first concentrates the flavor, adds a degree of caramelization, and also makes it much easier to separate the flesh from the skin.

Be sure to use "pie" or "sugar" pumpkins for this recipe—they are the small, elliptical ones that look like Cinderella's carriage. You could substitute butternut or another winter squash too, with satisfactory results, but by all means do not use the orange jack-o'-lantern gourds. They are nothing but water, seeds, and stringy fiber. If possible, prepare this pumpkin soup 1 or 2 days ahead of serving, and allow the flavors to deepen.

Preheat the oven to 350°F.

Split the pumpkin in half, and scrape out the seeds and fibers. Place the pumpkin halves, flesh side down, in a roasting pan lined with parchment or Silpat. Pour in ½ cup water and bake 1½ hours, until the skin is deeply browned and flesh tender when pierced with a knife. Remove from oven and let rest until cool enough to handle. Scoop out the flesh, discarding the skin.

Put the bacon in a cold heavy pot, and cook over medium-low heat until it is deeply browned and crisp. Using a slotted spoon, remove the browned bacon pieces. In the fat remaining in the pot, sauté the onion, shallots, leek, and garlic over medium-high heat, stirring often, for 5 minutes. Add the thyme, bay leaf, salt, pepper, nutmeg, and pumpkin. Stir well, and sauté 5 minutes longer, stirring often, and taking care not to burn the vegetables. Add the chicken stock, bring to a simmer, and cook, stirring occasionally, for 20 minutes.

Remove the bay leaf from the pot, and purée the soup in a blender or food processor until perfectly smooth. Return the soup to the Dutch oven, and bring to a simmer. Add the sherry, and simmer gently for 3–5 minutes. Add the cream if desired, and heat through. Taste very carefully for seasoning, and add more salt, pepper, or nutmeg as needed. Serve with fresh gratings of nutmeg and grindings of pepper over the soup, and sprinkle on the reserved bacon pieces. Serve as is or add more cream, using as much as you like, or with semi-ripened cheese added to the dish.

USING SEMI-RIPENED CHEESE AS A GARNISH FOR PUMPKIN SOUP

Not a strictly Southern garnish, but a delicious addition to pumpkin soup is a wedge of semi-ripened cheese such as St.-André, Rebluchon, or even Camembert, placed in the bottom of the soup dish. The hot soup quickly softens the cheese, which has a nutty quality, and adds an interesting element to the soup—an unexpected enrichment that varies with each spoonful. I first tried this when cooking a special cheese dinner for Jonathan White, founder of Egg Farm Dairy. A full-circle event, because Jonathan was an engineer experimenting with butter-making when he met Miss Lewis, and she lamented to him that there was no more cultured butter to be found, since dairies were using only sweet, non-cultured cream. He began researching the subject and eventually founded Egg Farm Dairy. His first, now defunct, marketed product: cultured butter.

Silken Turnip Soup

MAKES ABOUT 2½ QUARTS, SERVING 8

- 4 tablespoons (½ stick) unsalted butter
- 2 medium onions, thinly sliced
- 4 medium turnips, peeled and thinly sliced (1½ pounds)
- 1 small baking potato, peeled and thinly sliced (½ pound)
- 2 teaspoons kosher salt
- 5 cups Chicken Stock (page 33)
- ½ teaspoon freshly grated nutmeg
- ⅓ cup thinly sliced basil leaves, or whole globe basil leaves, as garnish (optional)

In my childhood, turnip greens were considered the important part of the vegetable. The "roots" were almost incidental—we'd just cube them and boil them along with the greens. I no more imagined cooking a soup from turnip roots than putting them in a chocolate cake.

So it was a surprise to visit Miss Lewis when she was the chef at Gage & Tollner in New York City and discover her Turnip Soup. Puréeing the soup in an electric blender makes a creamy-looking and creamy-tasting soup, without any cream or milk. This remains one of our favorites, the one we make for Thanksgiving dinner and other fall feasts.

Heat the butter in a large heavy pot until it is hot and foaming. Add the onions and cook over medium heat, stirring often, for 5 minutes. Add the sliced turnips, potato, and salt, and stir well. Cover the pot tightly, reduce the heat to very low, and cook this way, stirring occasionally, for 20 minutes, or until the vegetables are tender. Add the chicken stock and cook, partially covered, at a simmer for 10 minutes longer.

Remove the soup from the stove and purée in batches, using an electric blender, until it is perfectly smooth. Return the soup to the stove, add the freshly grated nutmeg, and gently simmer for 10 minutes. Taste carefully for seasoning, adding more salt or nutmeg as needed. If the soup is too thick for your taste, you may add a bit more chicken stock to thin. Serve the soup hot, garnished with a little of the basil sprinkled on top of each serving, if you like.

Cream of Rutabaga Soup

MAKES ENOUGH TO SERVE 8

- 4 tablespoons (1/2 stick) unsalted butter
- 2 medium-sized yellow onions, peeled and sliced thinly
- 1 large rutabaga (about 1 1/2–2 pounds), peeled, halved, and sliced 1/3 inch thick
- 1 teaspoon dried thyme
- Kosher salt and freshly ground black pepper to taste
- 7 cups Rich Chicken Broth (page 34)
- 1 cup heavy cream
- 1/4 teaspoon freshly grated nutmeg, or more to taste

Like many Southerners, I learned to love "rooterbagers" as a child. In fall, neighbors would give my mother brown grocery bags full of fresh rutabagas, and she would cook them like turnips—roots and greens together. And through the winter, she served us boiled and mashed rutabagas.

Unfortunately, many people aren't familiar with rutabagas at all (in some places they're known as "yellow turnips"), or regard them as a lowly vegetable. But here, rutabagas imbue the soup with a rich, deep flavor, beautiful ochre color, and velvety texture. It's good to make the soup a day ahead, so the flavors have time to develop. Since rutabagas are high in fiber and starch, the soup may thicken a little with resting; if so, just thin it with a bit of chicken stock. Fresh nutmeg, which goes in with the cream, enhances the flavors of the soup. And if you are especially fond of it—as we are—dust each serving of hot soup with a fresh grating of nutmeg at the very last moment.

Melt the butter in a large nonreactive pan over medium heat until it is foaming but not browned. Add the onions and cook, stirring often, until they become translucent without coloring. Add the sliced rutabaga, dried thyme, and 1 1/2 teaspoons kosher salt. Stir well to distribute the seasonings and coat the rutabaga with the butter. Reduce the heat to low and cook, covered, stirring often, until the rutabaga becomes tender, about 20 minutes. Add the chicken broth and simmer, uncovered, for approximately 20 minutes longer. Taste the broth, and add more salt if it is needed.

Purée the soup in a blender until it is silky smooth. Return it to the stove and bring to a gentle simmer. Stir in the cream, nutmeg, and a few grindings of black pepper. After adding the cream, cook only until the soup is heated through. Taste carefully for seasoning and adjust if needed with more salt or a few gratings and grindings of nutmeg and pepper. Serve hot in heated soup bowls.

Chestnut Soup

MAKES ENOUGH TO SERVE 6

- 2 tablespoons unsalted butter
- 3 tablespoons bacon fat (see box)
- 1 medium onion, peeled and coarsely chopped (about 1 cup)
- 2 small shallots, finely chopped
- 1 cooking apple, such as Winesap or Granny Smith, peeled, cored, and chopped
- 2 pounds fresh chestnuts, shelled and peeled (3½ cups) (see box)
- 1 teaspoon dried thyme
- 1 bay leaf
- 1 teaspoon salt
- ¼ teaspoon freshly grated nutmeg
- 1 cup semisweet white wine, such as Gewürztraminer
- 4 cups Chicken Stock (page 33)
- Freshly ground black pepper
- 3 tablespoons brandy (optional)
- 1 cup heavy cream

Miss Lewis, whose grandfather had a grove of chestnut trees in Freetown, has loved chestnuts and cooked with them since childhood. However—though there was a chestnut tree across from the house where I grew up—I never tasted chestnuts before I met her. In the years since, I've come to share her love for their unique earthy flavor and appeal, and we use chestnuts whenever they are in season.

I particularly like chestnuts in this suave and satiny soup, enhanced with apple, bacon, sweet wine, and enriched with cream. It makes a fine prelude to Roast Duckling Stuffed with Oysters and Red Rice (pages 106–107); equally good with a simple supper of raw oysters.

Melt the butter and bacon fat in a large saucepan or Dutch oven. Sauté the onion and shallots in the butter and rendered bacon fat for 5 minutes, or until translucent. Add the apple, chestnuts, thyme, bay leaf, salt, and nutmeg, and cook, stirring often, for 5 minutes. Add the wine and cook, tightly covered over low heat, for 15–20 minutes, until the chestnuts are very tender. Make sure that you stir often and that the chestnuts do not burn. Add the chicken stock and bring to a boil, then reduce to a low simmer and cook, uncovered, for 20 minutes.

Remove the bay leaf, and purée the soup in a blender or food processor until very smooth, then return to the pot. Taste carefully for seasoning and adjust with salt, freshly ground black pepper, and nutmeg as needed. Bring to a simmer, and add the optional brandy. Simmer for 3–5 minutes to cook off the raw alcohol, and stir in the heavy cream. Heat through, and taste again for seasoning. Serve hot.

BACON FAT

In our kitchen when I was growing up, there was an old coffeepot that my mother kept by the stove, into which she would always pour the leftover bacon fat. We used it in lots of ways—in cornbread, for greasing pans, for cooking vegetables and eggs and anything that needed that extra flavor. So, if you want the real Southern taste, be sure to save your bacon fat. If you store it in a closed container in the refrigerator, it will keep indefinitely. Should you not have any available when a recipe calls for it, just cook up some bacon. Five slices will yield about 1/4 cup fat.

HOW TO PEEL CHESTNUTS

Early in our acquaintanceship, I was desperately looking for several pounds of chestnuts to braise in a special duck dish at a *very* fancy dinner event in Florida. Without a word about what she was doing, Miss Lewis purchased the chestnuts in New York and had them shipped overnight to where I was cooking. Astonishingly, she'd shelled every nut, leaving me only the inner skin to remove. It was a true act of friendship but, I came to understand, not such a hardship for her: Miss Lewis loves to peel chestnuts as well as cook them.

Here's our method for shelling and peeling.

Cut off the outer shell with a sharp paring knife and, working in batches, drop 6–8 at a time into a pot of barely simmering water for 2 minutes. Remove with a slotted spoon, one at a time, and with the tip of a paring knife, dislodge and peel off the membrane.

Salads and Dressings

The salads and dressings in this chapter are not all unique to the South. But the versions here reflect, in distinct ways, Southern tastes, culinary customs, or ingredients. A few are historic: for instance, the Caveach is a recipe we discovered in a two-hundred-year-old cookbook, *The Kentucky Housewife.* But most of these salads come out of our personal experience.

If there is a "flavor" to this chapter, it would probably be "sweet and sharp." Vinegar and sugar—staples in Southern kitchens—were essential for pickles and preserves, and these became dominant seasonings in everyday salads and dressings.

You'll also find those "salads" that Southerners always serve at social events: holiday dinners, picnics, barbecues, wedding and anniversary receptions, and, perhaps most important, church suppers. In both black and white communities, potluck meals at church—called "covered-dish suppers" or, when held outside, "dinner on the grounds"—invariably included many different versions of Deviled Eggs, Potato Salad, and "congealed salads," like Tomato Aspic. Coleslaw is a must at picnics and fish fries; Chicken Salad, in fancy Toast Cups, is a tradition at wedding receptions and ladies' lunches.

Some of the salads are contemporary, incorporating the increasing variety of seasonal (and organic) produce now available in the South, as elsewhere, from farmers' markets and specialty growers. Many spicy greens like arugula, mâche, and watercress, as well as heirloom tomatoes and radishes, are not "new" vegetables but rediscovered traditional varieties. (In Jefferson's garden book, he refers to corn sallet, which is known as mâche today.) And Miss Lewis's family gathered wild watercress and field cresses (she calls them "cressies") as their first fresh vegetables for both salads and cooking.

As Southerners, neither of us generally considers (or eats) salads as a separate course. We tend to think of them as vegetable dishes—the table might be filled with as many as a dozen such dishes, including relishes and condiments. And, as with most vegetables, we eat them on the same plate with main courses, letting all the juices mingle together. We especially like the sweet-and-sour salad juices mixed with the drippings of grilled meat, poultry, and fish—and that's how we recommend you enjoy them.

Edna Lewis in front of one of the last remaining chimneys of Freetown

Boiled Dressing

MAKES ABOUT 2 CUPS

- 1 cup cider vinegar
- 3 egg yolks
- 2 teaspoons granulated sugar
- 1 teaspoon dry mustard
- 2 teaspoons all-purpose flour
- ⅛ teaspoon cayenne pepper
- 1 teaspoon salt
- ½ teaspoon freshly ground black pepper
- 1 tablespoon unsalted butter
- ⅓ cup heavy cream

Boiled dressing was for many generations a staple of the Southern table: a versatile, long-keeping condiment that served as a sauce for hot vegetables, as a spread, and as a salad dressing. Miss Lewis's mother used it as a base for potato salad and drizzled it over salad greens too. Unfortunately, you hardly see it anymore: in the age of refrigeration, boiled dressing has largely been replaced by mayonnaise. But it is worth turning back the clock to enjoy its creamy sweet-and-tart flavor in potato salad or coleslaw, in deviled eggs, on a cold pork sandwich, or over hot boiled potatoes.

Pour the vinegar into a saucepan and bring to a boil. Put the egg yolks in a small mixing bowl and stir in the sugar, mustard, flour, cayenne, salt, and freshly ground black pepper. Slowly stir the boiling vinegar into the egg-yolk mixture. Pour the dressing back into the saucepan and cook, stirring constantly, over medium heat until it thickens and begins to bubble. Remove from the heat and add the butter, stirring until it is melted and absorbed into the dressing. Stir in the cream, and cool completely. Cover and refrigerate. Will keep 2 weeks.

A NOTE ABOUT SALT

In the recipes in this book we call for two different kinds of salt: kosher salt and sea salt. In most of the baking recipes we specify kosher salt. It has a clean flavor and works well for baking. Also, because of the shape of the grain, it measures a little differently from very-fine-grained salts. So if you are using another salt in place of kosher, cut back a little on the amount and taste carefully for seasoning.

There are a couple of recipes where we specify sea salt. Usually these are recipes involving large amounts of mayonnaise. The reason is that kosher salt, because of its unique structure, can cause mayonnaise to break. Sea salt dissolves more quickly and thus eliminates that problem. If a recipe doesn't specify a particular salt, assume it means kosher salt. Although there are many different kinds of fancy salts out on the market these days, kosher salt remains our faithful standby.

Mayonnaise

MAKES APPROXIMATELY 1¾ CUPS

- 1 tablespoon cider vinegar
- 1 tablespoon freshly squeezed lemon juice
- 1 teaspoon sea salt
- 1 teaspoon dry mustard
- 2 egg yolks
- 1½ cups vegetable oil or light olive oil, or a combination
- 1 tablespoon hot water

Whenever MeMaw—my maternal grandmother—would prepare her potato salad for holiday dinners, she'd first make mayonnaise. Though we had plenty of jarred mayonnaise and Miracle Whip dressing on hand (and used them lavishly), I realized then that a special dish needs fresh mayonnaise, made from scratch.

The mayonnaise here is the one Miss Lewis and I use. It takes just a few minutes to make and lasts a week—but it's gone much sooner than that. There's a bowl of it on the table at almost every meal in the summer, to dress fresh tomatoes and other cold vegetables. With some simple additions, we often use it as a sauce on hot foods, like grilled fish or roasted vegetables, and as a spread on sandwiches. It's also the base dressing for the Chicken Salad, Deviled Eggs, and Potato Salad in this chapter, and for the essential Pimento Cheese you'll find on page 5.

Why is mayonnaise so important? It's the ingredient that pulls all the elements of a dish together—not just binding them physically, but unifying all the flavors as well.

Put the vinegar, lemon juice, salt, and mustard into a bowl, and whisk or stir until the salt and mustard are dissolved. Add the egg yolks, and beat until smooth. Add the oil drop by drop at first, and then in a slow, steady stream, whisking or stirring constantly until all of the oil has been incorporated and you have a very thick emulsion. Stir in the hot water until smooth.

Refrigerated, homemade mayonnaise will keep for up to 1 week.

Scott Peacock as chef for the governor of Georgia

Chicken Salad

MAKES ABOUT 5 CUPS, ENOUGH TO FILL APPROXIMATELY
3½ DOZEN TOAST CUPS OR TO SERVE 6–8 AS A SALAD

- 6 cups Chicken Stock (page 33) or lightly salted water
- 2 whole chicken breasts, boneless, with skin
- 1 stalk celery, including some tender celery leaves, finely diced (½ cup)
- 3 Jerusalem artichokes, peeled and finely diced (⅓ cup) (optional)
- 1 tablespoon finely chopped chervil
- 1 tablespoon finely snipped chives
- 2 teaspoons finely chopped tarragon
- 2 teaspoons finely chopped parsley
- ½ teaspoon sea salt
- ½ teaspoon freshly ground black pepper
- 1 cup homemade Mayonnaise (page 57), or more to taste
- A few drops freshly squeezed lemon juice
- Additional chervil sprigs or snipped chives for garnish

Chicken salad, in my childhood, was both an everyday and a special-occasion food. My mother kept a bowl on hand in the refrigerator for making lunch sandwiches—just chunks of cooked chicken mixed with mayonnaise, which I still think delicious. At church receptions, or for weddings and anniversaries, chicken salad was "party food," often served in Toast Cups, crisp little shells fashioned from white bread. The salad can, of course, be served just with salad greens or in a sandwich.

Our chicken salad is good for all occasions: lunchboxes, ladies' luncheons, picnics, and our open house on Sunday afternoon, for which I make Toast Cups (see box). We use gently poached chicken breasts for their tender, buttery quality, and sweet herbs—tarragon and chervil—as essential seasonings. Chervil, in particular, must be very fresh, preferably just picked, to have any flavor: we keep a pot growing on our windowsill. The addition of Jerusalem artichokes is Miss Lewis's touch. They're not always available but they add a special sweetness and pleasing crunch to the salad when used.

Pour the chicken stock or lightly salted water into a saucepan with a tight-fitting lid. Bring to a boil and remove from heat. Immediately add the chicken breasts, taking care that they are fully submerged, then cover tightly with the lid and let stand off heat for 20 minutes. Check the chicken breasts to be sure they are cooked through by cutting into the thickest part of the breast with a sharp knife. If the cut part is pink, cover the pan and cook over very low heat for 3–5 minutes.

Remove the cooked chicken from the pan and allow to cool completely—be sure to save the stock. When the chicken has cooled, remove the skin and trim any remaining bits of fat or cartilage from the breasts. Cut the chicken into a ⅓-inch dice and put into a mixing bowl. Add the celery, optional Jerusalem artichokes, the herbs, salt, and freshly ground pepper. Mix well to distribute the herbs and seasonings evenly. Blend in the mayonnaise and lemon juice, and taste carefully for seasoning. Add more salt, pepper, or lemon juice if needed. If using toast cups, fill each one to heaping with chicken salad, and garnish by sprinkling with the chervil sprigs or snipped chives. Or serve on a bed of salad greens.

If not using immediately, refrigerate until needed, for up to 2 days.

TOAST CUPS ON A SUNDAY AFTERNOON

Miss Lewis has always loved having a Sunday-afternoon open house, with friends and sometimes strangers stopping by. In the 1940s and '50s, her bohemian set in New York would get together to talk or read poetry, and munch chicken salad in buttery toast cups and other delicious treats. We've revived the custom now in Atlanta—and here's how we make those toast cups.

You'll need slices of white bread, soft butter, and mini-muffin tins (or a regular muffin tin for larger cups). Cut the crusts off the bread and, using a rolling pin, compress and slightly stretch each slice. With a cookie or pastry cutter, cut out rounds of bread, each big enough to line the bottom and sides of a single muffin mold. Butter both sides of the bread circles, and press them into the molds. Bake in the tins in a 375°F oven until the toast cups are golden. Remove them from the tins, and fill with chicken salad (or our Shrimp and Jerusalem Artichoke Salad, page 76, chopped up finely).

Old-Fashioned Dressing

MAKES APPROXIMATELY 1/3 CUP

- 2 tablespoons granulated sugar
- 1 teaspoon salt
- 1/4 teaspoon freshly ground black pepper
- 1/4 cup cider vinegar
- 2 tablespoons peanut or vegetable oil

In the South, there is a distinct taste for sweet-and-sour combinations. Miss Lewis in Virginia, and I in Alabama, grew up with this simple dressing. In my house, it was mixed every day in summer for cucumber salads, with no oil added at all. Here I've added a small amount of oil, which helps coat leafy greens: it's excellent on tender lettuces like Black-Seeded Simpson, limestone, and Bibb. White vinegar is sometimes used in old-fashioned dressings, but I much prefer cider vinegar for its depth of flavor.

Put the sugar, salt, freshly ground black pepper, and vinegar in a clean pint jar. Screw the lid on tight, and shake well until the sugar and salt are dissolved. Add the oil, and shake vigorously to emulsify. Can be made ahead and left in a cool, dark place for up to 2 weeks. Be sure to shake well again before using.

Coleslaw

MAKES ENOUGH TO SERVE 6

THE SLAW

- 1 large head green cabbage, cored and very finely shredded
- 3 kirby cucumbers, peeled, seeded, and sliced paper-thin
- 3 tablespoons kosher salt

THE DRESSING

- ½ cup white vinegar
- ½ cup granulated sugar
- ½ teaspoon salt
- 1 tablespoon Dijon mustard
- ¼ cup vegetable oil
- ¼ cup heavy cream
- 2 tablespoons sour cream
- Salt and freshly ground pepper to taste

I had to make coleslaw for the first time in my life—and lots of it—when I became chef for the governor of Georgia in the late 1980s. Barbecues are big in Southern politics, and if you're doing barbecue, you must have coleslaw.

Here is the coleslaw I developed then and have made at home and in restaurants where I've cooked ever since. I based it on an unusually fine-textured sweet-and-sour slaw made by a cook friend in Tallahassee. The key to its texture is salting, resting, and squeezing the shredded cabbage to get rid of excess liquid. Then you toss the shreds with a hot vinegar-sugar syrup, which softens and flavors them, and fold in sweet and sour creams. Although I've sometimes had to hand-squeeze nearly 100 pounds of cabbage for big parties, it's always worth the effort. In addition to barbecue, this is delicious with fried foods, like our fish, soft-shell crab, or chicken (see Chapter IV).

You can make the slaw just a few hours before serving, but it is even better if you start a couple days ahead: the salted cabbage can drain over one night, then steep in the sweet-sour dressing the next, before you mix in the creams.

Mix together the shredded cabbage and sliced cucumber in a large colander. Toss well with the 3 tablespoons salt, and leave to wilt for 20 minutes. Squeeze the slaw firmly by handfuls to extract as much liquid as possible, then use your fingers to toss and loosen the squeezed slaw. Toss it into a large bowl.

To make the dressing: Bring the vinegar, sugar, and salt to a boil in a small saucepan over medium heat, stirring just until the sugar is dissolved. Boil for 3 minutes, and whisk in the Dijon mustard and oil. Pour the hot dressing over the reserved slaw, and stir well to blend. Allow to cool slightly before stirring in the heavy cream and sour cream. Taste carefully for seasoning, and add salt and freshly ground black pepper to taste as needed. Serve cold or at room temperature.

Tomato Aspic

MAKES EIGHT 4-OUNCE MOLDS OR ONE 5-CUP MOLD, ENOUGH TO SERVE 8

THE JUICE

6–8 medium very ripe tomatoes, peeled and roughly chopped (4 cups)

1 medium onion, finely chopped (1 cup)

1 small stalk celery, preferably with some celery leaves, finely chopped (1 cup)

1 small clove garlic, smashed

3 bay leaves

5 whole peppercorns

5 whole cloves

3 teaspoons kosher salt

3 cups water

THE SEASONINGS

1 tablespoon granulated sugar

1 tablespoon cider vinegar

1 tablespoon freshly squeezed lemon juice

1 teaspoon kosher salt, or more to taste

2 envelopes (2 tablespoons) unflavored gelatin

¼ cup cold water

Tomato aspic should be light and delicate. But all too often, it is rubbery, a solidly congealed ring of canned tomato juice, with assorted items like shredded carrots, chopped celery, or hard-boiled eggs suspended inside. Typically served with a dollop of commercial mayonnaise, it's a dish to ignore or endure as politely as possible.

But the version we give you here is refreshing and full of tomato flavor. Miss Lewis and I developed it during a week of cooking in my mother's kitchen in Alabama. We had an abundance of juicy tomatoes supplied by my farmer uncles, and Miss Lewis—who loves tomatoes—was in heaven. She insisted we make our aspic from the fresh tomatoes (and nothing else), carefully seasoned, lightly jelled, and set in individual molds.

The aspics make a lovely appetizer on their own or with Deviled Eggs (page 65) or Shrimp and Jerusalem Artichoke Salad (page 76). But they can also be served on a platter, along with other cold summer vegetables. Homemade Mayonnaise (page 57) is a traditional accompaniment, but the aspic is so flavorful you don't need it. (You can also make one large mold, by increasing the gelatin, as detailed in the recipe.)

Put the ingredients for making the juice in a nonreactive saucepan and bring to a simmer, uncovered, over moderate heat. Simmer gently for 20–30 minutes, until the tomatoes have broken down and given up their juice. Take care not to cook longer than necessary; you want to maintain as fresh a flavor as possible. When the tomatoes have finished cooking, carefully strain them through a fine-meshed strainer, pressing gently with a wooden spoon or spatula to extract all of the juice from the vegetables but without forcing vegetable pulp through. Measure the juice; you should have approximately 4½ cups of liquid, though a little more or less will not make much difference.

Flavor the juice with the sugar, vinegar, lemon juice, and salt. Taste carefully. Depending on their ripeness and flavor, tomatoes can vary greatly in sweetness and acidity. Also, remember that aspic is a dish served cold, and cold temperature will dull the seasoning slightly. When it is well seasoned, return the flavored juice to the stove and bring back to a gentle simmer.

Mix the gelatin with the water until softened. Add the softened gelatin to the simmering liquid, and stir well for 2–3 minutes to dissolve the gelatin completely. Remove from the heat, and set the pan in a bowl of ice water, stirring constantly until the liquid chills and begins to thicken. This is an important step—otherwise your aspic may have an uneven color and texture.

When it is properly cooled, pour the aspic into lightly oiled custard cups or small molds. Cover and refrigerate several hours or overnight before serving. To unmold, run the tip of a sharp knife around the edge of the aspic and invert onto a serving dish. If the aspic is stubborn about releasing, placing a hot, damp cloth over the bottoms of the molds for a few moments should do the trick.

NOTE This recipe makes an aspic that is delicately jelled and is best suited to small molds. If you wish to make your aspic in a single larger mold, increase the amount of gelatin by ½–1 tablespoon. You will have an aspic that is firm enough to unmold and maintain its shape.

Jackson's Store, Lahore, Virginia, 1977

Potato Salad

MAKES 10–12 SERVINGS

- 5 large all-purpose potatoes
- 3 tablespoons cider vinegar
- 2 teaspoons sea salt
- 6–8 grinds of black pepper
- ½ cup finely chopped onion
- 6 hard-boiled egg yolks, pushed through a fine sieve
- 1½–2 cups homemade Mayonnaise (page 57)

Potato salad is highly personal. At a Southern church supper, there might well be a half-dozen different potato salads, reflecting the tastes of various cooks—and a bit of competitive spirit. There'd be a salad sprinkled with paprika; another garnished with whole deviled eggs, with more deviled eggs folded in. One salad would be studded with chopped onions and green peppers; another with chopped olives; sweet-pickle relish folded into a third. And the potatoes would be sliced, diced, or stirred into a chunky mash.

Here's the potato salad that we like the most, one in which you really taste potato and good mayonnaise, with a slight embellishment of finely chopped onions. We enrich homemade mayonnaise with sieved egg yolks—an idea we got from an old Mississippi cookbook. We put the chopped onions in the bottom of the bowl and dump the hot potatoes over them, which slightly cooks and softens them—a trick my grandmother MeMaw used for chopped green peppers in her potato salad.

The salad is best eaten the day it is made, as the onions get stronger over time. Since the potatoes absorb mayonnaise and seasonings while they cool, you want to mix in more mayonnaise at the beginning than might seem necessary. Taste and adjust the seasonings just before serving too.

This makes a large batch, so just cut the quantities in half if you want less.

Scrub the potatoes thoroughly, and put them in a pot. Cover well with cold water, and cook over moderate heat, partially covered, until they are tender when pierced with a knife but not bursting and mushy. Drain, and set aside to cool slightly. When slightly cooled, peel the potatoes and cut into ½-inch cubes. You should have about 8 cups.

Toss the cubed potatoes into a large mixing bowl. Sprinkle the cider vinegar, salt, black pepper, and chopped onion over them. Using two large forks or spoons, gently toss the potatoes to distribute and mix in the seasonings. In a separate mixing bowl, stir together the sieved egg yolks and 1½ cups of the mayonnaise. Add this to the potatoes and carefully mix in as before. Add more mayonnaise if needed, and taste carefully for salt and pepper.

Deviled Eggs

MAKES 12 EGGS

1 dozen large eggs
1 tablespoon kosher salt
1½ tablespoons cider vinegar
½ teaspoon sea salt, or more to taste
1 teaspoon granulated sugar
½ cup homemade Mayonnaise (page 57)
2 tablespoons heavy cream
2 teaspoons finely chopped chives, chervil, or tarragon, or a mixture of 2 or more (optional)

I have always adored deviled eggs. The ones I helped my mother and grandmother prepare, with sweet-pickle relish (a Peacock family favorite) mashed into the yolks, were served at holiday meals on a glass plate with a carrying handle, each paprika-sprinkled oval resting in a hollow.

But Miss Lewis shook things up when she introduced me to her eggs. She sliced the top third off each egg, leaving a small upright cup which she then filled with a suave mixture of sieved egg yolks, homemade mayonnaise, cream, sugar, and vinegar. Pure and undoctored compared with the deviled eggs of my childhood, with an unexpected sweetness, they're now my favorites.

I've given a method here for hard-cooking eggs: letting them sit in boiled water (off the heat) for exactly 10 minutes. They reach the perfect consistency for deviled eggs and egg salad, just this side of "hard-boiled," with yolks that are soft and waxy rather than dry and crumbly. It is important to stop the cooking with cold water right at the 10-minute mark, and to crack the shells immediately to release the sulfur that can discolor the yolks. Leave the eggs in the water to chill—and it's easier to peel them in the water too.

Put the eggs in a large saucepan, and pour in enough water to cover them by 2 inches. Add to the water 1 tablespoon salt and 1 tablespoon of the vinegar. Bring the water and eggs to a hard boil over high heat. Immediately remove them from the heat and cover. Let sit covered for exactly 10 minutes. Pour off the hot water, and immediately run cool tap water over the eggs to cool them and stop the cooking. Shake the pan as you do so, to crack the eggshells gently all over.

When cool enough to handle, carefully peel the eggs. Once the eggs are peeled, slice the top third of the egg off crosswise, and with a spoon remove the yolks from each egg, leaving the egg "cups." Using a wooden spoon or spatula, rub the egg yolks through a fine sieve into a mixing bowl. Blend in the remaining vinegar, sea salt, sugar, and mayonnaise until the mixture is very smooth. Blend in the heavy cream. Taste carefully for seasoning, adding more salt, vinegar, or sugar if needed. If the filling mixture is too dry, you may add a bit more mayonnaise or heavy cream.

Use a teaspoon or pastry bag to fill the egg cups. Arrange the filled eggs on a plate, and sprinkle, if desired, with the finely chopped herbs on top.

Salad of Cucumber and Radishes

MAKES ENOUGH TO SERVE 6 AS A SMALL SALAD BEFORE, WITH, OR AFTER THE ENTRÉE, OR 4 AS A HEARTIER DISH

THE DRESSING

- 2 tablespoons granulated sugar
- 1 teaspoon salt
- ½ teaspoon freshly ground black pepper
- 1 heaping teaspoon Dijon mustard
- 2 tablespoons cider vinegar
- ¼ cup extra-virgin olive oil

THE SALAD

- 3 large red-meat radishes
- 4 icicle or Easter-egg radishes
- 4 large kirby or pickling-variety cucumbers
- 2 bunches arugula, washed and picked (box, page 71)
- 2 bunches watercress, washed and picked (box, page 71)
- Salt and freshly ground pepper to taste

These days, organic farmers and farmers' markets throughout the South are making available an unprecedented array of traditional and heirloom vegetables. By following the maxim "What grows together, goes together," we have lots of possibilities for delicious seasonal combinations. As an example, here's a late-spring salad consisting of two different heirloom radishes, two types of tender greens, and kirby cucumbers.

The individuality of vegetable varieties become clear when you taste them together. Both of these radishes have distinct spiciness and texture, as well as a unique shape, size, and color. Red-meat radishes are pale green outside, snow white inside with a batiklike burst of purplish red. Icicle radishes are elongated like carrots; small Easter-egg radishes come in a range of red and purple hues. Even if you can't find these varieties in your market and use nothing but regular bunch radishes, this will be a lovely salad. The cucumbers cool the spicy radish and peppery greens, and the sweet mustardy dressing brings everything together.

Make the dressing: Put the sugar, salt, pepper, mustard, and cider vinegar in a nonreactive mixing bowl, and stir until the sugar and salt are dissolved. Slowly whisk the olive oil in.

Using a very sharp knife, slice the radishes as thinly as you can into rounds. Trim the ends of the cucumbers, and slice them thinly lengthwise into ribbons. Soak the radish slices and cucumber in ice water for 10 minutes to crisp them. Remove and blot dry with paper toweling. Toss in a large bowl with the arugula, watercress, and dressing. Season carefully with salt and pepper. Serve immediately.

Red Onion, Cucumber, and Tomato Salad

SERVES 4–6

- 1 large red onion, peeled and sliced into ½-inch wedges
- 4 kirby cucumbers, peeled and sliced into ⅓-inch rounds
- 3 large vine-ripe tomatoes, cored and sliced into ½-inch wedges
- ½ teaspoon salt, plus more for soaking onion
- ½ teaspoon freshly ground black pepper
- ¾ cup cider vinegar
- 6 tablespoons granulated sugar
- 2 tablespoons vegetable oil
- 1 tablespoon finely snipped parsley

This trio of summer vegetables is delicious when tossed together and chilled in an old-fashioned sugar-vinegar dressing. A common dish in my childhood, it is served today as my mother did, as a cold vegetable dish on the table rather than as a separate salad. (I love to put it on the same plate with grilled food, letting the juices run together.)

The salad is simple, fast, and convenient to make in advance. Soaking the onions first in salted water makes them milder and more digestible. You can then dress the vegetables and refrigerate them, from 30 minutes up to several hours. If your tomatoes are very ripe, though, add them only at the last, so they don't get mushy.

Soak the red-onion wedges in a small bowl of salted ice water for 20 minutes, then drain well.

Put the chilled onion wedges, sliced cucumbers, and tomato wedges in a large bowl, and season generously with salt and freshly ground pepper. Whisk together in a small bowl the vinegar, sugar, ½ teaspoon salt, ½ teaspoon freshly ground pepper, and vegetable oil until the sugar is completely dissolved. Pour the dressing over the vegetables. Toss the salad well, and refrigerate for 30 minutes. Taste carefully for seasoning, adjusting as needed, and add the snipped parsley before serving.

FIELD PEAS

Field peas are a distinct but sometimes confusing family of legumes, with many varieties known by different names in different regions of the South. Like sweet green peas (which we call "English peas"), field peas are picked in the pod, then taken out and cooked fresh. But they are starchy rather than sweet, and are harvested in summer rather than spring.

Probably the best-known type of field pea is the black-eyed pea. Though most non-Southerners know it as a dried pea, it is easy to find fresh black-eyed peas in summer in most parts of the South. Where I come from, we also have pink-eyed peas, silver Crowder peas, purple Crowder peas, white peas (also known as lady peas), zipper peas, and others. And—even though it is called a bean rather than a pea—the "butter bean" is one of my very favorite field peas.

Clockwise from top: purple Crowders, butter beans, white acre or "lady" peas, pink-eyed peas, speckled butter beans, black-eyed peas

Though you won't come upon this variety everywhere, not even in all parts of the South, you should find one or two kinds of fresh field peas at farmers' markets, most commonly black-eyed and Crowder peas. Be aware that varietal names are colloquial and may well be different from those I use. Even the generic name changes: in California, these legumes are called "shell peas," and some folks use the term "cow peas."

As an instance of how varied Southern cooking traditions are, Miss Lewis never knew of any "field pea" other than black-eyed peas and as a child rarely ate them, fresh or dried. They were grown primarily as a cover crop to replenish the nitrogen in the cornfields.

Tomato–Field Pea Salad with Garlic Mayonnaise

MAKES ENOUGH TO SERVE 6

- 1¼ cups mixed field peas and beans, at least 3 varieties if possible
- Salt and freshly ground black pepper to taste
- 4 vine-ripe tomatoes, cut into ½-inch wedges

THE DRESSING

- 1 tablespoon plus 1½ teaspoons sherry vinegar
- 1 tablespoon plus 1½ teaspoons red-wine vinegar
- 1 teaspoon salt
- ¼ teaspoon freshly ground black pepper
- 1 teaspoon Dijon mustard
- 1 tablespoon finely chopped shallot
- ½ cup plus 1 tablespoon extra-virgin olive oil

THE GARLIC SAUCE

- 1 small clove garlic, rubbed to a paste with a pinch of sea salt
- ½ cup homemade Mayonnaise (page 57)
- 1–2 tablespoons boiling water, if needed

In southern Alabama, field peas are one of the most important fresh vegetables of summer. And despite the heat, we ate them every day in season, cooked until tender and served hot (as we do with Lady Peas, page 150, and Butter Beans, page 178). But this salad—inspired by one I had at Chez Panisse, prepared by a chef from South Carolina—uses field peas in a distinctly different way. They're blanched briefly, chilled, tossed with heirloom tomatoes, dressed with a vinaigrette, and drizzled with a garlicky mayonnaise. Nontraditional but delicious, it is a salad that makes a fine light meal by itself. Also, as with other saucy salads, it's great on a plate with grilled meat or fish, such as Grilled/Broiled Quail or Squab (pages 108–109).

Try to use at least three varieties of field peas in the salad (see box), to appreciate their different flavors, textures, shapes, and colors. If you are fortunate enough to have several varieties of tomatoes, such as heirloom Cherokees, Brandywines, and Green Zebras, use them all. Cherry tomatoes are fine too, either whole or sliced in half.

Boil the mixed peas and beans in a large pot of boiling salted water until tender but al dente, about 8 minutes. Drain immediately, and refresh in a bowl of salted ice water. As soon as the peas are chilled, drain well and put them into a bowl with the tomato wedges.

Make the dressing: Put the sherry and red-wine vinegars, the salt, freshly ground black pepper, mustard, and shallot into a small nonreactive mixing bowl. Stir until the salt is completely dissolved, and slowly whisk in the extra-virgin olive oil. Taste for seasoning, and adjust with salt and freshly ground black pepper as needed.

Make the garlic sauce: Stir the garlic into the mayonnaise, and slowly stir in a little boiling water until the sauce is thinned to a drizzling consistency. Refrigerate until needed.

When you are ready to serve, season the peas and tomatoes with salt and freshly ground black pepper to taste. Pour enough of the dressing over the vegetables to coat them, and gently toss to mix the salad. Drizzle the garlic sauce generously over the salad, and serve, passing additional garlic sauce with the salad.

Sliced Cucumbers Dressed with Vinegar and Sugar

MAKES ENOUGH TO SERVE 6–8

- 1 cup cider vinegar
- ½ cup granulated sugar
- ½ teaspoon salt
- ½ teaspoon freshly ground black pepper
- 4 kirby cucumbers, peeled if waxed and thinly sliced (about 4 cups)

Cucumber slices soaked in this vinegar dressing make a crunchy, fresh relish that is common throughout the South. Starting in early May, my mother would prepare a dish of cukes, picked right outside the kitchen door, to go with lunch, every day all through summer. She'd serve the cucumbers after just a few minutes of marinating, but I like them better after they've been chilled in the dressing for at least an hour. They are great with sandwiches, cold vegetables, grilled meats—indeed, at almost any summer meal.

Put the vinegar, sugar, salt, and pepper in a nonreactive mixing bowl, and stir until the sugar is dissolved. Add the cucumber slices, and toss well to mix. Cover, and chill for 1 hour. Taste carefully, and adjust seasoning if needed. Serve very cold.

WASHING SALAD GREENS

For crisp, flavorful salads, wash the greens using this two-bath method. It rinses away dirt while invigorating and firming the leaves: the first immersion, in salt water, draws liquid out of the plant cells, and the second, ice-water bath crisps them. This technique is especially effective for arugula, watercress, endive, and other tender greens that easily wilt, but I use it for every kind of lettuce as well.

- Set up two baths, each containing at least 1½ gallons of cold water, using a double sink or two large bowls, basins, or pots.
- Add salt to one bath: 1 tablespoon salt for each gallon of water. Add enough ice to the second bath to chill the water thoroughly.
- Separate whole lettuce leaves from the head; remove tough stems from watercress and other small-leaved greens.
- Working in batches that don't crowd the water baths, carefully submerge greens in the salt water, and gently tumble and rinse them for 30 seconds to 1 minute (you will feel them get limp).
- Lift the greens from the bath, draining off water through your fingers, then immerse and tumble them in the ice-water bath for up to a minute.
- Lift greens, and transfer to a salad spinner; pack loosely, no more than half full. Rotate the spinner gently and slowly to dry the leaves; too-vigorous spinning can crush them.
- To store clean greens, either lay them on paper towel or kitchen towel and roll up gently, then store in a plastic bag, or use a large, covered plastic salad-keeper, first lining the bottom with a layer of paper towel.

Caveach: A Cold Fish Salad

MAKES ENOUGH TO SERVE 6–8

1½ pounds mackerel fillets, skin on, completely deboned (or other fish; see headnote)
1 teaspoon salt
½ teaspoon freshly ground black pepper
¾ cup vegetable or olive oil
¾ cup all-purpose flour

THE DRESSING

⅓ cup olive oil
2 tablespoons finely chopped garlic
1 shallot, sliced very thinly into rings
½ cup freshly squeezed lime juice
⅓ cup freshly squeezed lemon juice
⅓ cup red-wine vinegar
¼ cup freshly squeezed orange juice
2½ teaspoons salt
½ teaspoon freshly ground black pepper

This is a fresh and fast version of a very old method for pickled fish, which we discovered in two nineteenth-century Southern cookbooks. In *The Carolina Housewife,* we found a recipe for caveach of mackerel, and in *The Kentucky Housewife,* a similar caveach using catfish. We guess (but can't be sure) that "caveach" was a corruption of *escabeche,* the Spanish word for "pickle" (and pickled fish specifically). Also, we can't be sure that "caveach" was ever very popular, since the various *Housewife* cookbooks, starting with *The Virginia Housewife* in 1808, often included European recipes that no one necessarily prepared. Neither of us had ever encountered any such dish anywhere in the South.

Nevertheless, the original caveach inspired this "salad" of marinated fried fish and crunchy vegetables. Citrusy and piquant, it makes a refreshing first course or cocktail hors d'oeuvre, especially in summer. You can use almost any kind of fish fillet, including catfish, bluefish, or firm-fleshed snapper, tuna, or grouper. After the fillets are fried, they marinate in a vinegary, spicy dressing and are ready to serve in a couple of hours—but are even better the next day.

Cut the mackerel fillets crosswise into 2-inch pieces, and season with the salt and freshly ground black pepper. Heat the oil in a skillet until very hot but not smoking. Dredge the pieces of mackerel in the flour, and carefully pat gently to remove any excess before adding to the hot oil, skin side up. Cook the fish until golden brown, about 2–3 minutes, then turn and cook for 1 minute longer, skin side down. Transfer the fish to a cooling rack or crumpled paper towels and allow to cool. Meanwhile, prepare the dressing and garnishes.

Make the dressing: Gently heat the olive oil in a nonreactive saucepan, then add the chopped garlic and shallot. Cook the garlic and shallot for about 1 minute, taking care that neither browns, then add the lime juice, lemon juice, red-wine vinegar, orange juice, and the salt and pepper. Bring to a full boil and remove from heat.

THE GARNISH

2 tablespoons capers, rinsed

2 hot peppers (fingerling, jalapeño, Scotch bonnet, etc.), or more to taste, finely chopped

3 green onions or scallions, trimmed and thinly sliced

2 tablespoons chopped parsley

1 large red onion, sliced into rings 1/3 inch thick

3/4 cup coarsely chopped celery

1 cup whole olives, black or green

Arrange the cooked mackerel in a single layer, skin side up, in a nonreactive baking dish or casserole that will just hold the pieces. Scatter over the fish the capers, chopped hot peppers, green onions, parsley, red onion, celery, and olives, then pour the hot pickle over all.

If serving the same day, allow the fish to marinate for 2–3 hours at room temperature. Otherwise, refrigerate and serve within 2–3 days. May be served cold or at room temperature.

Wilted Salad

MAKES ENOUGH TO SERVE 4–6

- 6 slices bacon
- 1 cup cider vinegar
- ⅓ cup granulated sugar
- 1 teaspoon salt
- ½ teaspoon freshly ground black pepper
- 8 cups crisp, flavorful salad greens, such as romaine, watercress, Bibb, or Boston lettuce, or a mixture of the above, washed and thoroughly dried and torn in pieces
- 1 bunch arugula, prepared as above (optional)
- 4 spring onions or scallions, washed, trimmed, and very thinly sliced
- 1 tablespoon finely snipped chives
- 1 tablespoon finely chopped parsley
- Additional salt and freshly ground black pepper to taste

Wilted salad is one of those dishes about which Southerners wax nostalgic, perhaps because it was traditionally a highly seasonal dish, made with early-spring salad greens. These would be "wilted" under a hot dressing of bacon fat, vinegar, and sugar, with crumbled bacon tossed in. In Miss Lewis's family, it was almost a ritual to make wilted salad with the first leaves of Black-Seeded Simpson lettuce and wild watercress. My mother made it, too, during the few weeks when we had Bibb lettuce, before it bolted. Today, I like to wilt a mix of two or three mild lettuces, plus arugula for a kick. The salad makes a fine separate course, but is also wonderful on a plate with grilled meat or fish.

Cook the bacon in a frying pan until crisp. Remove the bacon from the pan, and set aside. Add the vinegar, sugar, salt, and black pepper to the bacon fat left in the frying pan. Stir well to blend, and bring to a vigorous boil.

While the dressing is coming to a boil, break the salad greens into large pieces and put them into a large stainless-steel or ceramic bowl. Add the optional arugula, sliced onions, chives, and parsley, and crumble the reserved bacon over the greens. Season with additional salt and a few grinds of black pepper. Toss gently, then pour the boiling dressing over. Toss well, and season to taste with more salt and grindings of black pepper. Serve at once.

BLT Salad

MAKES ENOUGH TO SERVE 4

- 1 head iceberg lettuce
- 8 slices good-quality bacon
- 4 slices White Loaf Bread (pages 202–203)
- 4 large, perfectly ripe tomatoes, cored and cut into 1-inch pieces
- Kosher salt and freshly ground black pepper
- 1/3–1/2 cup Mayonnaise (page 57)

During tomato season in Alabama, when we had really ripe tomatoes from my mother's garden, she would make this delicious salad for my sister and me. Though it didn't have a name, we considered the crisp cold lettuce, crisp warm bacon, and crunchy toast mixed with juicy tomatoes and mayonnaise a great treat.

Years later, as a restaurant chef, I prepared this as a summertime special and dubbed it the "BLT Salad." Customers loved it, too, and many protested when I took it off the menu after good tomatoes went out of season.

Cut the head of lettuce in half and remove the core. Put the halves in a bowl of ice water to wash and chill. Drain well, and tear into 1-inch pieces. Roll the pieces in paper toweling or spin gently in a salad spinner to remove all water. Store in the refrigerator until ready to use.

Cook the bacon in a skillet or in the oven until crisp, and simultaneously toast the bread.

Put the torn lettuce in a large bowl along with the cut tomato pieces. Crumble the bacon and add to the bowl. Cut the toast into 1-inch squares and add. Toss and season the salad liberally with kosher salt and freshly ground black pepper. Add enough mayonnaise to dress the salad generously, and serve immediately.

Shrimp and Jerusalem Artichoke Salad

MAKES ENOUGH TO SERVE 4 AS A LUNCHEON COURSE, 6 AS A FIRST COURSE

THE SHRIMP

3 tablespoons pickling spice or crab and/or shrimp boil

1/4 cup cider vinegar

4 tablespoons kosher salt

1 1/2 pounds large shrimp (21–25 per pound), peeled and deveined

THE SALAD

1 large stalk celery, tender green leaves included, chopped (1/2 cup)

4 small Jerusalem artichokes, diced (1/2 cup)

4 hard-boiled eggs, finely chopped

5 green onions or scallions, washed and trimmed, very thinly sliced

2 teaspoons freshly squeezed lemon juice

Kosher salt and freshly ground black pepper to taste

1/2 cup Mayonnaise (page 57), or more to taste

Leaves of Bibb lettuce, washed (optional)

Lemon wedges (optional)

1 tablespoon finely chopped parsley

My grandfather kept a boat in Florida when I was a little boy. We'd drive to the coast on Fridays, spend the days on the water and the nights on the boat, and be home in time for church on Sunday morning. We always ate out on these trips, and I always ordered shrimp salad. Restaurants were the only place I could find it: though fresh shrimp were abundant in the region, they (and fish in general) were rarely cooked at home (people considered fish smelly).

The use of Jerusalem artichoke in this salad, as in our Chicken Salad, is inspired by Miss Lewis. It's a favorite vegetable of hers, cooked or raw, especially when it has been sweetened by frost, which converts starch to sugar. Here it adds a pleasant crunch and, with the natural sweetness of the shrimp, provides a contrast to the sharp green onion and the vinegar used in cooking the shrimp.

Bring to a boil 1 gallon of water in a large nonreactive pot. Add the pickling spice, vinegar, and kosher salt and simmer for 5 minutes. Add the shrimp and stir well. Cook for 2–3 minutes, just until the shrimp are barely cooked through and tender. Drain the shrimp in a colander, and set aside to cool.

Put the cooled shrimp in a large mixing bowl. Add the celery, Jerusalem artichokes, hard-boiled eggs, green onions, lemon juice, 1/2 teaspoon kosher salt, and 1/2 teaspoon freshly ground black pepper. Stir well to distribute the vegetables and seasonings. Fold in the mayonnaise, and taste carefully for seasoning. Season with additional salt and freshly ground black pepper if needed.

May be served over lettuce leaves with wedges of fresh lemon. Garnish with a little chopped parsley sprinkled over.

Asparagus with Cucumber Dressing

MAKES ENOUGH TO SERVE 4 AS A SUBSTANTIAL STARTER OR 6 AS A SIDE DISH

- 3 tablespoons kosher salt
- 2 pounds fresh asparagus, trimmed of woody cut ends, washed in cool water and drained
- A large bowl of ice water with 3 tablespoons kosher salt stirred in, for shocking the asparagus
- 2 spring Vidalia onions, or 1 leek, split lengthwise, then cut very thinly crosswise and washed

THE DRESSING

- 1/4 cup white-wine or cider vinegar
- 1 1/2 teaspoons kosher salt
- 1/2 teaspoon freshly ground black pepper
- 1 teaspoon prepared Dijon mustard
- 3/4 cup extra-virgin olive oil
- 1 1/2 cups kirby cucumbers, peeled, seeded, and finely diced
- 1 tablespoon each finely chopped chervil, basil, chive, and parsley
- 1 teaspoon finely chopped tarragon

This salad celebrates the spring delights of asparagus, cucumbers, young Vidalia onions, and tender, sweet herbs, all of which become available by mid-April in Georgia.

When I was chef at the Georgia governor's mansion, I would often make this salad for the First Lady's formal luncheons. I'd blanch and slice the onion greens into fancy ribbons and tie each serving of asparagus into a precious little bundle. These days, I much prefer the natural patterns of asparagus just heaped on a platter. If you can't get young Vidalia onions, use a leek instead. You can prepare the asparagus and dressing a day ahead, but add the herbs and diced cucumbers to the dressing just prior to serving. Otherwise, the cucumbers will release too much liquid and the herbs will discolor.

Bring a gallon of water to a boil in a large saucepan. When the water is at a rolling boil, stir in 3 tablespoons kosher salt. Add the trimmed and washed asparagus, and cook 2–3 minutes, depending on the size and age of the asparagus. The asparagus should bend gently under its own weight when held by the cut tip, but retain a bright-green color and resist somewhat to the bite. When you have judged the asparagus to be done, use a long pair of tongs or a skimmer to transfer the cooked asparagus to the waiting ice bath, reserving the cooking liquid. It is important that the ice bath be salted as indicated; otherwise, you will rinse away the flavor of the asparagus. Leave the asparagus in the ice bath until vibrant green and completely chilled, then drain well and store refrigerated until needed (may be cooked 1 day before using).

Meanwhile, put the sliced and washed spring Vidalia or leek in a small metal bowl and ladle over 1 1/2 cups of hot water from the asparagus to wilt the onion gently and make it digestible. When it is wilted and cooled, drain well, and squeeze out all excess liquid by rolling in a tea towel and pressing firmly.

Make the dressing: Put the vinegar, salt, black pepper, and mustard in a mixing bowl, and stir to dissolve the salt. Slowly whisk in the olive oil until emulsified. Blend in the leek or onion, diced cucumbers, and herbs. Taste carefully. You may need to add more salt, since the onion and cucumbers eat up the seasonings.

To serve the salad, arrange the asparagus on a serving platter or individual plates, and spoon over the cucumber dressing. Serve immediately.

IV CENTERPIECE DISHES—EVERYTHING IN ITS SEASON

Fish, Seafood, Poultry, and Meat

Although this chapter offers over two dozen of our favorite "centerpiece" dishes—grilled trout and fried crab cakes; roast chicken and baked ham; slowly braised lamb shanks and oxtails—they don't represent the kind of cooking we do now every day. In fact, we probably have a meaty main course only two or three times a week (and that's counting Tuesday, the day I fry chicken at the restaurant and always bring some home). A more typical supper is made up of vegetable dishes (and cornbread) with a little meat, if at all, as a flavoring: the Smoked Pork Stock in which we cook greens, for example, or a handful of chopped-up country ham in a pan of butter beans or spinach.

We both grew up in homes where meat was not a given but, like vegetables that changed with the harvest, something to be enjoyed in its season. This was especially true for the Lewis family in Freetown, where the cycle of self-sufficient farming meant certain meats were available only at certain times—fresh pork at hog-butchering, cured hams and bacons months later; now and then a sheep or a young chicken culled from the flock. Fish and seafood were also of the season—shad and its delectable roe a few weeks in springtime; oysters at Christmas; fresh trout and catfish when a neighbor man shared his catch.

A couple of generations later, my family's sources of food were much greater, but life around Hartford was still rural enough to teach me that meat didn't just come from the supermarket. When pigs and steers were slaughtered, our empty freezers were filled with pork sides and beef quarters; the autumn quail hunt brought these tiny birds to the table; bags of oysters came from the Gulf in the fall too. In summer, a good day's fishing would bring in enough bream, crappie, and catfish from local ponds and streams to occasion a full-fledged fish fry. This was a real treat, and a major undertaking, often involving several families, outdoor cookers, and a dozen or so side dishes. Not something you did every day!

The meat and poultry sections of this chapter reflect another distinction of the Southern kitchen—the primacy of pork and chicken. Since colonial days, when pigs were left to roam the woods for acorns and chestnuts (and peanut-fattened hogs became world-renowned Smithfield hams), they have been, along with the economical chicken, the main source of meat for Southern cooks. And as years of monitoring customer preferences in restaurants has taught us, these are still, by far, the most popular meats in the South today. Thus the predominance of pork (both fresh and cured) and chicken recipes here, though just a small sample of the ways they're prepared across the region.

Lue Stanley Lewis, Edna's brother, 1977

Grilled Bacon-Wrapped Mountain Trout with Green Onion Sauce

MAKES ENOUGH TO SERVE 6

- Six 12–14-ounce freshwater trout, cleaned with heads and tails left intact
- 4–6 tablespoons rendered bacon fat
- Salt and freshly ground black pepper
- 12 fresh basil leaves
- 6 slices excellent-quality bacon, not too thick

THE SAUCE

- ½ cup thinly sliced green onions or scallions, including the tender green
- 1¼ cups homemade Mayonnaise (page 57)

In this recipe, fresh basil leaves are tucked inside the fish; the trout are wrapped in bacon (have your bacon at room temperature to make it more malleable); then the fish are grilled, yielding a crisp skin and moist, sweet flesh. The simple mayonnaise-based sauce is a delicate touch, drizzled over the trout as they come off the grill so the heat of the fish will release the flavor and aroma of the green onions. This was a signature dish when I was Chef at Horseradish Grill.

Gently wash the fish under cool running water, then thoroughly pat dry with paper towels. Lightly brush the inside of the fish with bacon fat. Sprinkle generously with salt and freshly ground pepper, and lay 2 basil leaves in the cavity of each fish. Close the fish, and brush the outside with more bacon fat. Sprinkle the outside of the fish generously with salt and pepper. Starting at the head, wrap a slice of bacon around each fish, and secure the bacon with a toothpick. (Fish may be prepared up to this point 24 hours in advance.)

Grill the fish over medium-hot coals or under the broiler for approximately 5 minutes, then gently turn the fish and cook the other side. After 8 minutes total, check the fish for doneness by using a knife to pry the cavity open gently to see if the flesh is opaque, indicating that it is cooked through. Do not overcook.

Meanwhile, to prepare the sauce: Stir the sliced onions into the mayonnaise, and season with salt and freshly ground black pepper to taste. If the sauce is too thick to drizzle, thin with 1 or 2 tablespoons of hot water. (May be made 1 day ahead.)

When the fish are done, drizzle the green-onion sauce over them and serve.

Fried Soft-Shell Crab with Brown Butter and Capers

MAKES ENOUGH TO SERVE 4 AS A MAIN COURSE

Fresh soft-shell crabs are so good that they are best cooked simply, either pan-fried or deep-fried, as here. You may ask the fishmonger to clean them, but be sure they are alive when you buy them, and cook them as soon as you can. Or take them home alive, keep them refrigerated in a box, and clean them just before cooking: cut off the eyes, lift up the apron, and remove the spongy gills, then rinse quickly and blot dry.

Crabs are a delicacy and shouldn't be drowned in heavy sauces. This brown-butter-and-caper sauce is a light and flavorful accompaniment that takes just a few moments to make.

THE CRABS

- 6 cups peanut or vegetable oil
- 2 cups all-purpose flour
- ¼ cup cornstarch
- 1 tablespoon salt
- ¾ teaspoon freshly ground black pepper
- ¾ cup milk
- 8 medium to large soft-shell crabs, cleaned (see headnote)

THE BROWN BUTTER

- 8 tablespoons (1 stick) unsalted butter
- 2 tablespoons capers, lightly rinsed and drained
- 2 tablespoons freshly squeezed lemon juice
- ½ teaspoon salt

Slowly heat the oil in a large, deep frying pan until it is 350°F.

While the oil is heating, stir together the flour, cornstarch, salt, and pepper until well blended. Pour the milk in a shallow bowl.

Once the oil has reached the right temperature, dip half the crabs, one at a time, into the milk, and then dredge lightly in the flour mixture. Shake off any excess flour, and gently ease the crabs, shell side down, into the hot oil. Cook until the crabs are a rich golden brown on one side, about 3–4 minutes, then turn them and continue cooking until browned on the other, about 2–3 minutes longer. Carefully transfer the crabs to a draining rack or thickly crumpled paper towels, and keep them warm while you fry the second batch and prepare the brown-butter sauce.

Heat the butter in a nonreactive skillet until it is foamy and begins to brown. Watch it carefully, and let it cook only until it is a rich, nutty brown. Remove from heat and add the capers and lemon juice carefully, because the lemon juice may cause the hot butter to splatter. Add the salt and taste for seasoning.

Serve the crabs hot with the brown butter and capers drizzled over.

Honestly Good Crab Cakes with Spicy Dipping Sauce

MAKES 8 CRAB CAKES—ENOUGH TO SERVE 4 AS AN ENTRÉE OR 8 AS A FIRST COURSE

Nowadays crab cakes show up everywhere, and far too often they are all gussied up. These cakes are simple and pure: good crabmeat, a bit of onion and scallion, seasonings, and a minimal amount of bread crumbs and eggs to hold the cakes together. Instead of a rich butter or cream sauce for crab cakes, we like this Spicy Dipping Sauce, because its sharpness accentuates the richness of the crabmeat. It's delicious, too, with fried oysters, or any fried fish.

- 1 pound jumbo-lump crabmeat
- 1 small onion, finely chopped (½ cup)
- 4 scallions or green onions, thinly sliced (¼ cup)
- 1 cup fresh bread crumbs
- ¾ teaspoon salt
- ½ teaspoon freshly ground black pepper
- ¼ teaspoon cayenne pepper
- A few drops freshly squeezed lemon juice
- 2 eggs, lightly beaten
- 4 tablespoons (½ stick) unsalted butter, melted
- 1 cup all-purpose flour
- 8 tablespoons (1 stick) unsalted butter

Carefully pick over the crabmeat and remove any bits of cartilage and shell. Put the crabmeat in a mixing bowl, and add the onion, scallions, bread crumbs, salt, pepper, cayenne pepper, and lemon juice. Toss lightly but thoroughly to blend. Pour the eggs and melted butter into the crabmeat, and mix until well blended. Taste the crab carefully for seasoning, and add more salt, pepper, cayenne pepper, or lemon juice as needed.

Use a ⅓-cup measure to divide the crab into 8 portions. If there is any leftover mixture, divide it evenly among the 8 portions. Shape the crab portions into round cakes ½ inch thick and approximately 2 inches in diameter. Dredge each cake lightly in the flour, and pat lightly on each side to remove all excess flour.

Heat the 8 tablespoons butter in a large skillet until hot and foaming. Put the crab cakes into the pan, leaving ½ inch between them (you may need to cook the cakes in two batches). Cook over moderate heat for 4 minutes on each side, or until golden brown all over. Remove the crab cakes from the pan, and drain on a rack or crumpled paper towels before serving.

Serve the crab cakes hot.

Spicy Dipping Sauce

MAKES 1½ CUPS, ENOUGH FOR 8 CRAB CAKES

- 1½ cups cider vinegar
- 1 teaspoon salt
- ½ cup very thinly sliced green onions or scallions, including tender green
- ⅓ cup finely chopped shallots
- 3 cloves garlic, minced
- 2 teaspoons coarsely cracked black peppercorns
- ¼ cup chopped parsley

Put the vinegar and salt in a nonreactive mixing bowl, and stir until the salt is dissolved. Add the green onions, shallots, garlic, and cracked black peppercorns. Let stand at room temperature for 30 minutes. Stir in the chopped parsley and taste for seasoning, adding more salt if needed. Serve immediately.

NOTE If you don't add the parsley, spicy dipping sauce will keep 5 days refrigerated. Add the parsley shortly before serving, so that it does not turn brown in the vinegar.

Whole Red Snapper Roasted Greek Style

MAKES ENOUGH TO SERVE 2 AS A DINNER ENTRÉE OR 4 AS A LUNCH

- Two 1½–2-pound whole red snapper, scaled, gutted, and gills removed
- 1 tablespoon dried Greek oregano, crumbled (see headnote)
- 2 teaspoons kosher salt
- 1 teaspoon freshly ground black pepper
- 2 whole lemons, 1 for juicing, 1 for slicing
- Pure olive oil

THE STUFFING

- Generous 2 cups 1-inch bread cubes cut from day-old sturdy bread, crusts removed
- 2 tablespoons unsalted butter, melted
- 2 tablespoons extra-virgin olive oil
- 2 teaspoons finely minced garlic
- 2 tablespoons chopped parsley
- Kosher salt and freshly ground pepper to taste

In the Florida Panhandle, near the part of Alabama where I grew up, Gulf red snapper is prized and very popular. And in this region, as throughout the South, many small cafés and restaurants are run by people of Greek descent. They mostly serve traditional Southern food, but the influence of Greek cooking surfaces in some dishes, like this delicious roasted red snapper.

Plan on a whole fish for each serving—this may seem like a lot for one person, but as an entrée it really isn't—there's a lot of discarded head and bones. No one has ever complained to me that it is too much to eat. The preparatory steps are simple and can be done ahead of time. Season and stuff the fish early in the day, store it wrapped in plastic, and then roast it in the evening. Be sure to use dried Greek oregano to season the fish, since ordinary oregano can be harsh and could spoil the flavor. In most cities, Middle Eastern markets sell dried harvested wild Greek oregano, still on the stem. But if you can't find it, use high-quality dried thyme.

Preheat the oven to 425°F.

Rinse the fish under cool running water to remove any scales, blood, or viscera. Carefully blot dry, inside and out, with paper toweling. Use a sharp kitchen knife and extend the cavity of the gutted fish down the length of the backbone almost to the tail, so that the entire fish, except for the head, is almost butterflied. Close the fish, and cut vertical slashes, four or five, down the length of the body. Proceed down the length of the fish, spacing the slashes about an inch apart down both sides of each fish.

Mix together in a small bowl the crumbled oregano, salt, and pepper. Rub the seasoning into the fish's cavity, inside the slashes, and sprinkle any remaining over the surface of the fish.

Extra-virgin olive oil for drizzling over the roasted fish

1 teaspoon chopped parsley for garnish

Lemon wedges to serve with the roasted fish

Prepare the stuffing: Put the cubed bread into a mixing bowl. Pour the melted butter and extra-virgin olive oil over, and add the garlic, parsley, and salt and pepper. Toss well to distribute the seasonings. Taste carefully, and adjust seasoning if needed.

Return to the fish. Squeeze lemon juice liberally inside each fish. Divide the stuffing, and put half into the cavity of each fish. Don't be afraid to use a little force if needed to fill the cavity and press the sides of the fish down to regain its shape. Squeeze lemon juice over the fish generously, then cut thin lemon slices and insert into the slits on the topside of the fish. Place on a lipped baking pan lined with parchment or a Silpat, drizzle with pure olive oil, put into the middle of preheated oven, and roast for approximately 20 minutes, until the fish is cooked and the skin begins to crisp and color. Remove from the oven, and carefully transfer to large plates. Drizzle with a little extra-virgin olive oil, sprinkle lightly with chopped parsley, and serve with lemon wedges.

Frogmore Stew

MAKES ENOUGH TO SERVE 6

- 1½ pounds spicy smoked sausage
- 2 medium green bell peppers
- 2 teaspoons vegetable oil
- 8 cups Chicken Stock (page 33)
- Salt and freshly ground black pepper to taste
- 3 bay leaves
- 1 teaspoon dried thyme, preferably Spice Islands brand
- 18 small new potatoes, cut in half
- 2 medium onions, peeled and sliced lengthwise into ⅓-inch wedges (leave the root intact to hold the slices together)
- 3 ears corn, shucked and silked, each cut into 4 pieces
- 1 large tomato, peeled, seeded, and cut into ½-inch pieces
- 36 large fresh shrimp, heads on if available
- 1 tablespoon chopped parsley

There are no frogs in Frogmore stew. And traditionally it isn't even a stew but a "boil" of shellfish, sausage, and vegetables, named for Frogmore Plantation, in the South Carolina Low Country. Like crawfish or crab "boils," an authentic Frogmore stew is a highly social outdoor event. All the components are cooked together in a huge cauldron of boiling water flavored with lots of Old Bay seasoning, then scooped up with a large strainer and dumped onto newspaper-covered tables, where everyone gathers around and feasts.

This unconventional version is more delicate and refined. The shrimp, sausage, potatoes, and fresh corn are gently simmered in chicken stock, resulting in a complex and deeply flavored both, which you can serve either ladled over the meats or vegetables, or in bouillon cups on the side.

Preheat the oven to 425°F.

Put the sausage in a baking pan. Rub the peppers with the oil, and put them in the pan, too. Roast in the preheated oven until the sausage is browned and cooked through and the peppers begin to blister, about 20 minutes. You may need to turn both the sausage and the peppers occasionally to ensure even cooking. Remove from the oven, and set aside until cool enough to handle. Cut the sausage into ½-inch pieces on the bias, and the peppers into ½-inch chunks.

Pour the chicken stock into a large nonreactive Dutch oven or heavy pot, and bring it to a boil. Lower the heat to a simmer, and season the stock with salt and freshly ground black pepper. Add the bay leaves, thyme, potatoes, and onions, and cook, partially covered, for 10 minutes. Add the sausage, bell pepper, corn, and tomato, and simmer, uncovered, until the potatoes and corn are done, about 10 minutes. Taste the broth for seasoning, and season with salt and freshly ground black pepper as needed. It should be highly flavored. Add the shrimp, and cook only until they are cooked through, 3–5 minutes. Remove from the heat, and sprinkle the parsley on top. Serve immediately in heated soup plates, making sure that everyone gets an even amount of the shrimp, sausage, and vegetables, with some of the broth ladled over.

Shad with Shad Roe Stuffing

MAKES ENOUGH TO SERVE 4

Four 6-ounce fillets of shad, bones removed by the fishmonger

Kosher salt and freshly ground black pepper

Juice of ½ lemon

1 tablespoon unsalted butter

THE STUFFING

3 slices smoked bacon

2 pairs shad roe

Kosher salt and freshly ground black pepper

3 tablespoons unsalted butter

½ cup finely chopped yellow onion

½ teaspoon dried thyme, preferably Spice Islands brand

1 teaspoon finely chopped garlic

2 cups ½-inch bread cubes cut from excellent bread (brioche would be wonderful, but any good, firm white bread will do)

2 tablespoons finely chopped parsley

Juice of ½ lemon

Lemon wedges for garnish

Shad and shad roe have always been a spring treat for Miss Lewis, when, each April and May, these ocean fish leave the Atlantic and swim into the fresh waters of Virginia to spawn. I knew nothing of shad, however, until I read Miss Lewis's description (in *A Taste of Country Cooking*). Intrigued, I found a fishmonger who could supply fresh roe and boned shad fillets. The fish has such a complex bone structure that it was often discarded after the roe was taken, but a new technique of filleting yields an almost boneless side of fish—though it's a good idea to check for pin bones that the fishmonger might have missed. These fillets, now widely available, are held in place by the skin and, since they can be opened and closed like a book, are excellent for stuffing.

In this recipe, shad fillets are filled with a highly seasoned roe-and-bread stuffing, then baked. The buttery fish and strong-flavored roe are delicious together, but you can always prepare and enjoy the roe separately and season and bake the fish, following the recipe, without any stuffing. This is a very rich dish and should be served with something a bit astringent, like Wilted Salad (page 74).

Preheat the oven to 325°F.

Open the folds of the shad fillets, and season inside and out generously with salt and a little freshly ground black pepper and squeezes of lemon juice. Leave the folds open, and set aside.

Prepare the stuffing: Cook the bacon until crisp in a medium sauté pan over moderate heat. Remove the bacon. Rinse the shad roe and pat dry with paper toweling, season well with salt and a little pepper, and put in the same pan. Sauté over medium-high heat about 4 minutes on each side, until well browned and just cooked through. Remove the roe, and set aside to cool. Discard all but 1 tablespoon of the bacon fat from the pan. Add 3 tablespoons butter and heat until melted and bubbling. Add the onion and cook gently, stirring often, until tender, about 5 minutes. Add the dried thyme, chopped garlic, and ½ teaspoon salt. Continue cooking gently for another 5 minutes.

Meanwhile, put the bread cubes in a mixing bowl and crumble the bacon and the cooked roe into the bowl. Add the sautéed onion, parsley, and the juice of ½ lemon. Toss well, and season with kosher salt and a minimal amount of freshly ground black pepper. Mix well, and taste carefully for seasoning. Divide the stuffing between the four fillets. Fill between the two lateral folds generously, and pull the sides up over the stuffing to close—don't worry if they will not close all the way. Transfer the filled fillets to a parchment- or Silpat-lined baking pan. Dot the tops of the fillets with the remaining tablespoon of butter and bake in preheated oven for about 15–20 minutes, until the shad is cooked through. Serve immediately with wedges of lemon.

OYSTER SEASON IN HARTFORD

In my hometown of Hartford, tucked deep in the southeastern corner of Alabama, just an hour or so from the Gulf Coast of Florida, the famous sweet Apalachicola oysters are harvested beginning in late October. The first big burlap bags of ice and oysters, still in their shells, arrive at makeshift oyster bars that spring up around town. You can sit at a bar and eat your fill of raw oysters as they are shucked in front of you and placed on the half-shell on large plastic cafeteria cups. In a town where there are no restaurants (just one barbecue stand), the opening of the oyster bars is always a big event. We had oysters at home, too, through the winter months, sometimes even for breakfast. And it was a tradition to have oysters for supper, always outdoors, on the evening after our midday Thanksgiving and Christmas feasts. A couple of families would get together and order a "Croker sack" of Apalachicolas from the oyster bar. Wearing thick rubber shucking gloves, my father and the other men would shuck the oysters, and we'd sit outside and eat them raw by the bushel, on saltine crackers, with catsup, mayonnaise, and Tabasco for condiments. Sometimes, my mother and the other women would also fry up oysters in the kitchen and bring them outside so we could relish them both ways.

Fried Oysters

MAKES ENOUGH TO SERVE 4 AS A FIRST COURSE

- 6 cups fresh peanut oil, or enough to come 3 inches up the sides of a deep saucepan
- 1 cup white cornmeal
- ¼ cup all-purpose flour
- 1 tablespoon cornstarch
- 1 teaspoon sea salt
- ½ teaspoon freshly ground black pepper
- 2 dozen oysters, shucked and in their liquor
- Kosher salt and freshly ground black pepper for seasoning the oysters

In my childhood, Apalachicolas were the only oysters we knew, so they were the ones my mother fried. But any of the varieties recommended for oyster stew (box, page 4) would be good in this recipe, cornmeal-coated and deep-fried. Miss Lewis and I serve fried oysters with Spicy Dipping Sauce (page 85) and Coleslaw (page 61).

Pour the peanut oil into a pot suitable for frying, and set over low heat. Meanwhile, mix together the cornmeal, flour, cornstarch, sea salt, and pepper in a flat dish. Drain the oysters, and season them generously with salt and a few grindings of black pepper.

Gradually raise the heat under the oil until the oil has reached 340°F. Dredge the oysters in the cornmeal mixture, and carefully lower them into the hot oil. Cook in two batches for 2–3 minutes, until golden and crisp, using a slotted spoon or skimmer to move them gently in the oil for even cooking. Remove to a draining rack or crumpled paper towels to drain, then serve immediately.

A Fish Fry for Porgy

MAKES ENOUGH TO SERVE 4–6 PEOPLE,
DEPENDING ON THE SIZE OF THE FISH AND THE APPETITE OF YOUR GUESTS

6 cups peanut oil, or enough to come 3 inches up the sides of a large pot, for frying

THE DREDGE

2 cups white cornmeal
¼ cup all-purpose flour
2 tablespoons cornstarch
2 tablespoons sea salt
1 teaspoon freshly ground black pepper
¼ teaspoon cayenne pepper

THE FISH

12–18 small freshwater fish, cleaned, gutted, heads removed, rinsed under cool running water, and drained well
Kosher salt and freshly ground black pepper

A fish fry in the South is a social event involving at least a couple of families or a church or civic group. It's an outdoor ritual of high summer, centered on big cast-iron pots set on portable butane burners. (When just our family had fried fish and fixings at home, we would *not* call it a fish fry.)

The best fish for a fry is the fresh catch-of-the-day from local streams, creeks, and lakes—though if fishing luck is bad or the crowd quite large it is sometimes augmented with fish that has been caught before, cleaned, and frozen in blocks of ice. Different types of small fish are fried, typically bream, crappie, Nile perch, small catfish, whiting, or Virginia spots. They're fried whole, dressed (only the head removed), which makes them particularly flavorful and succulent. The flesh is easy to pull off the bone.

Fixings for a fry are traditional too. Some are absolutely essential: Hush Puppies (page 218), sliced tomato, sliced raw onion, both sweet *and* dill pickles, Coleslaw (page 61), and iced tea. Not required—but nice to have—are potato salad and fried potatoes, corn on the cob, and homemade ice cream.

The title "A Fish Fry for Porgy" refers to Porgy in the George Gershwin opera *Porgy and Bess,* which is set in Charleston; there is a fish fry in the second act. Miss Lewis came to love the character of Porgy while she was at Middleton Place, outside Charleston, where the opera was sometimes staged at the Spoleto Festival. I love the music and the fact that the opera was a vehicle for the wonderful Southern soprano Leontyne Price.

Pour the peanut oil into a heavy pot for frying, and begin to heat gently.

Mix together the cornmeal, flour, cornstarch, sea salt, and peppers in a shallow dish. Season the fish generously inside and out with salt and a few grindings of black pepper. When the temperature of the oil has reached 340°F, dredge the fish quickly in the cornmeal mixture and shake off any excess. Slip one at a time into the hot oil, taking care not to overcrowd the pot. You will need to cook the fish in batches. Fry the fish until golden brown and crisp all over, about 5–7 minutes. Remove from the oil, and place on a draining rack or crumpled paper towels to drain. Serve immediately.

Sautéed Frogs' Legs with Brown Butter and Capers

MAKES ENOUGH TO SERVE 4 AS A FIRST COURSE OR LIGHT SUPPER

- 8 pairs medium-sized frogs' legs
- Kosher salt and freshly ground black pepper
- 1 cup all-purpose flour
- 1 tablespoon cornstarch
- 4 tablespoons (½ stick) unsalted butter
- 1 recipe brown-butter-and-caper sauce (page 83)

Frogs' legs *do not* taste like chicken, but they are delicate and tender, and make a wonderful appetizer or a light supper. Look for legs that are pink, almost translucent, with the veins just barely visible. Medium-sized legs are best, about the length of a chicken leg; any larger and they can be rather coarse in flavor and texture. We like to serve them right from the stove on small plates, topped with brown-butter sauce (page 83). By the way, if you can't find fresh frogs' legs, high-quality frozen ones can be used. Defrost slowly in the refrigerator overnight.

Rinse the frogs' legs under cool running water, and pat dry with paper toweling. Season them generously with salt and a few grindings of black pepper on both sides.

Mix together the flour and cornstarch in a pie plate, or some other flat dish. Heat a large skillet over medium-high heat. Add the butter, and heat until melted and bubbling. Dust the frogs' legs very lightly with the flour mixture, and pat well to remove all excess flour. Place them in the pan, and cook 3–4 minutes, or until golden on one side. Turn the legs, and continue cooking until golden brown on the other side. Remove from the pan to a draining rack or scrunched paper towels to remove any excess cooking fat. Serve immediately with a little brown-butter-and-caper sauce spooned over.

Grandmaw Peacock's Chicken and Rice

MAKES ENOUGH TO SERVE 4–6

Grandmaw Peacock's version of this Deep South country dish was my favorite of all the things she made. The chicken is cooked very slowly to release a pure rich essence that infuses the rice. Starchy short-grain rice, which Grandmaw used, gives the dish a creamy, moist, puddinglike consistency, but long-grain rice is fine too.

- 1 large chicken (3½–4 pounds), cut into 10 serving pieces (2 drumsticks, 2 thighs, 2 wings, 1 whole breast, quartered) plus back and neck
- Sea or kosher salt to taste
- 2 tablespoons unsalted butter
- 1 small whole onion, peeled
- 1 small, leafy celery rib
- 5 cups water
- 1½ cups white rice, long- or short-grained

Wash the chicken pieces, and dry well with paper towel. Trim the tips from the chicken wings and discard. Season the chicken pieces very generously and thoroughly with the salt.

Heat the butter in a heavy Dutch oven or heavy pan over moderately low heat until it becomes frothy but not brown. Add the chicken pieces to the pot, and with a wooden spoon toss them about to coat them with the hot butter. Cook slowly, turning the pieces occasionally, until they are a pale-golden color, about 5 minutes. Add the onion and celery rib to the pot, and cover tightly. Reduce the heat to very low, and cook this way for approximately 20 minutes.

At the end of 20 minutes, remove the lid from the pot. You will be surprised by the amount of liquid released by the chicken and vegetables. Pour in the 5 cups of water. Increase the heat slightly, and cook, partially covered, for an additional 35 minutes.

With a long slotted spoon or tongs, remove the onion and celery and discard. For a more refined dish you may choose to remove the back and neckbone pieces as well.

Taste the broth carefully. It should be highly flavored and seasoned. Indeed, it should be on the salty side, because the rice will absorb a great deal of the seasoning. Stir in the rice and cover. Continue cooking at a low simmer for 30–45 minutes longer.

When most of the broth has been absorbed by the rice but the contents are still a bit soupy, remove the pan from the heat and allow to rest completely, covered, for 10 minutes before serving.

Grandmaw Peacock

BRINING FOR POULTRY AND MEAT

Brining poultry or pork—that is, soaking it in a saltwater solution before cooking—serves a twofold purpose: it helps the flesh retain moisture and seasons it all the way through. To make the brine, stir kosher salt into cold water until dissolved, in the proportion of ¼ cup salt to 1 quart of water. (Don't use table salt in this formula, by the way; it will be too salty.) Mix enough brine to cover the poultry or meat completely in a (nonreactive) bowl or pot. Store refrigerated for the times specified below:

- Cut-up chicken (Country Captain, Smothered Chicken, Fried Chicken): brine for 8–12 hours
- Whole chicken for roasting: brine for 8–24 hours (after 24 hours, the chicken can become too salty)
- Whole turkey for roasting: brine for 24–48 hours
- Pork chops: brine for 2 hours
- Pork loin: brine for 8–24 hours
- Pork shoulder: brine for 24 hours

Country Captain and Crispy Thin Onion Rings

MAKES ENOUGH TO SERVE 4 GENEROUSLY, 6 REASONABLY

- One 3½-pound chicken, cut into 8 pieces and brined for 8–24 hours (box, page 95)
- 1 teaspoon dried thyme, preferably Spice Islands brand
- Freshly ground black pepper
- ¼ cup vegetable oil
- 6 slices bacon
- 2½ cups chopped onion
- 1 cup chopped celery, preferably with leaves
- 2 cups diced green bell pepper
- 1 tablespoon finely chopped garlic
- 2 cups drained and chopped canned tomatoes
- ¾ cup tomato juice, reserved from the canned tomatoes
- 2 tablespoons unsalted butter
- 2 tablespoons plus 2 teaspoons curry powder (recipe follows)
- ⅓ cup currants
- 2 bay leaves
- Salt to taste

Though its exact origins are unknown, this traditional curried-chicken dish has long been associated with Georgia—Savannah in particular, since it was a port for the spice trade. Good spices are the key to a great Country Captain, and we have our own formula for curry powder (box, page 98). Be sure to use fresh whole spices and grind them just before mixing.

Country Captain is a good dish for entertaining, because guests can embellish their dinner with an assortment of condiments and garnishes, including currants, peanuts, crumbled bacon, chutneys (see Chapter I), and delicious Crispy Thin Onion Rings, for which you'll find instructions. Coconut Rice (page 169) is our preferred accompaniment, though plain cooked rice is good, too.

Rinse the brined chicken pieces, and thoroughly pat dry with paper towels. Sprinkle with dried thyme and 5 or 6 grinds of black pepper. Heat the vegetable oil in a large sauté pan over high heat until quite hot but not smoking.

Place the chicken pieces in the hot oil, skin side down, and cook, turning once, until a deep golden brown on both sides. Remove the chicken pieces and set aside. Pour out the cooking oil from the sauté pan. Return the pan to the stove over moderately low heat, and cook the bacon slices until deeply colored and quite crisp. Remove bacon and reserve for use as a condiment in the finished dish. Add the chopped onion to the pan, and cook, stirring occasionally, for 2–3 minutes. Add the chopped celery and bell pepper, and continue cooking for approximately 5 minutes longer. Stir in the garlic, and cook 2–3 minutes before adding the chopped tomatoes and reserved tomato juice. Cook at a low simmer, partially covered, for 10 minutes, stirring often.

Heat the unsalted butter in a small pan until hot and foaming. Stir in the curry powder and cook, stirring continuously, for 2 minutes. Add the cooked curry powder, along with the currants and bay leaves, to the simmering tomato-vegetable mixture. Season well with salt and grinds of black pepper. Simmer, tightly covered, for an additional 30 minutes, stirring occasionally.

When the sauce has finished cooking, taste carefully for seasoning, adding more salt and pepper if needed. Spoon about 1 cup of the sauce into the bottom

CONDIMENTS FOR CURRY

- Crumbled bacon
- Thinly sliced green onion
- Crispy Thin Onion Rings (recipe follows)
- Currants or raisins
- Toasted coconut
- Finely chopped white of hard-boiled egg and the sieved yolk of same, served separately
- Chutney, 1 or more varieties
- Chopped peanuts

of an ovenproof casserole or baking dish that is just large enough to hold the browned chicken pieces comfortably in a single layer—it's all right if they touch. Arrange the chicken pieces over the sauce, then spoon the remaining sauce over all. Place a piece of parchment paper directly on top of the chicken, and a single layer of foil directly on top of the parchment. Put the cover on the baking dish or a double thickness of foil, sealing tightly. Bake in a preheated 325°F oven for approximately 1½ hours, until chicken is quite tender. Taste sauce again for any final seasoning adjustments.

Serve the chicken hot with the sauce spooned over it, along with rice and four or more curry condiments.

Crispy Thin Onion Rings

SERVES 4–6 AS A GARNISH FOR COUNTRY CAPTAIN

- 2 small onions
- 1 cup all-purpose flour
- ¾ teaspoon salt
- ½ teaspoon freshly ground black pepper
- ¼ teaspoon cayenne pepper
- Oil for deep-frying

Peel and slice the onions crosswise into 1⁄16-inch-thick rings. Sift the flour, salt, pepper, and cayenne pepper onto a sheet of wax paper, and toss to mix. Dredge the onion rings in the seasoned flour, and carefully shake off any excess flour. Heat at least 3 inches of oil in a heavy pot or skillet to 365°F, and fry the onion rings in batches for 1 or 2 minutes, until a deep golden brown. Drain on a rack or crumpled paper towels, and sprinkle lightly with salt. Serve hot or at room temperature.

MAKING YOUR OWN CURRY POWDER

1 tablespoon ground ginger
1 teaspoon chili powder
½ teaspoon ground cumin
1 teaspoon ground cardamom
½ teaspoon turmeric
1 teaspoon paprika
1 teaspoon ground coriander
1 teaspoon ground cinnamon
¼ teaspoon ground cloves
¼ teaspoon cayenne pepper, or less if desired

Mix the ingredients together, and store in a small, tightly sealed jar. Make in small batches as needed for a fresher, more vibrant flavor.

Roast Chicken

MAKES ENOUGH TO SERVE 3 OR 4

- One 3½-pound chicken, brined (box, page 95)
- 4 tablespoons (½ stick) unsalted butter, softened
- 1½ teaspoons salt
- 1 teaspoon freshly ground black pepper
- ¾ teaspoon dried thyme, preferably Spice Islands brand
- 1 small onion, peeled and quartered
- ½ cup water

Here is Miss Lewis's excellent and easy method for a moist and flavorful roast chicken *and* a delicious rich sauce. Start with a brined bird, put a bit of water in the roasting pan when you begin roasting, then pour off the accumulated juices and fat after 40 minutes. This method yields an intensely flavored base for the sauce (and reduces fat splattering in the oven). We also like to rub butter and dried thyme (and salt and pepper) into the chicken before roasting: the butter, salt, and pepper are essential, but you can substitute other herbs that you like.

Preheat the oven to 425°F.

Rinse the brined chicken, and dry thoroughly, inside and out, with paper towels. Mix together the softened butter, salt, pepper, and dried thyme until well blended. Rub the butter mixture over the chicken and inside the cavity as well. Truss the chicken with butchers' twine, making sure you secure the wing tips and tie the legs so that the whole bird is in a tight, plump form.

Place the chicken on a wire rack in a roasting pan that will hold it comfortably. Put the quartered onion and water on the bottom of the roasting pan. Set the roasting pan on the middle rack of the preheated oven, and roast for 40 minutes without opening the oven door. After 40 minutes, remove the roasting pan and carefully pour off the fat and juices from the bottom of the pan into a small bowl; reserve. Return the chicken to the oven for approximately 20 minutes longer, or until the juices from the thigh run clear when pierced. Remove from the oven, and transfer the chicken and the onion to a warm platter. Tent with foil while you prepare the sauce.

Skim off any visible fat from the bottom of the roasting pan, as well as from the roasting juices reserved in the bowl. Set the pan over high heat, and pour the juices in, scraping the bottom of the pan with a large spoon to dislodge any browned bits and caramelized juices. Boil hard for 2 or 3 minutes, until the juices have reduced slightly. You should have just a small amount of delicious sauce. Taste critically, and adjust the seasoning if needed.

Bring the chicken to the table and carve, portioning out light and dark meat as wanted plus a quarter of the onion, and spooning a little sauce over each serving.

Roast Turkey with Giblet Gravy and Cornbread-Pecan Dressing

12-POUND TURKEY MAKES ENOUGH TO SERVE 8–10

18-POUND TURKEY MAKES ENOUGH TO SERVE 12–14

- One 12–18-pound turkey, brined for 24 hours (box, page 95)
- 6 tablespoons (3/4 stick) unsalted butter, softened
- 1 teaspoon salt
- 3/4 teaspoon freshly ground black pepper
- 2 teaspoons dried thyme
- 2 tablespoons lemon juice
- 1/4 cup freshly squeezed orange juice
- 6 slices thick-sliced bacon
- 1 large onion, cut into quarters
- 2 stalks celery, cut into large pieces
- 2 bay leaves
- 4 cloves garlic, unpeeled
- 2 cups Chicken Stock (page 33)

Brining for a whole day is only one of the reasons this turkey is so moist and delicious. It also gets a generous rub with highly seasoned butter, and aromatic vegetables and herbs tucked into the bird's cavity. All of these flavors mingle in the turkey and the pan juices which are used in the giblet gravy. Instead of stuffing the bird, we bake the cornbread-pecan dressing in a separate pan, which allows the turkey to roast more quickly and reduces the danger of drying out the breast meat while cooking the stuffing to a safe temperature. Turkey roasting does require an accurate instant-read meat thermometer, since temperature is the only reliable indicator of doneness. As a general guideline, a 12–18-pound unstuffed turkey will take 3–4¼ hours of roasting at 325°F. Use a thermometer to be sure when done.

Make the Cornbread (recipe follows) ahead so it is ready for the stuffing.

Preheat the oven to 325°F.

Once the turkey is brined, rinse it well with cold water and pat it dry, inside and out, with paper towel. Mix together the softened butter, salt, pepper, dried thyme, and lemon and orange juices. Rub the turkey inside and out with the seasoned butter. Lay the bacon slices across the breast, and fill the cavity with the onion, celery, bay leaves, and garlic. Truss the turkey tightly, and put it on a rack in a roasting pan. Pour the chicken stock into the roasting pan, and set in preheated oven.

While the turkey is roasting, prepare the broth for the Giblet Gravy (recipe follows), since that will take over 2 hours of cooking. Also, make the stuffing (recipe follows), which can bake alongside the turkey for the last 30 minutes of roasting and the 15–20 minutes while the bird is resting.

Roast the turkey 45 minutes undisturbed, then baste it every 15 minutes with the pan juices, and cook until the thickest part of the breast reaches an internal temperature of 160°F and the thigh juices run clear. Remove from the oven, and let rest for 20 minutes before carving.

While the turkey is resting, degrease and deglaze the roasting pan, using the pan drippings for the giblet gravy.

Giblet Gravy

MAKES ABOUT 6 CUPS, ENOUGH TO SERVE 12–18 PEOPLE

THE GIBLET BROTH

- 2 tablespoons unsalted butter
- Neck and giblets reserved from turkey
- 1 carrot, peeled and diced
- 1 small onion, diced
- 1 stalk celery, diced
- 1 teaspoon salt
- 3 whole black peppercorns
- 3 whole cloves
- 1 bay leaf
- ½ teaspoon dried thyme
- 3 parsley stems
- 1 cup white wine
- 3 cups water
- 4 cups Chicken Stock (page 33)

THE GRAVY

- 8 tablespoons (1 stick) unsalted butter
- 8 tablespoons all-purpose flour
- 6 cups reduced giblet broth
- Chopped turkey-neck meat and giblets reserved from giblet broth
- Pan drippings from roasting the turkey
- 3 tablespoons brandy
- Salt and freshly ground black pepper to taste

To make the broth: Heat the butter in a large saucepan until hot and foaming. Chop the turkey neck into ½-inch pieces and add it with the giblets to the hot butter. Cook the pieces, stirring from time to time, until they are deeply browned all over. Add the carrot, onion, celery, and salt, and cook, stirring often, for 5 minutes or longer, until the vegetables begin to brown. Add the peppercorns, cloves, bay leaf, thyme, and parsley stems, and continue cooking 5 minutes longer. Add the wine, water, and chicken stock, and bring to a gentle boil. Skim the broth, and lower the temperature so that the partially covered broth is barely simmering. Simmer for 2 hours, or until the giblets are tender. Strain the broth, reserving the neck and giblets. Return the broth to heat and simmer, uncovered, until reduced to 6 cups. While the broth is reducing, remove the meat from the turkey-neck pieces and chop it and the giblets finely. Reserve.

Make the gravy: Heat the butter in a large saucepan until melted. Stir in the flour, and cook over moderately high heat, stirring constantly, until a deep, even brown, about 8–10 minutes. Whisk in the reduced broth and simmer, stirring occasionally, until the gravy thickens—about 5 minutes. Add the reserved chopped neck meat and giblets, reserved pan drippings, brandy, ¾ teaspoon salt, and ½ teaspoon freshly ground black pepper, and simmer 5 minutes longer. Taste carefully for seasoning, and add more salt and pepper as needed. Transfer to a bowl or gravy boat, and serve with the turkey and dressing.

Cornbread-Pecan Dressing

MAKES ENOUGH TO SERVE 12–16

THE CORNBREAD

2 cups white cornmeal
1½ teaspoons salt
1½ teaspoons baking soda
2 cups buttermilk
3 eggs, lightly beaten
4 tablespoons (½ stick) unsalted butter

THE DRESSING

4 tablespoons (½ stick) unsalted butter
4 tablespoons bacon fat; or 5 slices bacon, cut into ½-inch pieces, fried, to yield the fat
3 medium onions (about 2 cups chopped)
4–5 stalks celery (about 2 cups chopped)
2 large shallots, finely chopped
2½ teaspoons dried thyme
1 tablespoon plus 1 teaspoon rubbed sage
3 cups pecan halves, toasted
4 tablespoons (½ stick) unsalted butter, melted
1 cup Chicken Stock (page 33), or more as needed
4 eggs, lightly beaten
Salt and freshly ground black pepper to taste

To make the cornbread: Heat the oven to 450°F.

Put the cornmeal, salt, and baking soda into a mixing bowl, and stir with a wire whisk until blended. Add the buttermilk and eggs, and whisk until well blended. Put the butter into a 10-inch cast-iron skillet or 9-by-9-inch baking pan, and heat in the oven until the butter is melted and bubbling. Remove from the oven, and swirl the butter to coat the skillet or pan, then stir the butter into the cornbread batter. Turn the batter into the skillet or pan, and bake 20 minutes or longer, until the cornbread is golden brown and crusty. Remove from the oven, and turn out onto a cooling rack and allow to cool completely. Tear the cooled cornbread into large (1½-inch) pieces, and allow to sit, uncovered, overnight to dry out. (Alternatively, you may put the cornbread pieces on a baking sheet in a warm oven for 30 minutes to dry out.)

To make the dressing: Preheat oven to 325°F. Heat the butter and bacon fat in a heavy skillet, then add the onion, celery, and shallots and cook slowly for 5 minutes. Add the thyme and sage, and continue cooking, stirring often, until the vegetables are tender but not browned, about 15 minutes. Toss the cornbread pieces with the toasted pecan halves and the cooked vegetables in a large bowl until well mixed. Pour in the 4 tablespoons melted butter, the chicken stock, and eggs. Toss well to blend, and season generously with salt and freshly ground black pepper. Turn into a buttered 9-by-13-by-2-inch casserole and cover with foil. Bake for 30 minutes. Remove the foil and continue baking until golden brown, about 15–20 minutes. (If you like your dressing on the wet side, baste with additional chicken stock once the foil is removed.)

Chicken Baked with Delicate Herbs and Bread Crumbs

MAKES ENOUGH TO SERVE 3 OR 4

This is a very old hearth recipe from Virginia. The unusual "marinade" of butter and sweet fresh herbs imparts rich flavor to the chicken, and additional herbs infuse the bread-crumb coating. Delicious either hot or at room temperature, this is a good dish to bring to a picnic or covered-dish supper. You'll need lots of fresh herbs, however: if you can't find all the varieties called for in the recipe, use more of whatever you have.

- One 3–3½-pound chicken, cut into 8 pieces
- 8 tablespoons (1 stick) unsalted butter, melted
- 3 tablespoons finely snipped parsley
- 3 tablespoons finely snipped tarragon
- 3 tablespoons finely snipped chervil
- 3 tablespoons finely snipped chives
- 2 small cloves garlic, minced
- 1½ teaspoons salt
- ½ teaspoon plus ¼ teaspoon freshly ground black pepper
- 2½ cups soft fresh bread crumbs

Rinse the chicken pieces, and pat dry with paper towels. Put the melted butter, 1 tablespoon each of the herbs, the garlic, 1 teaspoon of the salt, and ½ teaspoon of the pepper in a shallow dish. Stir to blend, then add the chicken pieces, turning well to coat all over. Cover the dish, and marinate for 1 hour at room temperature, or refrigerated overnight.

Meanwhile, mix together the remaining 2 tablespoons of each herb, the bread crumbs, and the remaining salt and pepper. Cover and reserve.

When ready to cook, preheat oven to 325°F.

Uncover the chicken pieces (if the butter has solidified, or if the chicken was refrigerated overnight, warm briefly in a low oven just until butter is melted). Spread the bread crumbs onto a piece of wax paper. Roll each chicken piece in the bread crumbs to coat. Arrange the chicken pieces so they are not touching in a large, lightly buttered baking dish. Bake the chicken in the preheated oven for 45–55 minutes, until the crumbs are golden brown and the chicken juices run clear. Serve hot or at room temperature.

Southern Pan-Fried Chicken

MAKES ENOUGH TO SERVE 4

- One 3-pound chicken, cut into 8 pieces, brined for 8–12 hours (box, page 95)
- 1 quart buttermilk
- 1 pound lard
- ½ cup (1 stick) unsalted butter
- ½ cup country-ham pieces, or 1 thick slice country ham cut into ½-inch strips
- 1 cup all-purpose flour
- 2 tablespoons cornstarch
- 1 teaspoon salt
- ½ teaspoon freshly ground black pepper

We have blended our best chicken-frying tips from Virginia and Alabama in this recipe: it requires a bit of extra effort, but the results are absolutely outstanding. The chicken gets two long soaks, Alabama-style, first in brine and then in buttermilk. The frying fat is a special mix—Virginia-style—of lard and sweet butter, flavored with a slice of country ham, which makes the chicken extra crispy and rich-tasting. The cornstarch in the dredge adds to the crispness too. Carefully cooked, fried chicken will absorb a minimal amount of fat. Be sure to pat off all excess dredge; fry evenly at the proper temperature; and drain the chicken well on crumpled-up—not flat—paper towels or a wire rack.

To prepare the chicken for frying: Drain the brined chicken and rinse out the bowl it was brined in. Return the chicken to the bowl, and pour the buttermilk over. Cover and refrigerate for 8–12 hours. Drain the chicken on a wire rack, discarding the buttermilk.

Meanwhile, prepare the fat for frying by putting the lard, butter, and country ham into a heavy skillet or frying pan. Cook over low heat for 30–45 minutes, skimming as needed, until the butter ceases to throw off foam and the country ham is browned. Use a slotted spoon to remove the ham carefully from the fat. (The ham pieces can be saved and used to make Smoked Pork Stock, page 39.) Just before frying, increase the temperature to medium-high and heat the fat to 335°F.

Prepare the dredge by blending together the flour, cornstarch, salt, and pepper in a shallow bowl or on wax paper.

Dredge the drained chicken pieces thoroughly in the flour mixture, then pat well to remove all excess flour.

Slip some of the chicken pieces, skin side down, into the heated fat. (Do not overcrowd the pan, and fry in batches if necessary.) Cook for 8–10 minutes on each side, until the chicken is golden brown and cooked through. Drain thoroughly on a wire rack or on crumpled paper towels, and serve.

Fried chicken is delicious eaten hot, warm, at room temperature, or cold.

Tomato Gravy

MAKES APPROXIMATELY 2 CUPS GRAVY, ENOUGH TO SERVE 4–6

- 2 tablespoons bacon fat or fat from frying chicken (preceding recipe)
- 1 cup finely diced onion
- 2 large cloves garlic, finely minced
- 1 teaspoon salt
- ½ teaspoon freshly ground black pepper
- 1½ teaspoons dried thyme
- 1 tablespoon all-purpose flour
- 1 pound tomato, fresh or canned, peeled, seeded, and chopped into ⅓-inch pieces (¾ cup)
- ½ cup milk
- ½ cup heavy cream

We love to serve creamy tomato gravy along with fried chicken, using a bit of the flavorful frying fat after the chicken is done, and either fresh tomatoes or good-quality canned ones, depending on the season. The gravy is a very old Deep South recipe and was often prepared as part of a hearty breakfast, just spooned over hot biscuits. For nonchicken uses, prepare the gravy with bacon fat in place of chicken-frying fat, and substitute milk for the chicken stock.

Heat the bacon or chicken-frying fat in a heavy nonreactive skillet, and add the diced onion. Sauté over medium-high heat for 5 minutes, stirring often. Add the garlic, 1 teaspoon of the salt, the freshly ground black pepper, and thyme, and cook for another 5 minutes. Sprinkle the flour over and cook, stirring well, for another 2 minutes. Stir in the chopped tomato and the remaining ½ teaspoon salt, and cook 5 minutes longer. Slowly stir in the milk and heavy cream and bring to a simmer. Simmer gently for 5 minutes. Taste carefully for seasoning, adding more salt and freshly ground black pepper as needed.

Serve hot.

Roast Duckling Stuffed with Oysters and Red Rice

MAKES ENOUGH TO SERVE 4

THE STUFFING

3 tablespoons unsalted butter
1 cup shucked, drained fresh oysters, oyster liquor reserved
Salt and freshly ground pepper to taste
¾ pound smoked spicy sausage, such as andouille
3 tablespoons bacon fat (box, page 51)
½ cup chopped onion
¾ teaspoon dried thyme, preferably Spice Islands brand
¼ cup chopped green bell pepper
1 small hot green chili, seeded and minced
½ teaspoon coarsely ground chili pepper, or to taste (optional)
1 tablespoon chopped garlic
1 tablespoon tomato paste
1¼ cups drained canned whole tomatoes
About ½ cup Chicken Stock (page 33)
1 cup long-grain rice

One 5–6 pound duck

In Alabama, we never put stuffing in poultry; even cornbread dressing for Thanksgiving turkey was baked in a separate dish. When we started cooking together, though, Miss Lewis once used Red Rice (page 197) as a stuffing for a suckling pig. It was so delicious I decided to try it with poultry—first with goose and then with duck—and *that* tasted delicious. The meat is moist and well seasoned, and the flavor is even better after it has soaked up the duck juices and essences.

I've added to the basic red rice stuffing oysters, which were once so plentiful and cheap they were common in stuffings in the Old South. Though they are much more expensive now, you only need a cup of oysters—plus all their "liquor"—for this recipe. (If they're beyond your budget or you can't find them, just leave them out.) The chili peppers add quite a bit of heat here; if it's too much for you, use less.

This is an excellent dish for a holiday dinner or other special occasions during the cool season. With the rich stuffing, even a smallish duck can serve four quite easily. To balance the rich bird, serve sautéed spinach or a salad of sharp greens alongside.

Preheat the oven to 325°F.

Heat 2 tablespoons of the butter in a large sauté pan until foaming. Quickly sauté the oysters, seasoning lightly with salt and pepper, just until the edges begin to curl—about 1 minute. Transfer to a colander set over a bowl to cool and drain. If the oysters are large, cut them in half. Add the reserved oyster liquor to the drained juices.

Pour ½ inch of water into a heavy skillet, add the sausage, and cook, uncovered, about 10 minutes (you may have to add more water). Now let the water cook off and the sausage turn deep brown and firm. Cool right in pan, and cut diagonally into ½-inch slices and set aside. Heat the bacon fat in the skillet, and add the onion. Sauté until translucent, about 10 minutes. Add the thyme, bell pepper, chilis, and ground chili. Cook until the vegetables are well cooked but not deeply colored, about 10 minutes. Stir in the garlic, and cook 3 minutes, stirring often to avoid coloring. Add salt and pepper to taste, tomato paste, and tomatoes; continue cooking about 3 minutes.

Measure the reserved oyster juices, and add enough stock to make 1¼ cups. Add this to the vegetables. Cover and simmer gently, stirring frequently, about 15 minutes. Adjust seasonings.

Melt the remaining tablespoon of butter in a large, heavy nonreactive pan. Add the rice, and cook over medium heat for 2 minutes, stirring constantly, until the grains are all coated. Add the sausage and the tomato mixture to the rice, and cover tightly. Cook over medium-low heat until the rice is tender, about 20 minutes. Toss in the oysters, adjust seasonings, and let cool completely before stuffing the bird.

Wash and dry the duck. Remove the giblets and other innards from the cavity of the duck. Remove excess fat from the two cavity openings. Tuck any extra neck skin into the neck cavity. The giblets may be saved for soup or stock, and the fat may be used for rendering or for a pâté.

Spoon as much of the stuffing into the duck as will fit, and use skewers to secure the skin closed. Any extra stuffing can be spooned into an ovenproof casserole dish and placed in the oven with the stuffed duck for the last 30 minutes of roasting.

Rub the duck with salt and sprinkle it with pepper, prick the skin of the breast and sides with a knife to allow rendered fat to drip out, then place the duck on a rack in a roasting pan. It's ready for the oven.

Roast for 2 hours in the preheated oven, pouring fat off once or twice during cooking to keep spattering down. After 2 hours, turn up the heat to 425°F and roast another 10 minutes to crisp the skin.

Grilled/Broiled Quail or Squab

MAKES ENOUGH TO SERVE 4

- 4 squab or 8 quail, brined for 2 hours (box, page 95)
- Salt and freshly ground black pepper
- 1 teaspoon dried thyme, preferably Spice Islands brand
- 4 tablespoons olive oil
- 4 bay leaves
- 4 tablespoons brandy (optional)

Quail and squab are familiar items on the Southern table. As it's been for generations, quail hunting is still a big autumn activity across the South, though today the birds are farm-raised as well. Squab (a kind of pigeon) have long been raised domestically for meat. There are old plantations in the Carolinas and Louisiana with rather fancy roosting houses for squab known as "pigeon-aeries" which allowed the birds to fly in and out freely. Quail and squab are both available by mail order (see page 317). Quail are tiny, mainly a morsel of breast meat—and you'll need two per person. A plump squab, which weighs a bit less than a pound, makes a serving by itself.

The rich, almost red-meat flavor of quail and squab is the main reason for preparing these luxury-priced birds on occasion. But, as you will find with this recipe, cooking them is extremely easy, and conveniently quick too. Use it for either kind of bird, and for either outdoor grilling or inside broiling. We like to serve the birds right on top of a salad—such as our Tomato–Field Pea Salad (page 69). Spicy Eggplant Relish (page 6) and Candied Kumquats (page 15) are both delicious condiments for quail and squab. Be sure to save any trimmings or, if you can, cook up some extra birds, to make extraordinarily good Squab or Quail Hash (page 195) the next day or so.

Remove the giblets and any other innards from the body cavity of the squab. Using kitchen shears or poultry shears, cut closely along one side of the spine, then the other side, to remove the backbone. (Save it for making stock.)

Preheat the broiler.

Flip each squab over so it is breast side up, and, placing the heel of your hand at the center of the breast, press down firmly, breaking the breastbone and flattening out the bird. On each side of the bird, make a slit through the skin between the breast and the thigh on the lower part of the torso. Tuck the end of each drumstick through the slits, to hold the legs in place. Tuck the wings under the back to keep them in place. Liberally sprinkle salt, pepper, and thyme on both sides of the birds, and drizzle about a tablespoon of olive oil over each (or ½ tablespoon if using quail). Loosen the skin on the breasts of the birds by gently working your fingers under the skin at the neck. Tuck half a bay leaf under the skin on each side of the breast. Dribble the optional brandy over the squab, and set aside to rest for 30 minutes.

Place the birds about 6 inches below the heat element. Broil for a total of 15 minutes, flipping the birds onto their backs after about 10 minutes. Remove from the oven, and let rest 5 minutes before serving.

NOTE We prefer squab cooked medium-rare, and the time I've specified is for that. If you prefer your squab more cooked, allow another 5 minutes.

Thyme-Smothered Chicken

MAKES ENOUGH TO SERVE 4–6

- 4 chicken legs, 4 thighs, and 4 wings, brined for 8–12 hours (box, page 95)
- 3/4 teaspoon freshly ground black pepper
- 2 teaspoons dried thyme
- 4 tablespoons (1/2 stick) unsalted butter
- 3 large onions, peeled and sliced into 1/2-inch wedges
- 5 cloves garlic, crushed
- 1 bay leaf
- 1/2 teaspoon salt
- 1/2 teaspoon freshly ground black pepper

Traditionally, "smothered" poultry and meats are served with (and often cooked in) a heavy, flour-thickened gravy. Here, the chicken is cooked in its own juices, with plenty of onions, thyme, and butter. No water, stock, or flour is added, so both chicken and sauce are lighter and more intensely flavored. It's delicious served over stone-ground grits or rice.

Rinse the chicken pieces, and dry them thoroughly with paper towel. Sprinkle the chicken all over with the pepper and thyme. Heat the butter in a large covered skillet or Dutch oven until hot and foaming. Put the chicken pieces, skin side down, into the pan, and cook over moderately high heat until the chicken is a rich golden brown. Turn the pieces as needed until they are golden brown all over.

Remove the chicken from the pan. Immediately toss the sliced onions into the skillet and cook, stirring often, until the onions become limp and translucent. Use a wooden spoon to dislodge from the bottom of the pan any browned bits left from cooking the chicken. Add the garlic, bay leaf, salt, and pepper, stir well to distribute the seasonings, and cook for 5 minutes longer. Return to the pan the browned chicken pieces and any juices they have given off while resting. Bury them in the onions and cover. Cook, covered, over low heat, stirring occasionally, for about 1½ hours, until the chicken is fork-tender. Serve hot.

A NOTE ABOUT DRIED THYME

Although we generally prefer the flavor of fresh herbs in our cooking, one notable exception is thyme. Good quality dried thyme, such as Spice Islands brand, has a more focused and intense flavor, in our opinion, than fresh thyme, and we use it in all the recipes in this book. Spice Islands is a fairly common brand and can be found in most supermarkets.

AUTHENTIC SOUTHERN HAM: "VIRGINIA," "SMITHFIELD," OR "COUNTRY"

Not all country ham is "Virginia" ham, but this unique curing tradition started there. Virginia Indians are said to have used the method on venison centuries ago, and it was first developed for and applied to pigs on a large scale in the mid-1700s, in the tidewater town of Smithfield, Virginia. Ever since, "Smithfield hams" have set the standard for Southern hams. Today, however, only pork legs actually processed in that town (under the Gwaltney or Luter brand names) can be called "genuine Smithfield hams." But excellent long-cured "country hams" are produced in other parts of Virginia, North Carolina, Tennessee, Kentucky, and even some states outside the South. Different curing formulas and smoking and aging methods yield distinctly different hams—some are drier, saltier, and stronger-tasting than others—but you can use any real country ham in our recipes. (See the list of sources on page 317.)

Country hams—whether cured in Smithfield, Virginia, or elsewhere—are almost always available either uncooked or cooked. If you buy an uncooked ham, you will have to soak and boil it first, before baking. Most ham companies provide instructions for this initial desalting and cooking of their products; you can follow theirs or use the basic recipe for boiling we give here (see below).

Trim the ham before baking. Once you've boiled the ham—or if you've bought a ham that's cooked but not trimmed—remove the skin and all but a thin coating of the fat. Then proceed with the baking, or, if you prefer, just refrigerate the boiled ham. It will keep for months that way—ready to be sliced paper-thin to put in biscuits, or thick-sliced as steaks for frying or baking.

Carving a country ham: Start at the hock (or narrow, bony end of the ham), and slice down toward the bone. Make your first slice into the meat a few inches from the end, with the blade slanted toward the large end of the ham; make your next slices a bit farther from the hock (that is, moving toward the large end). Increase the angle of your slices as you go and—most important—keep your slices *extremely thin*! You will likely receive carving instructions with your ham, by the way. (Miss Lewis recommends the instructions provided by the Gwaltney company; she likes their hams, too.)

HOW TO COOK A COUNTRY HAM

There is more than one way to cook a country ham. Individual producers usually include directions and recipes they feel are best suited to the preparation of their particular hams. We have researched and tested many recipes, including some that call for soaking and simmering in either sweet milk or buttermilk to sweeten and tenderize the ham, and various prescribed methods for lengthy baking, up to 24 hours, at varying temperatures.

Most of the recipes in this book call for uncooked country ham, since it is the intensity of the cured, smoky, aged pork flavor that we value as a seasoning. However, when you are serving a whole baked country ham as the centerpiece of a meal or party buffet, or using slices to stuff biscuits, the following is the simplest and, we think, the best way to prepare a genuine country ham. It demands little attention during cooking, but does require some lead time for repeated soakings of the ham in water, and a rather large pot for slowly cooking the ham just beneath a simmer, or, as we say in the South, at a *mull.*

Scrub the country ham well under cool running water to remove any cure, pepper coating, or possible mold. (Do not be alarmed if there is mold growing on your ham; it is a natural occurrence and does not mean the ham is spoiled.) Put the ham into a container large enough to hold the ham, and cover it with cool water. Set the ham in a cool, safe place, and let soak for 3 days, changing the water once each day. This step is necessary to remove some of the salt and to rehydrate the ham.

Once the ham has been soaked, put it into a large pot with enough water to cover the ham, and gradually bring the water to a very slow simmer. Cover the pot, and adjust the heat so that the water is just percolating beneath a simmer. Check this several times during the first 20 minutes or so, until you are able to regulate the cooking speed, and once every hour after that, to ensure a slow, steady cooking. On average, a country ham takes 4–5 hours to cook using this method. You will know the ham is done when its top skin becomes covered in what will look like large blisters. Once this occurs, uncover and allow the ham to cool in the cooking pot, off the heat. Then pour off the cooking liquid and transfer the ham to a sheet pan or platter. At this point you have a country ham that is ready to be eaten as is, or baked following the recipe for Smithfield Ham Baked with Madeira (recipe follows).

Country ham cooked this way will keep for 2 months or longer refrigerated, and may be prepared this far in advance before baking if desired.

Smithfield Ham Baked with Madeira

MAKES ENOUGH TO SERVE 15–20 AS AN ENTRÉE

- 1 Smithfield ham, boiled and trimmed (preceding recipe)
- 3 tablespoons unsalted butter, cut into small pieces
- 1 bottle good-quality Madeira
- Fresh nutmeg for grating

You have lots of choices with a whole country ham (box, pages 111–113). You can buy it uncooked, leave it hanging in a cool place, and just slice off thin slivers and steaks to cook when you want or use small pieces to flavor other dishes. Alternatively, you can boil the ham and keep it in the refrigerator for months, all ready to eat. Or, once you've got a country ham and boiled it (or bought a cooked one), you can bake and glaze it with Madeira for a great holiday or big-party dish. It has not only the intense and authentic flavor of fine cured pork, but all the advantages a host could want: it can be prepared ahead; served hot, at room temperature, or cold; it makes a striking sight on the buffet; feeds twenty people and still yields plenty of leftovers. Serve with lots of condiments in the Southern style—butter, fig relish, fig preserves and strawberry preserves, and apple and pear chutneys (see Chapter I).

Preheat the oven to 350°F.

Put the fully cooked and trimmed ham on a roasting rack in a heavy roasting pan. Dot the surface of the ham with the small pieces of butter. Pour the Madeira into the roasting pan, and grate the fresh nutmeg generously over the ham.

Put the ham into the preheated oven. After 30 minutes, begin basting the ham every 15 minutes and cook for 1 hour longer, or until the ham is well glazed and caramelized and the fat is blistered. Watch carefully toward the end of cooking, because as the sugars in the Madeira concentrate from baking, the ham will glaze more quickly, and you will need to take care not to burn it.

Remove from the oven and allow the ham to rest for 15–20 minutes before cutting into very thin slices, starting at the hock end and proceeding toward the front of the ham (see box page 112 for how to carve a country ham).

If serving the ham warm, skim all fat from the roasting pan and serve the pan juices as a simple and delicious sauce.

Serve warm, cold, or at room temperature.

Country Ham Steak with Red-Eye Gravy

MAKES ENOUGH TO SERVE 4

- 4 uncooked country-ham steaks, center-cut, about 1/4 inch thick
- 2 tablespoons unsalted butter
- 3 1/2 cups strong, freshly brewed coffee

A cook from the mountains of northern Georgia taught me to cook country-ham steaks this way, which varies somewhat from most recipes, in which slices of country ham are fried briefly on each side in a cast-iron skillet, and then the skillet is quickly deglazed with a little water or coffee to make a fast and simple gravy. A ring of fat typically gilds the surface of the gravy, and many proclaim this the "eye" in red-eye gravy. There is, however, another school of lore that attributes the "red eyes" to the early-morning cook preparing the dish. Regardless of folklore, this recipe makes a tender country-ham steak not too salty, with a rich-tasting gravy that is the result of brief, gentle simmering in coffee.

The ham you will need for this preparation is uncooked country ham. You can slice it yourself from a whole ham, or buy presliced country-ham steaks, available in most supermarkets and through mail-order sources (page 317). Center-cut steaks with the bone in are handsome, but any cut, as long as it is no more than 1/3 inch thick, will do.

Rinse the ham steaks briefly under cool running water, and pat dry with paper towels. Heat the butter in a large covered skillet or frying pan until hot and foaming. Lay the ham steaks in the pan, and cook over medium-high heat for 2 minutes on each side. Remove the steaks from the pan, and pour in the coffee. Use a wooden spoon to dislodge any browned bits and pieces in the pan, and deglaze well. Return the ham steaks to the pan, cover tightly, and simmer gently for 20–30 minutes, until they are tender. Transfer the ham to a platter, and serve with the coffee or "red-eye gravy" passed separately.

Bay-Studded Pork Shoulder with Sauce of Wild Mushrooms

MAKES ENOUGH TO SERVE 6–8

THE PORK SHOULDER

1 bone-in pork shoulder (picnic or Boston butt), brined (box, page 95)

½ teaspoon salt

½ teaspoon coarsely cracked black peppercorns

1½ teaspoons dried thyme

3 cloves garlic, peeled and sliced thinly lengthwise

12 whole bay leaves

Long, slow oven-braising—in red wine or tawny port—is an excellent way to cook a big cut of pork so that it's moist and succulent. We first cooked a pork shoulder this way several years ago, on a Sunday visit to a friend's farm. We'd brought the pork and a bottle of port with us. We then took a walk through the woods and discovered a cache of wild mushrooms as well as wild blackberries ripening on the bushes. So we gathered what we could and, following the principle that what grows together goes together, we sautéed the mushrooms and added them to the sauce, and then, finally, tossed in the blackberries. The special flavors that they yielded are not essential, and if you don't have such treats at hand, you can serve it with just the defatted and reduced braising liquid. This pork is particularly good served with Old-Fashioned Creamy Grits (pages 170–171), and any leftover meat is delicious sliced and served cold with a salad or in a sandwich. Try to get a shoulder with the bone in and the skin attached. If, however, you can't find one, a boneless, skinless shoulder roast is still very good.

Preheat the oven to 325°F.

Rinse the pork shoulder and pat dry. Using a sharp paring knife, cut twelve slits in the skin side of the pork shoulder, about 1 inch wide and 1½ inches deep—the slits should be in three rows of four each, spaced equally apart.

Mix together the salt, cracked peppercorns, and thyme. Sprinkle approximately ⅛ teaspoon of the seasoning mixture into each slit, then insert 1 garlic sliver and 1 whole bay leaf. (The bay leaves should protrude from the shoulder so that you can easily remove them before serving.) Sprinkle any remaining seasoning all over the pork shoulder.

Scatter the sliced onions over the bottom of a baking dish or roasting pan that will just hold the meat. Place the seasoned pork shoulder on top of the onion slices, and pour the wine into the bottom of the pan. Lay a piece of parchment

2 large onions, peeled and thickly sliced
1 bottle (750 milliliters) red wine or ruby or tawny port

THE WILD MUSHROOM SAUCE

2 tablespoons unsalted butter
2 cups mushrooms, or a mixture of wild and cultivated mushrooms, cleaned and cut into ⅓-inch slices (or, if very small, trimmed and left whole)
Salt
Freshly ground black pepper
1 shallot, minced
2 small cloves garlic, minced
2 tablespoons finely snipped parsley
Reserved liquid from cooking the pork shoulder
½ cup heavy cream

paper directly on top of the pork shoulder, and wrap the pan tightly with a double thickness of foil. Put in the preheated oven to cook for 4½–5 hours, until the meat is very tender when pierced with a sharp knife. Remove from the oven and allow to cool slightly.

If you have a roast that has its skin intact, raise oven temperature to 425°F. If not, disregard.

Remove the onions and cooking liquid from the roasting pan, and strain through a fine-meshed sieve, pressing gently on the onions with the back of a wooden spoon to extract as much liquid as possible. Skim any visible fat from the surface of the cooking liquid, and reserve for the sauce.

Meanwhile, remove the bay leaves from the pork shoulder and discard. Using a sharp knife, carefully separate the skin (rind) from the top of the pork shoulder, and remove in 1 piece. Transfer the pork shoulder to a heated serving platter and keep warm.

Gently scrape any soft fat from the underside of the pork rind. Place the rind on a baking sheet and put into the 425°F oven until crisp and deep golden brown, about 10 minutes. While the rind is crisping, make the wild-mushroom sauce.

Heat the butter in a large skillet until hot and foaming. Add the mushrooms, and cook over high heat, stirring occasionally, until they begin to brown, about 5–10 minutes. Season with salt and a small amount of freshly ground black pepper. Add the minced shallot and garlic and snipped parsley, and cook for an additional 3–4 minutes, stirring often. Pour in the reserved cooking liquid, and boil until the liquid is reduced by one-half. Add the heavy cream and simmer briefly. Taste carefully for seasoning, and adjust if needed. Serve hot.

To serve, cut the crisped pork rind into ½-inch strips and arrange on top of the pork shoulder. At the table, slice the pork shoulder thinly against the grain, and serve with a piece of crisped pork rind (or crackling) on the side and the wild-mushroom sauce spooned over the sliced meat.

Thyme-Scented Loin of Pork with Muscadine Grapes and Port

MAKES ENOUGH TO SERVE 8–10

One 6–8-pound pork loin, boned, and brined for 8–24 hours (box, page 95)
2 tablespoons unsalted butter
2 teaspoons dried thyme
Salt and freshly ground black pepper
A few gratings of nutmeg
5 whole bay leaves
2 ribs of leafy celery, chopped
1 large onion, thinly sliced
2 shallots, thinly sliced
1 clove garlic, thinly sliced
2½ cups muscadine, scuppernong, or Concord grapes
2 cups port wine
1 tablespoon unsalted butter, cut into ¼-inch pieces
1 cup light Chicken Stock (page 33)
2 tablespoons brandy or cognac
3 tablespoons unsalted butter, cold, cut into pieces

Pork loin today tends to be so lean that it is easily overcooked, becoming dry and losing flavor. Preparing a loin this way—brined and then roasted with aromatic vegetables—helps to ensure a moist, tender, and delicious roast. An instant-read thermometer is handy, because you want to take the pork out when it just reaches 140°F.

Muscadine grapes—especially the scuppernong variety—are Southern natives, popular as a table grape but also used in a traditional sweet wine. Here, they lend their pungent, spicy flavor to a rich sauce for serving with the roast. Concord grapes are a fine substitute if muscadine are not available.

This roast makes wonderful leftovers, which we like to serve cold with Clemson blue cheese, roasted pecans, fresh or dried figs, and good mustard.

Rinse the pork loin, and dry thoroughly with paper toweling. Tie the loin tightly every 2½ inches with butchers' twine so that it will keep a nice round shape while cooking. Heat the 2 tablespoons butter in a large sauté pan over high heat until hot and foaming. Place the pork loin, fat side down, in the pan, and cook until a deep golden brown. Turn the meat, and brown on all sides, including the ends. Remove from the pan, and set aside to cool.

When the pork loin is cool enough to handle, season it all over with dried thyme, salt, pepper, and gratings of nutmeg. Position the loin fat side up, and tuck the bay leaves underneath the butchers' twine down the length of the loin. Place on a rack in a roasting pan, and arrange the vegetables and grapes around the meat. Pour 1½ cups of the port into the bottom of the roasting pan, and sprinkle the ¼-inch pieces of butter over all. Cook in a preheated 350°F oven for 40 minutes to 1 hour, until the internal temperature of the meat reaches 140°F. *Take great care not to overcook.* Remove from the oven, and put the meat on a warm platter tented with foil to rest for 15 minutes. Meanwhile, prepare the sauce.

Place the roasting pan with all of the vegetables and aromatics on top of the stove over high heat. As the juices begin to simmer, use a wooden spoon to stir and scrape the bottom of the pan to dislodge any caramelized bits of meat juices and vegetables—there probably will not be too much, though, because of the amount of port. Use the back of the spoon to press the grapes and vegetables and break them up a bit into the simmering pan—this will help to release more juice and flavor from them. Continue cooking for about 5 minutes. Strain through a fine-meshed strainer into a sauté pan, again pressing with the spoon to extract as much liquid as possible. Discard the solids, and carefully skim the juices and wine to remove any fat that may be floating on the surface. Add the remaining ½ cup port and the stock to the pan, and bring to a fierce boil over high heat. Cook until reduced by approximately a third in volume, skimming any scum that rises to the surface. Add the brandy or cognac, and continue to boil until the sauce begins to concentrate and become a bit syrupy; it should lightly coat the back of a metal spoon when dipped into the sauce. At this point, begin to add the 3 tablespoons butter in pieces, boiling until each piece has melted and boiled into an emulsion before adding the next. When all the butter has been incorporated, remove from the heat and taste for salt. Whisk in a few grains if needed. You should have a rich, sweet-tasting sauce with rounded flavors of the meat juices, grapes, and vegetables. Reserve and keep warm.

Remove the twine and bay leaves from the pork loin. At the table, carve thin slices on the bias, and serve several slices to each person with a little of the sauce spooned over the slices. Pass any remaining sauce separately.

Scuppernong grapes

Baked Pork Chops with Cranberries

MAKES ENOUGH TO SERVE 4

- 4 pork chops cut from the loin, 1/2 inch thick, brined for 2 hours (box, page 95)
- 4 tablespoons lard or unsalted butter, or a mixture of both
- Salt and freshly ground black pepper
- 12 ounces fresh cranberries, rinsed and picked over
- 3/4 cup granulated sugar

A simple, flavorful supper dish that Miss Lewis used to make at Café Nicholson in the 1940s. Layer pork chops and sugared cranberries in a casserole and bake—the tart berries tenderize the meat and render a delicious sauce. It's a good way to prepare chicken too.

Preheat the oven to 350°F.

Rinse and dry the pork chops with paper towels. Heat the lard or butter in a heavy sauté pan until quite hot. Brown the pork chops on each side in the hot fat. Remove from the pan, and season well on each side with salt and pepper.

Put a third of the cranberries in the bottom of a small baking dish that will hold the pork chops in two layers. Sprinkle 1/4 cup of the sugar over the cranberries. Lay two of the pork chops side by side on top of the sugared cranberries. Top with half of the remaining cranberries, and sprinkle another 1/4 cup of sugar over all. Top with the two remaining pork chops, the same as before, and the remaining cranberries and sugar. Place a piece of parchment directly on top of the cranberries, and a piece of foil directly on top of the parchment. Cover the baking dish with a tight-fitting lid, or wrap with a double thickness of foil to seal tightly.

Bake in the preheated oven for about 1 hour, until pork chops are tender. Taste the cooked cranberries carefully, and add a little salt and black pepper if needed. Serve the pork chops hot with the cranberry sauce spooned over.

Garlic Braised Shoulder Lamb Chops with Butter Beans and Tomatoes

MAKES ENOUGH TO SERVE 4

- 4 lamb shoulder chops, cut ½ inch thick (about 8 ounces each)
- 2 tablespoons unsalted butter
- 2 large onions, cut into ⅓-inch slices
- 6 cloves garlic, cut into thin slivers
- 1½ teaspoons salt
- ¾ teaspoon freshly ground black pepper
- 3 medium-sized tomatoes, peeled, seeded, and cut into ½-inch pieces
- ½ cup red wine
- 2 bay leaves
- 1⅓ cups fresh butter beans, cooked in lightly salted water until barely tender, about 20 minutes
- 2 teaspoons finely chopped parsley

Shoulder lamb chops are one of those underappreciated cuts of meat which, if cooked properly, yield delicious flavor. Long, slow cooking is essential—the chops braise in wine with tomatoes, onion, and garlic for a couple of hours; then butter beans are added and cooked for an additional ½ hour. In summer, use fresh tomatoes and beans (or field peas). In winter, use canned tomatoes and cooked dried lima beans soaked with 1½ teaspoons dried thyme. Shoulder lamb chops don't yield that much meat, but they are inexpensive. Double the recipe for meat lovers.

Preheat the oven to 325°F.

Trim the lamb chops of any visible excess fat. Rinse the chops under cool running water, and pat thoroughly dry with paper towel. Heat the butter in a heavy skillet or frying pan until hot and foaming. Sauté the lamb on both sides over medium-high heat until deeply browned, about 6 minutes per side. Transfer the lamb to a casserole or baking dish just large enough to hold it in a single layer. Pour off all but 2 tablespoons of the fat. Add the onions to the pan, and stir well to coat in the cooking fat. Sauté for 5 minutes. While the onions are cooking, use a wooden spoon to scrape the bottom of the skillet and dislodge any browned bits and lamb juices. Add the garlic slivers and stir well. Season with ½ teaspoon of the salt and ½ teaspoon of the freshly ground black pepper. Cook for 10 minutes longer, stirring often, then stir in the chopped tomatoes and remove from the heat. While the onions and garlic are cooking, season both sides of the lamb chops with the remaining salt and pepper.

Spoon the onions and garlic over the lamb chops, pour on the red wine, and add the bay leaves. Place a piece of parchment paper directly over the lamb and onions, and place a piece of foil, shiny side down, directly on top of the paper. Cover the cooking vessel tightly with a double layer of foil, shiny side down, and if the dish has a lid put it on now. Bake in the preheated oven for 1¾ hours. Remove from the oven, and carefully uncover. Use a large, flat spoon to skim off the fat that has pooled on the surface. Carefully stir in the butter beans and re-cover with the parchment and foil. Return to the oven for 30 minutes.

Taste the sauce carefully for seasoning, and season with salt and freshly ground black pepper as needed. Sprinkle the chopped parsley on top and serve.

Slow-Cooked Oxtails

MAKES ENOUGH TO SERVE 4–6

- 5 pounds beef oxtails
- ½ cup lard, or a mixture of lard and butter
- 1½ teaspoons dried thyme, preferably Spice Islands
- Kosher or sea salt as needed
- Freshly ground black pepper as needed
- 2 large onions, chopped (2 cups)
- 2 large stalks celery, with leaves, chopped (1 cup)
- 1 medium carrot, thinly sliced (½ cup)
- 2 large cloves garlic, minced
- 1 cup peeled, seeded, and chopped tomatoes, fresh or canned
- ½ cup Chicken Stock (page 33) or water

The rich flavor and luscious texture of oxtails develops through patient, slow cooking. We cook them in the oven, with vegetables and seasonings, for almost 4 hours, until the meat is meltingly tender. Serve over grits or rice.

Rinse the oxtails, and dry well with paper towels. Heat the lard in a large sauté pan until it is quite hot but not smoking. Brown the oxtails in the hot fat, turning until deeply browned on all sides. Remove to a baking dish just large enough to hold the oxtails comfortably in a single layer. Sprinkle the dried thyme and salt and pepper over the meat.

Pour off all but 3 tablespoons of the cooking fat from the sauté pan. Add the chopped onions and cook over medium-high heat, stirring and scraping the bottom of the pan with a large wooden spoon to dislodge any flavorful browned bits. Add the celery, carrots, and garlic, and continue cooking, stirring often, until the vegetables begin to brown. Add the tomatoes, and season with salt and pepper. Reduce heat, and simmer for about 10 minutes.

Check the vegetables for seasoning, and adjust if needed; then spoon them over the oxtails. Pour the stock or water over all. Place a piece of parchment paper directly on top of the oxtails and vegetables, and a piece of foil directly on top of the parchment. Cover the baking dish with a tight-fitting lid or a double thickness of foil wrapped to cover tightly. Place in a preheated 300°F oven, and bake for 3½–4 hours, until oxtails are very tender. Spoon off any visible pools of fat, check for seasoning, and serve hot over rice or grits.

Pigs' Feet in Savory Tomato Sauce

MAKES ENOUGH TO SERVE 6

6 whole pigs' feet

1 teaspoon salt

2 medium onions, chopped (1½ cups)

6 whole black peppercorns

Water to cover the pigs' feet

THE SAVORY TOMATO SAUCE

¼ cup peanut oil or light olive oil

1 tablespoon unsalted butter

1 cup chopped onion

1 teaspoon minced garlic

1 teaspoon salt

½ teaspoon freshly ground black pepper

½ teaspoon dried thyme

2 cups peeled, seeded, and chopped tomatoes, fresh or canned

The wonderful Bessie Smith immortalized pigs' feet in her gritty love song "Gimme a Pig's Foot and a Bottle of Beer." Though they take a long time to cook—4 hours or so of slow simmering—the rich, succulent morsels of meat they yield are worth the wait. There's little actual work in the initial long cooking, and it can be done a day or two ahead. We love them this way, served with lima beans and Simple Boiled Cabbage (page 152).

Be sure to buy whole—not split—pigs' feet for this recipe. And save (and freeze) the leftover cooking liquid in which the feet are first simmered. It's delicious as a soup base or for cooking beans.

Rinse the pigs' feet well, and put them in a large pot with the salt, onions, and whole peppercorns. Add enough water to cover the pigs' feet by 2 inches. Partially cover the pot, and cook at a gentle simmer for 3 hours. While cooking, start the tomato sauce.

In a deep nonreactive sauté pan or Dutch oven, heat the oil and butter together until the butter begins to foam. Add the onion, garlic, salt, pepper, and thyme, and cook over moderately low heat for about 30 minutes, stirring frequently. Add the tomatoes, and stir well to blend. Simmer, partially covered, for 30 minutes. Taste carefully for seasoning, and add salt and pepper as needed. Reserve.

When the pigs' feet have cooked for 3 hours, transfer them along with 3 cups of their cooking liquid to the cooked tomato sauce. Stir gently to blend in the liquid. Partially cover, and cook at a very low simmer for 1 hour, until the pigs' feet are very tender.

Lamb or Veal Shanks Braised with Green Tomatoes

MAKES ENOUGH TO SERVE 4

4 lamb shanks, about 1 pound each, or veal shanks

Kosher salt

1 teaspoon freshly ground black pepper

3 teaspoons dried thyme—2 for the veal, 1 for the braising vegetables

4 tablespoons (½ stick) unsalted butter

2 large yellow onions, cut into ½-inch dice (about 3 cups)

1 stalk celery, thinly sliced (½ cup)

1 medium carrot, diced (½ cup)

1 tablespoon finely chopped garlic

3 medium green tomatoes, cored and cut into ½-inch chunks (2½–3 cups)

3 bay leaves

½ cup white wine

1 cup Chicken Stock (page 33) or water

If the frost comes before all your tomatoes have ripened, take advantage of those green tomatoes to make this rich braise. The flavor and acidity of the tomatoes are a good foil for shanks. If you can't get green tomatoes, substitute canned San Marzano plum tomatoes, although the dish won't taste the same.

The dish calls for lamb shanks, but we have made it with veal shanks too with excellent results. Either way, it's delicious served with Yellow Rice (page 168).

The technique is the same with either kind of meat, though with veal shanks you'll want cross-cut "ossobuco" sections at least 1½ inches thick; 2 or 3 inches is better. For an unusual treat, try to get a whole, uncut veal shank—long like a lamb shank but much larger. You'll need a big pot, but the results are terrific.

In Alabama, where I grew up, and in Georgia, where both Miss Lewis and I now live, the growing season is 10 months long. Consequently, we are blessed with two crops of tomatoes—a summer crop that ripens in early to mid-June, and an autumn crop that is ready for harvest in mid- to late October and stretches into the first frost. Because the fall tomatoes ripen less quickly and there is always a bounty of green tomatoes left on the vine as cold weather approaches, cooks have devised many different ways to use green tomatoes—pickles, preserves, chutney, and pie, to name a few, in addition to the widely known fried green tomatoes.

This recipe is especially good because the slightly tart flavor of the green tomatoes, which mellows as it cooks, is a good foil to the rich succulence of the slow-cooked shanks. The acidity of the tomatoes also helps to tenderize and release the flavor of the shanks as they cook.

Preheat the oven to 325°F.

Rinse the shanks well, and pat them with paper towel until completely dry. Trim the shanks of any excess fat, and rub 1 tablespoon salt, the pepper, and 2 teaspoons of the dried thyme into them so they are well seasoned.

Heat a large sauté pan over high heat, add the butter, and heat until melted and bubbling but not colored. Place the shanks in the pan and cook, turning on all sides, until deeply browned all over.

Remove the browned shanks from the pan, and transfer them to a baking dish just large enough to hold them.

Pour off half of the fat from the sauté pan, then immediately add the chopped onions, celery, and carrot. Sprinkle on 1½ teaspoons salt and the remaining dried thyme. Stir well to distribute the seasonings and cooking fat. Using a wooden spoon, dislodge any caramelized bits from the sauté pan and stir them into the vegetables—the moisture released by the sautéing of the vegetables will help to facilitate the deglazing. Continue sautéing the vegetables until they begin to brown—about 10 minutes. Add the garlic, green tomatoes, and bay leaves, and stir well. Cook for 2 minutes longer, and pour in the wine and chicken stock. Bring to a full boil, and cook for 2 minutes. Remove from heat, and taste carefully for seasoning. Adjust as needed with salt and pepper. Spoon the vegetables over the shanks, and place a piece of parchment paper directly over them. Cover tightly with a double thickness of aluminum foil, shiny side down. (Don't omit the parchment; the acidity of the tomatoes in direct contact with the foil could impart a metallic flavor.)

Cook on the middle rack of the preheated oven for 1½ hours, or until a paring knife inserted into the thickest part of the meat pierces and releases easily. Remove the foil and parchment and cook, basting occasionally, for ½ hour longer, or until the shanks begin to glaze and take on a rich, caramelized color. Remove from the oven and spoon off any visible fat. Taste the vegetables and sauce carefully, and adjust seasoning if needed. Serve the shanks hot with the braising vegetables spooned over.

NOTE Can be prepared up to 3 days in advance. To reheat, place in a preheated 325°F oven for ½ hour, or until completely heated through.

Braised Beef Short Ribs

MAKES ENOUGH TO SERVE 8 FOR LUNCH OR 4 AS A HEARTY DINNER MAIN DISH

- 8 beef short ribs
- 1 tablespoon kosher salt
- 1 teaspoon freshly ground black pepper
- 1 teaspoon dried thyme, preferably Spice Islands brand
- ¼ cup peanut oil or lard
- 3 large yellow onions, peeled and sliced into ½-inch wedges (about 4 cups)
- 3 bay leaves
- 12 whole cloves garlic, peeled
- 28 ounces canned whole tomatoes (preferred) or 8 very ripe garden tomatoes, cored and peeled
- 1 cup Chicken Stock (page 33) or water
- ½ cup red wine

Miss Lewis was quoted once as saying, "I figured out a long time ago that beef has no flavor." And while it's true that she rarely cooks or eats beef, she does love short ribs, especially these short ribs. They're prepared almost exactly like the lamb or veal shanks, though here red tomatoes are used, along with lots of onion. During the final, uncovered cooking, the liquid reduces to an intense sauce, which just coats the meat.

Butchers cut short ribs two ways, either between the bones, so each chunk has one rib, or across the bones, so each piece has several small bony sections connected by meat. Both kinds of ribs are fine for this, though I prefer the latter cut—known as "flanken"—because the exposed bones and cartilage release more flavor and body into the dish.

Serve with rice or grits or, for what I consider a perfect meal, with Whipped Rutabagas (page 158), Braised Cabbage (page 153), and Our Favorite Sour Milk Cornbread (page 210).

Preheat the oven to 325°F.

Rinse the short ribs under cool water, and pat them dry with paper toweling. Sprinkle the salt, pepper, and ½ teaspoon of the dried thyme all over the ribs. Heat the oil or lard in a large, heavy-bottomed skillet until hot, then add the ribs in batches without crowding, and cook, turning as needed, until they are deeply browned on all sides. Transfer the browned short ribs to a baking dish or casserole just large enough to hold them, and set aside.

Carefully pour off all but 2 tablespoons of the cooking fat from the skillet, and immediately add the onions to the pan. Sprinkle 1 teaspoon salt over the onions, and stir well. Cook the onions over medium heat, and, using a wooden spoon, scrape the bottom of the skillet as they cook to dislodge any caramelized bits left from browning the ribs. Add the bay leaves, a few grindings of black pepper, and the remaining ½ teaspoon dried thyme. Stir well to distribute the seasonings. Add the whole garlic cloves and cook 3 minutes longer. Pour in the tomatoes, stock, and red wine, bring to a simmer, and cook for 5 minutes. Taste carefully for seasoning. The braising vegetables and liquid should be highly seasoned.

Pour the vegetables and liquid over the browned ribs, and spread the vegetables around so they are in an even layer. Cover with a piece of parchment paper and a double thickness of heavy-duty aluminum foil, shiny side down. Seal tightly, and put in the center of the preheated oven to cook for 1½ hours, or until a paring knife pierces the meat easily. Uncover, and bake 30 minutes longer, basting often, to caramelize the ribs. Remove from the oven and spoon off any visible fat. Taste the braising juices carefully for seasoning, and correct if necessary. Serve hot, with the vegetables and braising juices spooned over as a sauce.

NOTE If you chill the casserole, it's much easier to peel off the fat.

TO REHEAT: Put covered into a preheated 350°F oven for 25 minutes. Uncover and continue heating for 10 minutes longer.

Scott Peacock cooking in the hearth at Bullock Hall in Roswell, Georgia, on the occasion of Edna Lewis's 80th birthday

Tomatoes
Tomatoes
TOMATOES
CALIFORNIA STRAWBERRIES
Tomatoes
TOMATOES

V SPICY COLLARDS AND SWEET POTATOES

Vegetables and Side Dishes

Skillet Asparagus
Skillet Scallions
Creamed Scallions
Watercress Cooked in Pork Stock
Braised Spring Vidalia Onions
Roasted Beets in Ginger Syrup
Variation: Hot Buttered Roasted Beets
Cymling Squash in Light Tomato Sauce
Simmered Yellow Squash
Garlic Green Beans
Fresh Okra in Alabama
Roasted Okra
Corn on the Cob Boiled in the Husk
Fried Green Corn
Variation: Creamed Corn
Scalloped Tomatoes
Scalloped Green Tomatoes
Sauté of Heirloom Tomatoes and Okra with Bacon Garnish
Pole Beans Simmered in Pork Stock
Lady Peas Cooked in Pork Stock
Fried Eggplant
Simple Boiled Cabbage
Braised Cabbage
Substitutes for Pork Stock
An Assembly of Southern Greens Cooked in Pork Stock
Buying, Trimming, and Washing Greens
Spicy Collards in Tomato-Onion Sauce
Mashed Turnips
Whipped Rutabagas
A Note About Cooking Sherry
Savory African Squash
Sautéed Apples with Chestnuts
Deep-Fried Celery Hearts
Roasted Parsnips
Cardamom-Scented Whipped Sweet Potatoes
Sweetness in Sweet Potatoes
Lemon-Glazed Sweet Potatoes
Sweet Potato Casserole
White Sweet Potatoes Baked in Pastry
Plain Rice
Yellow Rice
Coconut Rice
To Prepare Coconut
Old-Fashioned Creamy Grits
Shrimp Paste and Grits

We are lucky as cooks in the South because of the abundance of fresh vegetables available much of the year. Where Miss Lewis and I now live in Georgia, we get locally grown asparagus, peas, and onions in early April, followed almost immediately by summer squashes and cucumbers; by June, we've got tomatoes and corn. In high summer, the supper table is crowded with bowls of okra, squash, eggplant, green beans, field peas (sometimes four or five different kinds!), beets, and other vegetables—not to mention salads, pickles, and relishes. And in the fall, there are sweet potatoes and other root vegetables, winter squashes, and greens.

In recent years, there's been a dramatic increase in the range of vegetables, as both new varieties of produce and traditional "heirlooms" have come to market—often organically grown and raised by local farmers. This development has been a boon to us and other Southern city-dwellers, who grew up with a taste for truly fresh homegrown vegetables. In Miss Lewis's childhood, the farming community of Freetown, Virginia, was self-sufficient, and the year was marked by the vegetables her family grew, harvested—or foraged.

My hometown of Hartford, Alabama, was in the midst of farm country, and the seasonal cycle of produce was part of my life, too. Every summer, I spent days sweating in our bean patch, picking butter beans, which we ate at every meal (and froze for the rest of the year). My father, who'd grown up on a farm, taught me about harvesting vegetables at just the right moment, when corn was at its sweetest and okra most tender. In the days before refrigeration, he told me, his family would "bank" their cabbage and sweet-potato crops through the winter by burying them in pits in the earth, then covering them with straw and canvas tarpaulins.

This chapter has an assortment of our favorite vegetable recipes presented in seasonal order, starting with springtime, but many can be prepared all year long.

Scott Peacock on his family's Alabama farm

Skillet Asparagus

MAKES ENOUGH TO SERVE 4–6

- 2 pounds asparagus
- 2 tablespoons unsalted butter
- Salt and freshly ground black pepper

Miss Lewis's mother cooked asparagus this way, in a covered skillet with just a bit of butter. It concentrates the flavor, rather than diluting it as steaming or boiling can. Choose thin to medium spears for this method, no more than ½ inch thick, and make sure they don't overcook (or burn). They should be still crisp and bright green.

Rinse the asparagus in cold water, and trim off the tough ends of the stalks. Put the butter in a heavy skillet with a tight-fitting lid, and heat until the butter is foaming. Lay the asparagus in the pan, and shake it from side to side to coat the asparagus gently with the melted butter. Cover tightly, and cook over medium heat for 3 minutes. Check the asparagus, and turn them as needed to make sure they cook evenly and don't burn. Continue cooking 5 minutes longer, or until the asparagus are tender but still crisp and bright green. Season to taste with salt and freshly ground black pepper, and serve hot.

Skillet Scallions

MAKES ENOUGH TO SERVE 4

4 bunches scallions (about 40 scallions)
3 tablespoons unsalted butter

Whole scallions make a simple and delicious side-dish vegetable, which may come as a pleasant surprise to those who use them only as a garnish or flavoring. Here and in the following recipe are two ways to skillet-cook scallions—braised in butter until they are brilliant green and tender; or in cream, to coat them with a very light veil.

Trim the scallions, removing the root tips and about 1 inch of the green tops. Remove any damaged greens or skins, and rinse thoroughly under cool running water. Drain well, but leave some water droplets clinging to the onions.

Put the butter in a heavy skillet with a tight-fitting lid, and heat until the butter is foaming. Lay the scallions in the pan, and shake the pan gently back and forth to coat the scallions in the hot butter. Cover the skillet and cook over moderate heat. Turn the scallions over after 3 minutes, and cook 2–3 minutes longer. Be careful not to overcook; the white part should be a bit resistant and the tops tender, shiny, and green. No seasoning should be needed.

Creamed Scallions

MAKES ENOUGH TO SERVE 4 HEARTILY

4 bunches scallions (about 40 scallions)
3/4 cup heavy cream
1 clove garlic, mashed to a paste with a pinch of kosher salt
Salt and freshly ground black pepper (optional)
1 tablespoon chopped parsley

Put the trimmed and cleaned scallions (see preceding recipe) in a heavy skillet with a cover, and cook over medium-high heat, shaking the pan from time to time to prevent scorching, for about 4–5 minutes, until the scallions begin to soften but remain bright green. Remove the cover, pour over the heavy cream, and add the garlic. Raise the temperature to high, and cook, uncovered, briefly, until the scallions are just tender through and the cream is lightly reduced. Taste for seasoning, adding a pinch of salt or grinding of black pepper if needed, though they seldom need additional seasoning.

Serve immediately with the parsley sprinkled over.

Watercress Cooked in Pork Stock

SERVES 4

- 4 bunches watercress
- 2 cups Smoked Pork Stock (page 39)
- Salt and freshly ground black pepper to taste

When Miss Lewis was young, wild "cressies" were the first fresh greens of the year for her family. The peppery field cresses would peek up through the snow in late winter, and her family would gather them and store them in a burlap bag hung from the porch. Watercress was sometimes eaten as a salad green, but the sharper field cresses were always cooked this way, in pork stock. Today, cultivated watercress is widely available, and, though milder than wild varieties, it is very good cooked too. (If you don't have pork stock, use one of the quick "substitutes" in box on page 153.)

Wash the watercress, and remove any yellow or damaged leaves. Trim off any woody stems.

Put the smoked-pork stock in a nonreactive saucepan and bring to a rolling boil. Drop in the watercress, and use a spoon to submerge it in the boiling stock. Boil, uncovered, for 10–15 minutes, until tender. Taste for seasoning, and add salt and freshly ground black pepper as needed. Remove the watercress from the stock with a slotted spoon and serve. (Save the leftover stock from cooking the cress. Freeze if needed, and use to add to soups or stews when appropriate.)

Braised Spring Vidalia Onions

MAKES ENOUGH TO SERVE 4

- 1 large bunch spring Vidalia* or large green onions (about 8 onions)
- 3 tablespoons unsalted butter
- Salt and freshly ground black pepper
- 1/3 cup Chicken Stock (page 33) or water

Spring Vidalias have sparkling white bulbs about the size of golf balls and beautiful green tops that are full of flavor. They are delicious when braised this way, in butter and a little cooking liquid. Spring Vidalias are now sold around the country, but you can use any large spring onions in their place, or even scallions in a pinch. We also like them raw—sliced into salads, or on buttered bread as a delicate tea sandwich.

Wash and trim the onions carefully, leaving about 6 inches of the green. Heat the butter in a large covered skillet until foaming but not browned. Add the onions, and roll them around in the butter so that they are coated all over. Season lightly with salt and pepper, then add the stock or water, and cover. Cook over very low heat, shaking the pan or tossing the onions periodically, until they are tender, about 5–7 minutes.

Remove the cover, and cook briskly, reducing the liquid in the pan so that it just coats the onions like a glaze. Taste for seasoning, and serve hot.

*Spring Vidalias are small and have the greens attached still. Any large green onion will do.

Roasted Beets in Ginger Syrup

MAKES ENOUGH TO SERVE 6–8 AS A SIDE DISH

- 8 medium to large beets
- 2 tablespoons vegetable or olive oil
- 4 or 5 grinds of black pepper

GINGER SYRUP

- 1 cup cider vinegar
- 1 cup granulated sugar
- 2 inches fresh ginger, peeled and sliced thickly
- 1 bay leaf
- 4 whole cloves
- ½ teaspoon salt

Roasting is a great way to cook beets, because it intensifies their natural sweetness. Roasted beets are particularly delicious in ginger syrup—our favorite way to eat them. You can heat the beets in the syrup and serve them as a side dish, or chill them and use them in salads. They can be enjoyed right from the roasting pan, or you can roast them in advance (a day or two ahead), then heat them in a skillet with butter and seasonings, just before serving.

Preheat the oven to 325°F.

Carefully wash the beets. If they still have their tops attached, remove and trim to approximately ½ inch above the beetroot. Place the beets in a casserole or baking pan that will comfortably hold them. A little crowding is okay. Drizzle the oil over the beets, and sprinkle with pepper. Cover with a layer of parchment paper followed by a double thickness of foil, and seal tightly. Place in the middle of the preheated oven, and bake for approximately 1 hour, until the beets are tender when gently pierced with the tip of a sharp knife. Remove from the oven, and allow to cool still covered.

When partially cooled but warm, peel the beets by gently rubbing them with paper toweling. The skins should slip off easily and without staining your hands. Trim as needed. If beets are small, you may wish to leave them whole; otherwise, slice into rounds or wedges, and set aside while you prepare the ginger syrup.

In a nonreactive saucepan, stir together all of the sauce ingredients. Cook at a simmer for about 20 minutes, until of a syrupy consistency. Remove from the heat, and cool. Strain the syrup and discard the solids.

Marinate the beets in the syrup, preferably a couple of hours or longer before serving. They may be served cold as a garnish for salads, or heated in their syrup and served as a side dish.

Variation: Hot Buttered Roasted Beets

MAKES ENOUGH TO SERVE 4–6

8 small or medium-sized beets
2 tablespoons unsalted butter
Salt and freshly ground black pepper to taste
A few drops of freshly squeezed lemon juice

Prepare, bake, and peel the beets as in the preceding recipe. If the beets are small, leave them whole; if larger, halve or quarter as needed.

When ready to serve, heat the butter in a medium-sized skillet until hot and foaming. Add the beets, salt, and pepper, and cook, stirring often, until heated through. Sprinkle with a squeeze of fresh lemon juice, and serve hot.

NOTE Beets can be baked and peeled up to 1 day before, then heated in butter and seasoned just prior to serving.

Cymling Squash in Light Tomato Sauce

MAKES ENOUGH TO SERVE 6–8

- 3 large cymling squash (about 1½–2 pounds)
- 1 teaspoon salt, plus more for the cooking water
- 2 tablespoons bacon fat
- 1 tablespoon unsalted butter
- 1 large onion, chopped (1 cup)
- 1 small stalk celery, with leaves, finely chopped (⅓ cup)
- 4 large cloves garlic, thinly slivered
- 1 teaspoon dried thyme
- ½ teaspoon freshly ground black pepper
- 2 cups tomato, peeled, seeded, and coarsely chopped
- ¾ cup Chicken Stock (page 33)
- 2 tablespoons finely chopped parsley

Cymling is the traditional name for pattypan squash—a favorite of Thomas Jefferson's, and Miss Lewis's family too. They have a more delicate flavor than zucchini or yellow squash, which is best preserved by simmering them whole, as we do here. You may also slice and braise cymling with onions, following the recipe for crookneck squash opposite.

Leave the cymlings whole, and cook them in simmering lightly salted water until they are just tender when pierced with the tip of a sharp knife. Drain the cymling and let cool. When cool enough to handle, with a teaspoon or melon-baller scoop out the seeds from the top center of each squash and discard them. Slice the cymling lengthwise into ⅓-inch slices, and serve as is or make the tomato sauce.

To prepare the sauce: Heat the bacon fat and butter in a heavy nonreactive skillet until the butter is foaming. Add the onion and celery, and stir well to coat in the cooking fat. Cook over medium heat, stirring often, until the onion and celery are just tender, about 10 minutes. Add the garlic, thyme, salt, and freshly ground black pepper, and cook for 5 minutes. Add the chopped tomato and chicken stock, and simmer gently for 20 minutes. Taste carefully for seasoning, and add more salt and pepper as needed. Add the sliced cymling to the sauce, and continue cooking for 5 minutes. Sprinkle on the parsley, and cook for 2 minutes longer. Taste again for seasoning, and adjust as needed.

Simmered Yellow Squash

MAKES ENOUGH TO SERVE 6–8

- 4 tablespoons (1/2 stick) unsalted butter
- 2 medium Vidalia onions, peeled and sliced into 1/3-inch wedges (2 1/2 cups)
- 9 yellow crookneck squash, washed, trimmed, and sliced crosswise into 1/3-inch slices (8 cups)
- 1 teaspoon salt, or more to taste
- 1/2 teaspoon freshly ground black pepper, or more to taste

Yellow crooknecks are a popular and prolific summer squash in the South. When simmered in their own juices, their flavor becomes clear and concentrated. Here the squash and onions must cook slowly and should not color at all. Stir often but carefully—especially when the squash approaches doneness—so the slices remain whole.

Heat the butter until foaming in a large saucepan or Dutch oven. Add the onion wedges, and cook over moderate heat for 5 minutes, stirring often. Add the sliced squash, salt, and freshly ground pepper, and stir well to coat the squash with the butter and seasonings. Reduce the temperature to low, and cook, covered, for 20 minutes or longer, stirring often, until the squash is very tender and yielding. Taste carefully for seasoning, and adjust if needed. Serve the squash hot.

Garlic Green Beans

MAKES 4–6 SERVINGS

Salt

1 pound green beans, washed and stemmed

2 tablespoons unsalted butter

1 large clove garlic, minced

1 tablespoon finely snipped parsley

Freshly ground black pepper to taste

This is a nice way to cook up fresh, crisp green beans. They are blanched in boiling water and shocked in ice water to maintain their bright color, then briefly sautéed in butter with minced garlic and parsley. For convenience, you can blanch and chill the beans and store them in the refrigerator for a day before sautéing and serving.

Fill a big pot with water and bring to a rolling boil. Add 1 tablespoon of salt and the stemmed green beans, and cook, uncovered, for 5 minutes, or until tender but resistant to the bite. Drain the beans, and immediately plunge into a bowl of lightly salted ice water to stop the cooking. As soon as the green beans are chilled, drain them.

Heat the butter in a wide skillet until hot and foaming. Add the green beans, and cook, tossing constantly, until heated through. Add the garlic, parsley, a generous sprinkling of salt, and a few grinds of black pepper, and continue cooking 1 minute longer. Serve immediately.

FRESH OKRA IN ALABAMA

These days, you can find "fresh" okra in supermarkets around the country, sometimes even in winter, with passable flavor and texture, though it was likely picked weeks before and thousands of miles away. But what you get is quite a different vegetable from the okra I picked as a little boy in Hartford.

My father, Franklin Peacock, would plant a patch of okra each spring in a field by our house. During summer vacation, starting when I was about 7, my sister and I had to pick the okra—twice a day, early in the morning and just before sunset. As my father taught us, the pods had to be just the right size and tenderness: too small and they lacked flavor, too big and they'd be tough. In the fierce heat, the pods grew rapidly. The small ones that weren't ready in the morning would be ready at dusk (by the next day they'd be too mature). My sister and I would go into the patch with tube socks over our hands and forearms—to protect us from the plant fuzz that scratched like fiberglass—wielding little jackknives. We were alone in the morning, but in the evening my father would come home from work and join us. That's when I learned just how picky he could be about okra.

The okra of that era also had to be eaten or processed right away. By the next day, the pods were like sticks. My mother cooked some of it for supper that night—cut crosswise, coated with cornmeal, and deep-fried—and some of it she put into the freezer in bags, to be pulled out and fried during wintertime. Most days, we had so much that my father would drive us down to the local IGA grocery so we could sell our harvest. We each had our pickings in a separate basket—my sister, more skillful and speedy, always had more. The grocer weighed our baskets and paid us, pennies per pound.

The money at the time seemed a reasonable reward for the effort of careful picking. But it never occurred to me that there were many other folks growing okra around Hartford at that time of year, or that the IGA man had many larger, cheaper sources of supply. Years later, I discovered that my father had made a deal: the grocer would pay us kids for the okra; my dad would then pay him back. It was just another lesson he wanted us to learn.

Roasted Okra

MAKES ENOUGH TO SERVE 4

- ½ pound okra
- 1 small (about 6 ounces) onion, preferably red
- 2 cloves garlic, sliced thinly
- 3 tablespoons olive oil
- 4 mint sprigs
- Salt and freshly ground pepper

Okra invariably is deep-fried where I come from—but roasting it makes it crisp yet tender, neither mushy nor slimy, and it takes only 5–10 minutes. Here I've flavored it with onion, garlic, and mint, but you can make delicious variations with fresh green beans, cherry tomatoes (or fresh tomato wedges), even oil-cured olives. Toss any (or all) of these ingredients together, season, let sit, and roast as directed. (If you have one, use a Silpat pad: it's an excellent heat conductor, makes the roasting quicker and the cleanup far easier.)

Preheat the oven to 375°F.

Rinse the okra under cold running water, and drain. Trim the tops off the okra by removing the stems, but don't cut the whole caps off. Cut the onion in half from stem to top, then again in thirds in the same direction. Put the okra, onion, and garlic onto a Silpat pad on a baking sheet, or on an oiled pan, and drizzle the olive oil over them. Tuck in the mint sprigs, sprinkle with ¾ teaspoon salt and freshly ground black pepper, toss all together lightly, and let the flavors mingle at least 20 minutes before roasting.

Place in the preheated oven to roast for 5–10 minutes.

Corn on the Cob Boiled in the Husk

MAKES ENOUGH TO SERVE 4 AS A CASUAL FIRST COURSE OR VEGETABLE ACCOMPANIMENT

- 4 fresh, plump, full ears corn in the husk
- 1 gallon water
- Unsalted butter, at room temperature
- 4 tablespoons kosher salt
- Salt and freshly ground black pepper

Picking corn off the stalk and immediately boiling up the ears—still wrapped in their husks—was once a summertime ritual in the South. I maintain that boiling in the husks makes for more flavorful corn. The presentation of ears still in the husk adds a bit of drama to a meal, too. I like to put out thick cloth napkins so everyone can peel the husks back, wrap the napkin around them, and use this as a handle when eating the corn.

Pull the husks from the tip of each cob to the base, but do not detach from the cob. Carefully remove all of the silks from the ear of corn (a kitchen towel rubbed briskly between the rows of kernels can be helpful). When the silks are removed, pull the husks back up over the corn, and tie the ends with strips of husk or string.

Put the water into a large pot and bring to a full boil. Add the ears of corn, and cook for 10 minutes. Carefully remove, and drain briefly. Serve with lots of butter, salt, and freshly ground black pepper.

Fried Green Corn

MAKES ENOUGH TO SERVE 4–6

- 5 ears fresh corn
- 3 tablespoons unsalted butter
- Salt to taste

The "green" in this recipe means that the corn is fresh, cut right off the cob, to distinguish it from dried corn, hominy or grits, and so forth. Southerners eat corn in so many different ways that we need all these names, the same way Eskimos have a multitude of words for "snow."

Fried corn is a delicious and traditional breakfast dish in summer, served with sliced tomatoes. It's good both ways—just fried in butter, or with a light cream sauce. In either case, don't let the corn kernels brown or they'll lose their delicate flavor.

Shuck the corn, and carefully remove all of the silks. Using a sharp knife, cut the corn kernels from the cob.

Melt the butter in a heavy-bottomed nonreactive skillet over medium heat until hot and foaming. Toss the cut corn into the skillet, and stir well to coat all over with the butter. Sprinkle salt over lightly, and continue cooking, stirring often, until the corn is tender, about 5–7 minutes. Taste for seasoning, and add more salt if needed.

Variation: Creamed Corn

MAKES ENOUGH TO SERVE 4–6

4 ears corn
4 tablespoons (½ stick) unsalted butter
½ teaspoon salt
Small pinch of freshly ground black pepper
1 tablespoon all-purpose flour
¾ cup half-and-half, or more as needed

Remove the husks and silks carefully from the corn. Using a sharp knife, cut the corn kernels from the cob. Reserve the cut corn, and discard the cobs.

Heat the butter in a large skillet or frying pan until hot and foaming. Add the corn kernels, salt, and pepper to the pan, and stir well to coat the corn with the hot butter and seasonings. Cook over medium heat for 5 minutes, stirring often, and taking care that the corn does not brown. Sprinkle the flour over the corn, stir well to blend, and cook for 2 minutes longer. Add the half-and-half, stirring well, and simmer for 3–4 minutes longer, until the corn is tender and the half-and-half coats the corn lightly. (Corn can vary greatly in starch content, so it may sometimes be necessary to use a bit more half-and-half to keep the sauce from being too thick.) Taste carefully for seasoning, and add more salt and freshly ground pepper as needed.

Scalloped Tomatoes

MAKES ENOUGH TO SERVE 4

- 6 large vine-ripe tomatoes, peeled and seeded, and cut into 1½-inch pieces
- 1 small onion, finely chopped (about ⅓ cup)
- 1 teaspoon salt
- ½ teaspoon freshly ground black pepper
- 2 teaspoons granulated sugar
- 4 slices white loaf bread, crusts removed, cut into ½-inch cubes
- 7 tablespoons unsalted butter, melted

This is a delicious old-fashioned casserole for high summer, when tomatoes are juicy and abundant. The toasted croutons soak up the juices of the tomatoes and give both a buttery flavor and crunchiness. The sugar in the recipe is intended to balance the acid of the tomatoes: use only as much as you need to achieve a nicely rounded flavor, not to sweeten the dish. Scalloped tomatoes are especially good with grilled or roasted meats or fish.

Preheat the oven to 375°F.

Put the tomato pieces and chopped onion into a large nonreactive bowl. Season with the salt, black pepper, and sugar, and toss well to distribute the seasonings. Scatter the bread cubes on a baking pan, and drizzle 4 tablespoons of the melted butter over them. Toast them in the oven until they are golden brown, 8–12 minutes.

Add the toasted cubes of bread to the tomatoes, and toss well. Taste the tomatoes carefully for seasoning and adjust, adding more salt, black pepper, or sugar as needed. Turn everything into a buttered 9-by-13-inch nonreactive baking dish, and drizzle the remaining melted butter over. Place a piece of parchment paper directly over the tomatoes, and cover tightly with aluminum foil. Bake for 35 minutes, then uncover and bake for 10 minutes longer.

Scalloped Green Tomatoes

MAKES ENOUGH FOR 4–6 SERVINGS

- 4 large green tomatoes, washed, seeded, and cut into ½-inch pieces
- 1 small onion, finely chopped (⅓ cup)
- 1 teaspoon finely minced garlic
- 1 teaspoon salt
- ½ teaspoon freshly ground black pepper
- 1 teaspoon granulated sugar
- 1 teaspoon dried thyme
- ¼ teaspoon freshly grated nutmeg
- 3 slices white loaf bread, crusts removed, cut into ½-inch cubes
- 7 tablespoons unsalted butter, melted

Green tomatoes have a meaty flavor and make an interesting variation on traditional scalloped tomatoes. If you have plenty of both green and ripe tomatoes, serve both versions side by side so you can appreciate their distinctive tastes.

Preheat the oven to 375°F.

Put the green-tomato pieces, onion, garlic, salt, pepper, sugar, dried thyme, and nutmeg in a large nonreactive bowl, and toss well to distribute the onion and flavorings. Scatter the bread cubes on a baking tray, and drizzle 4 tablespoons of the melted butter over them. Toast them in the oven until they are golden brown, about 8–12 minutes. Add the toasted bread cubes to the tomatoes, and toss. Turn everything into a buttered 9-by-9-inch nonreactive baking dish, and place a piece of parchment paper directly over the surface. Cover tightly with foil, and bake for 40 minutes. Remove the cover and bake 10 minutes longer, basting if needed. Serve hot.

Sauté of Heirloom Tomatoes and Okra with Bacon Garnish

MAKES 6 SERVINGS

This simple summer sauté is full of flavor, and color. The okra should be just tender and bright green, the onion cooked but still a bit crunchy, and the tomatoes just warmed through, with a very fresh taste. This is a nice way to use the different heirloom tomatoes from your own garden or varieties that you can find at farmers' markets, but any ripe, juicy garden tomato would be delicious.

- 5 slices bacon
- 4 cups okra, washed, trimmed, and sliced ½ inch thick (about 1 pound)
- 1 large onion, cut into ⅓-inch wedges
- ½ teaspoon salt, or more to taste
- ¼ teaspoon freshly ground black pepper, or more to taste
- 4 medium heirloom tomatoes, cut into ½-inch wedges (about 2½ cups)

Cook the bacon slices in a large skillet until crisp. Leaving the rendered bacon fat, remove the bacon from the pan and reserve. Add the sliced okra to the skillet, and cook, stirring frequently, over moderate heat for 10 minutes. Add the onion wedges, salt, and pepper, and continue cooking, still stirring, for 5 minutes. Toss in the tomato wedges, and reduce the heat to low. Cook, partially covered, just until tomatoes are heated through, 3–4 minutes. Carefully taste for seasoning, and adjust if needed. Serve warm, with reserved bacon slices crumbled over.

Pole Beans Simmered in Pork Stock

MAKES ENOUGH TO SERVE 8

- 2½ pounds pole beans
- 8 cups Smoked Pork Stock (page 39) or substitute (box, page 153)
- Salt and freshly ground black pepper to taste

Pole beans are a type of flat "string" beans. They're similar to common green beans but more fibrous (and with strings that need to be removed), and so need longer cooking. In the South, pole beans are picked from late spring into the fall and, like field peas, are cooked in pork stock. Because they vary in maturity and variety (sometimes they are called "broad beans"), there is no standard cooking time—it can take them up to 2 hours to become fork-tender!

Wash the pole beans under cold running water, and drain well. Using a paring knife, trim both ends of the beans, and carefully remove any strings. Bring the smoked-pork stock to a rolling boil in a large saucepan or Dutch oven. Add the pole beans, and use a spoon to push them down into the boiling stock. Cover, and reduce heat so the beans cook at a brisk simmer.

After 15 minutes, check the pole beans for tenderness and seasoning. They can vary greatly in the amount of time they take to cook, so it is important to check them early and often to gauge how quickly they are cooking. Season the beans with salt and pepper if needed, but taste both the beans and stock carefully, because smoked-pork stock can vary in saltiness. Continue cooking the beans until they are fork-tender. Drain, reserving the pork stock for another use. Serve the beans hot.

Lady Peas Cooked in Pork Stock

MAKES ENOUGH TO SERVE 6–8

- 4 cups shelled lady peas
- 2½ cups Smoked Pork Stock (page 39) or substitute (box, page 153)
- Salt and freshly ground black pepper to taste

Lady peas are a delicious small "field pea" particular to the Deep South; in my part of Alabama, they're called "white peas." Follow this method to cook any variety of field pea. Though it is best to buy them in the pod and shell them yourself—a fair amount of work but worth it—you will sometimes find them already shelled. Make sure they've been refrigerated and are fresh and shiny. Frozen field peas can also be cooked in this manner.

Carefully wash and pick over the shelled lady peas. Discard any that are damaged or "buggy." Put the peas in a pot, and pour the smoked pork stock over them. Bring to a boil over moderate heat. At this point the lady peas, like all field peas, will begin to throw off a significant amount of foam. Use a slotted spoon to remove the foam, and discard. When they stop foaming, reduce the heat to a low simmer and cook, covered, until the peas are quite tender but not mushy, about 30 minutes. Taste carefully for seasoning, and adjust as needed. Serve hot with some of the cooking liquid to moisten.

A variety of field peas sometimes known as Crowder

Fried Eggplant

1 large or 2 medium-sized eggplant

Kosher salt

1 egg, lightly beaten

1/3 cup buttermilk

3/4 cup fine-ground white cornmeal

2 tablespoons cornstarch

3/4 teaspoon salt

1/2 teaspoon freshly ground black pepper

Oil for frying

MAKES ENOUGH TO SERVE 4–6

Eggplant is often prepared in the South in place of meat, and frying is a favorite way to cook it. This is not a do-ahead preparation—fried eggplant should be served right away, while it is still crisp.

Remove the stem end from the eggplant. Cut the eggplant lengthwise into 1/3-inch slices. If your eggplant is large, you may wish to slice it crosswise. Sprinkle the slices generously on both sides with kosher salt, and place in a colander to drain for 20 minutes.

Meanwhile, whisk together the egg and buttermilk in a shallow dish. Mix together the cornmeal, cornstarch, salt, and freshly ground black pepper on a piece of wax paper.

When the eggplant has finished draining, press the slices between two layers of paper towel to remove any excess moisture. Heat 1 inch of oil in a heavy skillet until it is very hot but not smoking—350°F. Dip the eggplant slices first in the egg wash, and drain off any excess; then dredge each slice carefully in the cornmeal mixture, making sure that it is completely coated and patting off any excess.

Fry the eggplant in batches until it is crisp and a rich golden brown, 2–3 minutes on the first side and about 1 minute on the other. Remove the slices from the pan, allowing oil to drain from the slices into the pan before transferring to crumpled paper towels or a draining rack to drain further. Sprinkle lightly with salt and freshly ground pepper, and serve immediately.

Simple Boiled Cabbage

MAKES ENOUGH FOR 6

I grew up with plain boiled cabbage, cooked until tender—my mother kept the wedges held together with toothpicks. I still love it prepared this way, served with Hot Pepper Vinegar (page 14).

- 1 large head green cabbage
- 3 cups water
- 1 teaspoon salt, or more as needed
- ¼ teaspoon freshly ground black pepper, or more as needed
- 3 tablespoons cider vinegar

Slice the cabbage in half lengthwise. In the same manner, cut each half into three pieces, holding the cabbage by the root. Put the pieces in a large saucepan along with the water, salt, and pepper. Cover, and cook at a simmer until the cabbage is quite tender, 30 minutes or longer, until the wedges are easily pierced with a knife. Use a large slotted spoon to transfer the cabbage to a warm serving platter. Sprinkle the cider vinegar and a little of the cooking liquid over the cabbage. Season lightly with additional salt and pepper, if needed, and serve while hot.

Braised Cabbage

MAKES ENOUGH TO SERVE 6

- 3 tablespoons bacon fat, butter, or olive oil
- 2 medium onions, sliced ⅓ inch thick
- 1 large head green cabbage, washed, cored, and cut crosswise into 1-by-2-inch pieces
- Salt
- Freshly ground black pepper

Cabbage is delicious when simmered slowly in its own juices, with just a bit of fat and onions. You could use butter or olive oil here if you prefer (or even omit the onions), but bacon fat gives this dish a distinctive, Southern flavor.

Heat the bacon fat or butter in a large covered skillet or Dutch oven until hot. Add the onions and cook, stirring often, for 5 minutes. Add the cabbage, and season with 1 teaspoon of salt and ½ teaspoon of freshly ground black pepper. Stir the cabbage well, to coat with cooking fat and distribute seasonings. Reduce heat to low, and cook, tightly covered, for 30–40 minutes, stirring often, until cabbage is very tender. Taste carefully for seasoning, and adjust if needed.

SUBSTITUTES FOR PORK STOCK

Smoked Pork Stock (page 39) is the traditional cooking medium for greens—and the best—but if you don't have time (or the right pork) to make a finished stock, here are some alternatives:

- Use a small slice (about 2 ounces) of smoked, cured pork to make a quick stock: Boil the meat in 6 cups of water for ½ hour, tightly covered. Remove the meat, and season with salt and pepper,
- Cut four slices of good smoked bacon into small dice, and render slowly in a pan until deeply browned. Remove the bacon bits (use for another purpose), and put the fat and 6 cups of water in a saucepan. Simmer for 15–20 minutes, then season with salt and pepper
- Use Chicken Stock (page 33), vegetable stock, or lightly salted water (about 2 teaspoons salt per quart of water).

An Assembly of Southern Greens Cooked in Pork Stock

MAKES ENOUGH TO SERVE 6–8

- 8 cups Smoked Pork Stock (page 39) or substitute (box, page 153)
- 4 pounds mixed greens, such as turnip, mustard, rape, winter kale, watercress, escarole, and chard, carefully washed and stemmed (page 155)
- Salt and freshly ground black pepper to taste

Miss Lewis grew up with a tradition of cooking many types of greens in the same pot. In Alabama, I am sad to say, we were "segregationists" in this regard, cooking turnip greens almost exclusively, and always by themselves. In recent years, though, I've come to appreciate the wonderful flavor of different types of greens cooked together—cultivated and wild greens, "Southern" greens like turnip and mustard with more widely grown varieties like kale and chard.

The basic method given here can be followed for any combination of greens or just one type. (Collards, for instance, are best cooked separately, because they have a different texture and require considerably longer cooking time.) Most varieties of cultivated greens are widely available in supermarkets, and, increasingly, "wild" greens—such as cresses, pokeweed, rape, and purslane—can be found at farmers' markets.

Greens should always be accompanied by some type of Cornbread (pages 210, 213–214). And although they are delicious by themselves or simply moistened with some of the "pot likker," many Southerners serve greens along with thinly sliced white or green onions or scallions, and crushed red pepper or liberal dashes of Hot Pepper Vinegar (page 14).

"Pot likker" is the flavorful broth in which the greens have cooked. You can reserve it and use it to cook up another batch. After that it will have too strong a flavor. Or, as many Southerners do, enjoy the pot likker by itself with cornbread as a light supper.

Pour the smoked-pork stock into a large Dutch oven or heavy saucepan and bring to a boil. Add the prepared greens in batches, waiting until the first batch wilts into the stock before adding more. (This will seem like an enormous amount of greens, but they cook down considerably and quickly.)

Cook, uncovered, over high heat until the greens are just tender, about 15–20 minutes. Take care not to overcook the greens. They should be silky and tender but still vibrant green in color. During cooking, season as needed with salt and freshly ground black pepper. Greens are served highly seasoned.

When they are done, use a slotted spoon or strainer to remove them from the pot, draining off any excess liquid, and serve hot.

BUYING, TRIMMING, AND WASHING GREENS

- Buying greens: Greens should be fresh, young, and vigorous. Don't buy any that are yellow, wilted, or too large or thick. You can taste raw greens too: they should have a sharp flavor, like mustard or horseradish, but should not be bitter. Bitterness will not cook away.
- Trimming greens: For *turnip* or *mustard* greens: If the leaves are young and tender, simply cut away the thick base of the stem. If mature, strip the leaves off the stems and central rib, pulling from the top of the leaf downward (discard the stems). Small leaves can be left whole; larger ones should be torn in half or thirds.

  For *collards* and *kale:* Cut off the stems of young leaves at the base of the leaf. For large, thick collards, cut the entire stem and central rib from the leaf with a paring knife. Slice the leaves crosswise into ribbons about 1–1½ inches thick.
- Washing greens: Wash all types of greens carefully in at least two changes of cool water. Few things are less pleasant than getting a mouthful of gritty greens. Fill a sink full of water and drop in batches of the trimmed leaves, gently agitating to rinse off grit. Lift each batch out to a colander or bowl, then drain, taking care to remove any sand from the bottom of the sink, before refilling with clean water. Repeat the rinsing, until there is no longer any grit or dirt settling in the sink. Ruffled greens like turnip and mustard can hold a lot of sand; they may need more than two rinsings. (I have heard stories of some people putting these greens in their washing machines with a bit of borax, but I don't recommend that technique.)

NOTE *Greens can be trimmed and washed one day before cooking.*

Mustard, turnip, and collard leaves (left to right)

Spicy Collards in Tomato-Onion Sauce

MAKES ENOUGH TO SERVE 6

- 1½ pounds collard greens
- 6 cups Smoked Pork Stock (page 39) or substitute (box, page 153)
- ⅓ cup olive oil
- 1 large onion, chopped (about 1¼ cups)
- 1 tablespoon minced garlic
- ½ teaspoon crushed red-pepper flakes (more or less, according to taste)
- Salt and freshly ground black pepper
- 38 ounces canned whole, peeled tomatoes, drained, preferably San Marzanos

As a child in Virginia, Miss Lewis says, she didn't even know there was such a thing as collard greens. And though we knew them in Alabama, we thought of them as crude and didn't eat them. Now I love them, however, whether simply cooked in pork stock or finished, as here, in a spicy tomato sauce. (Miss Lewis will eat collards when I cook them, but seems to have no interest in preparing them herself.) Other greens are also delicious served in this sauce—especially escarole—but most will need far less cooking time than collards.

Wash and drain the collards (page 155). Remove the stems, beginning at the base of the leaf, and discard. Cut the collard leaves crosswise into 1-inch strips. Bring the pork stock or water to a rolling boil in a large Dutch oven, drop in the collard greens, and cook, uncovered, for 30–40 minutes, until tender. Drain the greens, and reserve the cooking liquid.

Heat the olive oil in a large skillet or Dutch oven. Add the onion and cook, stirring often, over moderate heat for 10 minutes, until the pieces are translucent and tender. Add the garlic and crushed red pepper, ½ teaspoon of salt, and ½ teaspoon freshly ground black pepper. Stir well to distribute the seasonings, and cook for an additional 5 minutes. Add the drained tomatoes and 1½ cups of the liquid reserved from cooking the greens. Simmer gently for 15 minutes. Taste carefully for seasoning, and adjust as needed. Add the drained collard greens, and simmer for an additional 10 minutes. Taste for seasoning again, and serve hot.

Mashed Turnips

MAKES ENOUGH FOR 6 SERVINGS

- 4 tablespoons (1/2 stick) unsalted butter
- 3 pounds white turnips, peeled and sliced into 1/2-inch rounds
- 1/2 teaspoon salt
- 1/4 teaspoon freshly ground black pepper
- 1/4 teaspoon freshly grated nutmeg

Baking turnips brings out their sweetness and intensifies their flavor. In this recipe, they go into the oven buttered and seasoned, so when they're tender just mash them up a bit and serve. If possible, buy turnips with the greens attached; the roots should be smooth and firm. If the greens have been removed, avoid any roots that have begun to sprout (an indication of age).

Preheat oven to 325°F.

Melt the butter in large baking dish by setting it in the oven until melted. Put the sliced turnips in the baking dish and toss with the melted butter, then sprinkle the salt, pepper, and nutmeg over them. Lay a piece of parchment paper directly on top of the turnips, and wrap the baking dish tightly with a double thickness of foil. Bake in the preheated oven until tender, about 1 hour. Remove from the oven, and use a fork or potato masher to mash the turnips coarsely. Taste carefully for seasoning, and adjust if needed. Serve the turnips hot.

Whipped Rutabagas

MAKES ENOUGH TO SERVE 4

- 1 large rutabaga (about 2¼ pounds), peeled and cut into 1-inch chunks
- 4–6 tablespoons (½–¾ stick) unsalted butter
- ¼ teaspoon freshly grated nutmeg
- Salt

Boiled rutabagas whip up nicely, because of their high fiber and starch content (which also makes them great for soup, page 49). And with their rich, earthy flavor—accented by nutmeg—whipped rutabagas are a wonderful fall and winter vegetable, especially on a plate with braised meats, such as beef ribs or lamb shanks, or roast pork or duck.

You can do the whipping by hand, but an electric mixer makes the task much easier. Even with a machine, though, rutabagas will never get completely smooth and light. They'll always have few lumps and a satisfying thickness. (Don't try this recipe with regular white turnips—they soak up too much water when boiled.)

Put the rutabaga pieces in a large saucepan and cover with water. Bring to a boil, then reduce heat, and simmer until the rutabaga pieces are fork-tender, about 30–45 minutes.

Remove from the heat, drain the rutabagas, and whip them with an electric mixer, along with 4 tablespoons of the butter, the nutmeg, and salt to taste. Add more butter if needed.

A NOTE ABOUT COOKING SHERRY

Throughout the book when we call for sherry in a recipe, we invariably mean Harvey's Bristol Cream. Although there are fancier sherries out there, and you can use them if you choose, we like Harvey's because it gives us the richness we are looking for with just the right amount of sweetness.

Savory African Squash

MAKES ABOUT 6 CUPS, ENOUGH TO SERVE 8

2 large African squash (about 2 pounds each), or 2 pounds other hard winter squash, peeled, seeds removed, cut into 1-inch cubes
1 teaspoon salt
½ teaspoon freshly ground black pepper
½ teaspoon freshly grated nutmeg
6 tablespoons (¾ stick) unsalted butter, cut into small pieces
3 tablespoons sherry (page 158)
4–6 tablespoons unsalted butter (optional)
¼–½ cup heavy cream, heated (optional)

Baked or mashed winter squash is traditional autumn fare in the South. We like "African squash," a flavorful variety that farmers around Atlanta have recently started to grow (supposedly from seeds smuggled from Africa). It looks a lot like butternut squash, and you can certainly use butternut or any other winter squash (including pumpkin) in this recipe. Because the moisture and starch content of squash varies, though, you may need more or less butter and cream. And though we like to whip the squash in an electric mixer until soft and smooth, you could purée it in a food processor or just mash it up by hand for a different texture.

Preheat the oven to 350°F.

Put the squash pieces into a large baking dish or casserole, and sprinkle over the salt, pepper, nutmeg, and small pieces of butter. Place a piece of parchment paper directly on top of the squash, then cover and seal the dish tightly with a double thickness of foil. Bake in the preheated oven for 1 hour or longer, until the squash is very tender. Remove the parchment and foil covering, stir the squash well, sprinkle the sherry over, and return the dish to the oven to cook for 15 minutes longer.

Transfer the squash to the large bowl of an electric mixer fitted with a whip attachment. Mix on low speed to break up the squash, and add as much of the optional butter as you wish. When the butter is incorporated, increase mixer speed and whip until smooth. Taste the squash carefully, and add more salt, pepper, and nutmeg as needed. If the squash is too stiff and dry in texture, you may add the optional cream bit by bit until the texture is silky and smooth. Transfer the squash to a warm serving dish, and serve hot.

Sautéed Apples with Chestnuts

MAKES ENOUGH TO SERVE 6

- 3 tablespoons unsalted butter
- 3 large cooking apples, such as Stayman, Winesap, Cortland, or Granny Smith, peeled and sliced into wedges ½ inch thick
- 2 teaspoons granulated sugar
- ½ teaspoon salt
- 1¼ cups whole chestnuts, cooked (Note, page 194)

This dish makes a delicious accompaniment to roast chicken, duck, or pork. It can also be made as a simple winter dessert by sweetening it with a bit more sugar or honey and perhaps a splash of sherry or cognac and serving with Rich Custard Sauce (page 249).

Heat the butter in a large, heavy-bottomed nonreactive skillet until it is hot and foaming. Add the apple slices and toss them well to coat them in the hot butter. Sauté over medium-high heat, turning the apple slices occasionally, until they begin to turn golden brown. Sprinkle the sugar and salt over, and add the chestnuts. Toss well, and continue cooking 3–5 minutes longer, until the chestnuts are heated through and start to caramelize. (Take care after you add the chestnuts to watch the apples closely; once the sugars begin to concentrate from browning, the whole process accelerates, and you may need to reduce the heat to avoid scorching.) Taste carefully for seasoning, adding more salt and sugar if needed.

Deep-Fried Celery Hearts

MAKES ENOUGH TO SERVE 8

2 celery hearts, quartered lengthwise
4 cups milk
½ onion, peeled
3 whole cloves
3 bay leaves
1 teaspoon salt
5 whole black peppercorns
¼ teaspoon dried thyme
⅛ teaspoon freshly grated nutmeg

6 cups peanut or vegetable oil for deep-frying

THE BATTER

⅓ cup milk from precooking celery hearts, cooled
1 egg plus 1 egg yolk
¾ cup all-purpose flour
2 cups fresh bread crumbs

An unusual and delicious way to cook an often overlooked, readily available vegetable. The celery hearts are poached in milk and spices before they're deep-fried, and you can use the aromatic liquid to make a marvelous cream sauce if you like.

Carefully wash the quartered celery hearts, and trim the root end as needed. With a vegetable peeler, carefully peel any particularly stringy outer stalks of the celery. Put the celery in a heavy saucepan with the milk, onion, and seasonings. Gently simmer, partially covered, until celery is very tender but not mushy, about 20–40 minutes depending on the age and maturity of the celery. When tender, gently remove the celery quarters to a plate to cool, taking care to keep them intact while transferring. Reserve the milk they cooked in.

To fry the celery hearts, heat the oil in a deep-frying pot that will hold the oil at a depth of at least 4 inches, to a temperature of 350°F. Blend together in a wide, shallow bowl ⅓ cup of reserved milk and the egg and yolk. Spread the flour out on one piece of wax paper and the bread crumbs on another. Dredge the cooled celery hearts lightly in the flour, then dip in the blended milk and egg, and roll in the bread crumbs to coat. Fry in the heated oil on all sides, turning as needed, until golden brown. Drain well on crumpled paper towels, and season lightly with salt. Serve hot.

NOTE Celery hearts are simply trimmed-down bunches of celery with the outer, tougher stalks removed. You can buy them already trimmed, but you would do better to get whole fresh bunches and save the outer stalks for soups.

Roasted Parsnips

MAKES ENOUGH TO SERVE 4–6

- 6 medium to large fresh parsnips, 1½–1¾ inches in diameter at the thick end
- 3 tablespoons unsalted butter, melted
- Kosher salt and freshly ground black pepper

Parsnips are commonly wintered over in the ground in the South, and thought of as both a fall and a spring vegetable. In any season, though, their rich, sweet flavor is intensified by roasting. Blanching them first brings the starch to the surface so in the oven they develop a crisp, golden exterior and a soft and creamy inside. These are a great complement to any roast meat or poultry, as well as an unexpected hearty breakfast treat topped with a little powdered sugar or honey. For a fancy touch, run the tines of a fork down the sides of the blanched parsnips before roasting. This will produce crisp, beautifully colored ridges—which are also effective for soaking up little streams of delicious meat juices.

Preheat the oven to 375°F.

Peel the parsnips and trim the ends. Slice in half lengthwise, and if they are especially large, halve each half lengthwise again. Bring 2 quarts lightly salted water to a boil. Drop the parsnips into the boiling water, and cook for 3 minutes. Drain in a colander, and allow the parsnips to cool until they are dry and cool enough to handle.

Transfer the parsnips to a nonstick roasting pan or lipped baking sheet lined with a silicone baking sheet (Silpat). Drizzle the melted butter over them, and sprinkle generously with salt and a bit of freshly ground black pepper. Toss the parsnips with your hands to ensure that they are well coated with the butter and seasonings. Spread them out in a single layer, and roast in the preheated oven for 20 minutes. After 20 minutes, check the parsnips and toss gently and rotate the pan so they cook evenly. Cook until the parsnips are a lovely golden color with bits of brown coloring on the cut angles, 10–15 minutes longer. Remove from the oven, and serve immediately.

Cooled roasted parsnips can be reheated in a 350°F oven.

Cardamom-Scented Whipped Sweet Potatoes

MAKES ENOUGH FOR 6 SERVINGS

- 6 medium-sized sweet potatoes (about 2½ pounds)
- ½ cup (1 stick) unsalted butter, at room temperature
- ⅓–1 cup heavy cream, heated
- ½ teaspoon ground cardamom
- ¼ teaspoon freshly grated nutmeg
- Salt to taste

The secret to intensely flavored sweet potatoes is slow cooking. For whipped potatoes, we bake them first in a low oven until very tender, then add just enough cream when whipping to give them a silky look and feel. Since sweet potatoes vary greatly in starch content (see box), you may need anywhere from ⅓ to a whole cup of hot whipping cream to get the right texture.

Preheat the oven to 325°F.

Put the sweet potatoes on a foil-, parchment-, or Silpat-lined baking sheet, and bake in the preheated oven for about 1½ hours, until very soft and tender. Remove from the oven and cool slightly. Peel the warm potatoes, and put them in the bowl of an electric mixer. Beat the potatoes until mashed, and add the butter, ⅓ cup of the heavy cream, cardamom, nutmeg, and ½ teaspoon of salt. Whip until smooth and creamy—you may have to add considerably more cream. Taste carefully for seasoning, and add more salt if needed. Serve hot.

NOTE Sweet potatoes are naturally fibrous, so if you want perfectly smooth whipped sweets, run them through a food mill before whipping.

SWEETNESS IN SWEET POTATOES

The starch and sugar content of sweet potatoes varies according to how long they have been stored. Older sweet potatoes tend to be darker, sweeter, and less starchy after cooking. Newly harvested potatoes usually appear lighter in color and, when cooked, will feel dry, starchy, and coarse on the tongue. Be prepared to use more milk, butter, or cream (and sugar) to moisten and sweeten them.

Lemon-Glazed Sweet Potatoes

MAKES ENOUGH TO SERVE 4

- 3 medium-sized sweet potatoes
- 1 cup water for the glaze
- 1 cup granulated sugar
- ½ teaspoon salt
- ¼ cup freshly squeezed lemon juice
- ½ teaspoon freshly grated nutmeg
- 2 tablespoons unsalted butter, at room temperature, for greasing pan

We don't usually boil sweet potatoes, because the flavor is diluted by the cooking water. This recipe, though, is an exception: whole sweet potatoes are simmered first, so that when sliced and baked they will absorb the sweet syrup glaze without drying out. The lemon in the syrup heightens the potatoes' flavor and balances the sweetness. If you have any leftovers, try them cold the next day: they're a great mid-morning snack with a strong cup of coffee.

Preheat the oven to 350°F.

Put the potatoes in a pot, and cover them with water. Bring to a boil, then simmer for 10 minutes, or until the potatoes are just tender but not soft. Drain the potatoes, and let them cool.

Meanwhile, put the water, sugar, and salt in a nonreactive saucepan, and bring to a vigorous boil, stirring just until the sugar is dissolved. Boil for 5 minutes, remove from heat, and stir in the lemon juice and nutmeg.

Butter a shallow baking dish. Peel the sweet potatoes, and cut lengthwise into quarters or sixths, depending on how large the potatoes are. Arrange the potato slices in the buttered baking dish in a single layer. Pour the lemon-flavored syrup over them, and bake in the preheated oven for 30–45 minutes, basting 2 or 3 times, until the sweet potatoes are glazed and begin to caramelize slightly. The edges of some may begin to darken, which is delicious.

Serve hot.

Sweet Potato Casserole

MAKES ENOUGH TO SERVE 12

This is a real Deep South sweet-potato dish. To Yankees it may seem more like a dessert, but the sweetness is a good foil to a salty ham or a pork roast, and the dish is traditional at the holiday table. It is also always welcome at a covered-dish supper. You can, of course, cut the ingredients in half and bake in a 9-by-9-inch pan if you want a smaller amount. There are many versions, but I prefer this one, with a pecan topping (you could use almonds or black walnuts instead). The potatoes are baked first, then peeled and blended with eggs and milk until they are smooth and pourable, then baked again with the topping; if you are using very starchy sweet potatoes, you may have to add more milk.

5 pounds small sweet potatoes (about 10 potatoes)
8 tablespoons (1 stick) unsalted butter
1¾ teaspoons salt
¾ teaspoon freshly grated nutmeg
⅓ cup honey
⅓ cup light-brown sugar
½ cup granulated sugar
3 eggs, lightly beaten
2 teaspoons vanilla extract
3 cups milk, heated
1 tablespoon unsalted butter, softened

THE TOPPING

1 cup light-brown sugar
1 cup all-purpose flour
½ teaspoon ground Ceylon cinnamon
½ teaspoon freshly grated nutmeg
¼ teaspoon salt
8 tablespoons (1 stick) unsalted butter, chilled
1 cup chopped pecans

Preheat the oven to 350°F.

Wash the sweet potatoes, and put them on a foil- or parchment-lined baking sheet. Bake in the preheated oven for 1–1½ hours, until they are very tender. Remove from the oven and allow to cool briefly, then peel. Put the peeled sweet potatoes into the large bowl of an electric mixer fitted with beaters or a whip attachment. Mix the hot sweet potatoes on low speed to begin mashing them. Add the butter, and mix until it is absorbed. Add the salt, nutmeg, honey, and both sugars, and mix until they are thoroughly blended. Add the lightly beaten eggs and vanilla, and beat on medium speed for 2 minutes. Reduce mixer speed to low, and slowly add the heated milk. When the milk is incorporated, taste carefully for seasoning, and add more salt or nutmeg as needed. Thoroughly butter a 9-by-13-by-2-inch baking dish with the softened butter, and pour the sweet-potato mixture into it.

Raise the oven temperature to 375°F.

Make the topping: Put the brown sugar, flour, cinnamon, nutmeg, and salt into a mixing bowl and mix well. Use your fingers to work the chilled butter into the mixture until it resembles oatmeal with some pea-size pieces of butter in it. Stir in the pecan pieces, and mix well. Sprinkle the mixture evenly over the top of the sweet potatoes, and bake in the 375°F oven for 30–45 minutes, until the topping is golden brown and crisp and the sweet potatoes are set but still slightly loose in the center. Serve hot.

White Sweet Potatoes Baked in Pastry

MAKES ENOUGH FOR 12 SERVINGS

- 2 cups water
- 2 cups granulated sugar
- 1 stick Ceylon cinnamon
- 1 teaspoon freshly grated nutmeg
- 3 tablespoons bourbon or cognac
- 1 teaspoon salt
- 4 tablespoons unsalted butter
- 2 recipes Basic Pie Dough (pages 242–243)
- 8 medium-sized white sweet potatoes (about 4 pounds), peeled and sliced lengthwise into ⅓-inch slices

Here is a different "sweet-potato pie"—not the traditional dessert, but a casserole of sliced white sweet potatoes baked in a pastry crust with a lattice top.

Miss Lewis got the idea for this recipe years ago from a neighbor whose husband grew white sweet potatoes. His wife, who was from Alabama, used to make a version of this dish, so when Miss Lewis realized I was from Alabama, too, she wanted us to re-create the recipe. But 10 years ago white sweet potatoes were difficult to find, even in the Deep South. To our surprise, a few years later, on a trip to Italy, we were walking through the Rialto Market in Venice and Miss Lewis spotted a small mound of white tubers labeled "Potatoes Americains." She quietly purchased several, packed them in her bag, and without my knowing smuggled them through customs, so that once back home we could make this splendid dish. But sweet potatoes seem to be coming back in vogue and are not so difficult to find now. They are lighter in color and less sugary than ordinary sweet potatoes, and are delicious and waxy when baked. If you can't find "white sweets," you can substitute regular sweet potatoes here with fine results.

Preheat the oven to 350°F.

Put the water, sugar, and stick of cinnamon in a medium saucepan and set over medium-high heat. Bring to a boil, stirring just until the sugar is dissolved, then cook 5 minutes. Remove from the heat, and stir in the nutmeg, bourbon (or cognac), and salt. Let cool completely. (The recipe can be prepared to this point the day before baking and stored, covered, at room temperature.)

Using 1 teaspoon of the butter, lightly butter the bottom and the sides of a 9-by-13-by-2-inch baking dish.

On a lightly floured surface, roll half of the dough out into a large rectangle (approximately 1⁄16 inch thick) that will fit into and overhang the sides of the baking dish. Gently transfer the rolled dough to the baking dish, and carefully fit it into the sides and corners. Use a knife or scissors to trim any overhanging dough, leaving a ½-inch border; reserve the trimmings for the filling.

Roll out the remaining batch of dough as you did the first. Using a knife or pastry wheel, cut it into ½-inch strips, lengthwise. Set aside fourteen of these strips to use for the lattice top; the remainder you will use as trimmings in the filling.

To assemble, arrange a layer of the sliced sweet potatoes in the bottom of the pastry-lined baking dish. It is okay if they overlap a bit. Scatter some of the reserved pastry trimmings over the potatoes. Top with another layer of sliced potatoes, and scatter reserved trimmings over, just as before. Continue layering until all of the potatoes are used. Remove the cinnamon stick from the cooled syrup, and pour it carefully over the potatoes. Cut the remaining butter into small pieces, and scatter over the final layer of potatoes. Now lay eight strips of pastry lengthwise over the top, leaving about ½ inch between, then arrange the remaining strips vertically on top, at an angle, to form a lattice pattern, trimming the strips as necessary for shorter pieces at the ends and longer pieces toward the center. Fold the edges of the pastry onto the rim of the dish all around, and crimp lightly to seal.

White sweet potato, left, and its more familiar rose-hued cousin, the regular sweet potato, right

Place the dish in the middle of the preheated oven, and bake for approximately 1 hour, or until the sweet potatoes are tender and glazed, and the pastry is a rich golden brown. (If the pastry begins to brown before the potatoes are tender, simply lay a piece of aluminum foil, shiny side up, over the top. This will prevent further browning of the crust.)

Serve hot or at room temperature.

Plain Rice

MAKES ENOUGH TO SERVE 4–6

- 1 tablespoon unsalted butter
- 1 cup short-grain, long-grain, or basmati rice
- 2 cups water
- 1½ teaspoons kosher salt

This is our basic everyday rice. When it is made with a starchy short-grain variety, it can produce a slightly "gummy" texture, which we like.

Heat the butter in a saucepan over medium heat until melted and foaming. Add the rice, and stir constantly for 2 minutes, or until the rice begins to turn translucent. Stir in the water and salt. Bring to a boil, and cover tightly. Cook over very low heat for 20 minutes. Remove from heat, fluff the rice with a fork, and serve.

Yellow Rice

MAKES ENOUGH TO SERVE 4

- ½ teaspoon saffron
- 2 cups Chicken Stock (page 33) or water, heated
- 1 tablespoon unsalted butter
- 2 tablespoons finely minced onion
- 1 cup rice
- 1½ teaspoons kosher salt

Yellow rice is often found on Southern tables, and often the color comes from a flavor packet (mainly turmeric) that's packaged with the rice. This Yellow Rice, however, is a beautifully tinted and flavored version made with real saffron (a bit expensive, but worth it in this case), minced onion, and (if you like) chicken stock. This is the rice to serve with Lamb or Veal Shanks Braised with Green Tomatoes (pages 124–125), or any other braised dish. I also like to serve Yellow Rice with sautéed or Breakfast Shrimp for Supper (page 186).

Crumble the saffron in a small bowl, and pour ¼ cup of the heated stock or water over it. Set aside to steep.

Heat the butter in a saucepan over medium heat until melted and foaming. Add the onion and stir well, cooking until softened but without browning. Add the rice and salt and stir well to coat with the butter and seasonings. Stir constantly until the rice begins to become translucent—about 2 minutes. Add all the heated liquid and the dissolved saffron. Stir well and bring to a boil. Reduce to a gentle simmer and cover tightly. Cook over low heat for 20 minutes. Remove from heat, fluff up the rice with a fork, and serve hot.

Coconut Rice

MAKES ENOUGH TO SERVE 4–6

- About 14 ounces canned or fresh coconut milk, unsweetened
- 1½ cups long-grain rice
- 1 small onion finely chopped (about ½ cup)
- 1 medium fresh tomato peeled, seeded, and finely chopped (⅔ cup)
- 1½ teaspoons salt

Coconut milk, onion, and fresh tomato make a delicious and unusual dish. It's easiest to use canned coconut milk (not sweetened coconut drink mix), but it is even better, and not much harder, if you make your own (see box).

Preheat the oven to 350°F.

Pour the coconut milk into a heavy-bottomed pot or casserole. Bring to a simmer, and add the rice, onion, tomato, and salt. Cover tightly with a lid or double thickness of foil, and put into the preheated oven for 30 minutes, or until the liquid has been absorbed and the rice is tender. Taste carefully for seasoning, and adjust if needed. Carefully fluff the rice with two dinner forks and serve.

TO PREPARE COCONUT

Wrap the coconut in a kitchen towel, and whack it several times with a heavy hammer until it splits open. Try to save any of the liquid inside. Pry out the coconut meat from the shell with a knife. Peel off the brown skin, and grate the white flesh. You should have about 2 cups.

To make coconut milk: Pour 3 cups of boiling water over the grated coconut, and add any reserved coconut liquid. Steep for 15 minutes, then strain off the milk.

Old-Fashioned Creamy Grits

MAKES ENOUGH TO SERVE 4–6

- 2 cups water, or more
- 2 cups milk, or more
- 1 cup stone-ground or regular grits
- Kosher salt
- ¼ cup heavy cream
- 2 tablespoons unsalted butter

Grits are a fundamental Southern food, and we want more people to try them and to enjoy them. I grew up with grits as a breakfast staple, plopped onto a plate with lots of melting butter, with bacon or ham and eggs alongside. My sister and I would stir jelly into our grits on occasion, too. And grits have long been enjoyed as a side dish at dinner and supper, with fried chicken or fish, or as "cheese grits," with grated cheese stirred in.

Still, I've found that many people—Southerners and non-Southerners alike—have little appreciation and even an unwarranted disdain for this great side dish. As a chef in the late 1980s, when I began serving grits as an accompaniment to roasted and braised meats—as one would rice or polenta—it was a shock to many, a thrill for others. Soon, however, grits became trendy, and pesto grits, sun-dried-tomato grits, and lemon-grass grits began showing up on restaurant menus. Miss Lewis's response to this was, "People should really leave grits alone."

Here are good grits, left pretty much alone. This formula, using milk, makes them a bit thicker and creamier than standard package directions call for.

Serve grits for breakfast with bacon and eggs, or for supper with Roast Chicken (page 99), Braised Lamb or Veal Shanks (pages 124–125), Braised Beef Short Ribs (pages 126–127), or Salmon Croquettes (pages 182–183).

Heat the 2 cups water and milk in a heavy-bottomed saucepan until just simmering.

While the milk is heating, put the grits in a large mixing bowl and cover with cool water. (If you are using regular grits, skip this step.) Stir the grits assertively so that the chaff floats to the top. Skim the surface carefully, and remove the chaff. Drain the grits in a fine strainer, and stir them into the simmering water and milk. Cook, stirring often, until the grits are tender to the bite and have thickened to the consistency of thick oatmeal. Regular grits are done in about 20 minutes, but stone-ground require an hour or a little more to cook, and you will have to add additional milk and water as needed. As the grits thicken, stir them more often to keep them from sticking and scorching.

Season the grits generously with salt, and stir in the cream and butter. Remove from heat, and let rest, covered, until serving. Serve hot.

NOTE Leftover grits can be reheated over low heat, stirring in a little hot milk or boiling water as needed to thin.

SHRIMP PASTE AND GRITS

Miss Lewis learned in the Low Country, near Middletown Place, about topping hot grits with a generous dollop of Shrimp Paste (page 4). I like to stir in the paste thoroughly, which gives the grits a lovely coral color. Serve as an appetizer or as a supper dish with hot buttered toast, or as a savory side dish. For every cup of hot grits, stir in about 1/4 cup or more Shrimp Paste, and sprinkle some chopped fresh chives on top, if you like them.

Supper Dishes, Good for Lunch and Breakfast, Too

Watching TV as a kid in the Deep South, I was often confused when people on the shows talked about having dinner—at night! For folks in Hartford (and for Miss Lewis and numberless others around the South), dinner was a daytime meal; come evening, we only had supper. Dinner also signified for me a meal with more formality and organization—not just big Sunday and holiday dinners, but the lighter dinners we'd have on Saturdays and during the summer, when my father and grandfather closed the store for an hour and came home to eat. Everything had to be ready and proceed pretty fast.

Supper was less formal and less hurried—a more relaxed, end-of-the-day occasion. The dishes in this chapter are just right for that kind of meal. Supper's also the time to make good use of leftovers—I can remember my mother surveying the dinner table and declaring which dishes would be saved for supper. Some of our favorites here rely on cooked ingredients—all of our hashes start with cooked chicken, duck, or quail, for example, and Red Rice can incorporate any kind of meat, seafood, or poultry.

Note that these are not "one-dish meals," though in general they need only a salad and cornbread or biscuits to make an ample supper. And don't relegate them only to suppertime. They are equally delicious in the daylight, as light dinner or "lunch" dishes, and some will serve as starch or vegetable side dishes.

Crossing mealtime categories is something I loved as a kid, when my dad would make "breakfast for supper"—pancakes, French toast, eggs and grits and bacon in the evening (for ideas, check out our pancakes in Chapter VII!). Likewise, some of these supper dishes are scrumptious served in the morning: try Breakfast Shrimp, of course, or Trout Roe with Scrambled Eggs; or put a poached egg over our Chicken Hash, with Corn Griddle Cakes on the side.

Okra Pancakes

MAKES APPROXIMATELY SIXTEEN 2-INCH PANCAKES, ENOUGH TO SERVE 4 AS A SUPPER OR 6–8 AS A SIDE DISH

- ½ cup stone-ground white cornmeal
- ½ cup all-purpose flour
- 1½ teaspoons salt
- 1 teaspoon Homemade Baking Powder (page 230)
- 1 egg, lightly beaten
- ½ cup water
- ½ teaspoon freshly ground black pepper
- ½ cup finely chopped onion
- 2 cups thinly sliced okra
- Oil for frying

These pancakes, pan-fried like fritters, are delightfully crispy, so even those who think they hate the "slimy" aspect of okra will enjoy them. As well as making a nice supper dish, they can be served as a bread or a side vegetable or even as a cocktail nibble. In place of okra, you might stir grated raw squash or cooked eggplant or sautéed winter greens into the batter. Just be sure to eat them right away, before they lose their crispness.

Put the cornmeal, flour, 1 teaspoon of the salt, and homemade baking powder in a mixing bowl, and stir well with a whisk to blend. In a separate bowl, whisk together the egg and water, then stir into the dry ingredients, mixing only until moistened. Sprinkle the remaining ½ teaspoon salt and the freshly ground pepper over the onion and sliced okra, and toss lightly. Fold the vegetables into the batter.

Pour 1 inch of oil into a heavy skillet and heat to 340°F. Spoon the okra batter by heaping tablespoons into the hot oil; do not overcrowd the pan. Fry until golden brown on one side, then carefully turn and continue frying until both sides are browned. Remove from the skillet and drain well on a draining rack or crumpled paper towels.

Corn Pudding

MAKES ENOUGH TO SERVE 6–8

- 4 ears corn, husked and stripped of silk
- ⅓ cup granulated sugar
- 1 teaspoon salt
- 1 tablespoon all-purpose flour
- 2 eggs, beaten
- 1 cup milk
- 1 cup heavy cream
- 3 tablespoons unsalted butter, melted
- ½ teaspoon freshly grated nutmeg

Corn pudding is a true Southern delicacy, and one of the great treats of summer. It can be served as a light supper dish, as an accompaniment to meat, or as a part of a vegetable plate. Use only the freshest corn, and bake until just set for the best texture.

Preheat the oven to 350°F.

Cut the corn from the cob, slicing from the top of the ear downward. Put the cut corn into a mixing bowl, sprinkle in the sugar, salt, and flour, and mix well. Mix the beaten eggs, milk, and cream together, and pour while stirring into the corn. Blend in the melted butter and nutmeg, and spoon into a buttered 6-cup casserole. Set the casserole into a pan of hot water, and bake in the preheated oven for 35–40 minutes, until golden brown and just set. Test for doneness by inserting the blade of a knife into the center of the casserole. As soon as it comes out clean, the pudding is done. Don't overcook.

Baked Eggplant with Peanuts

MAKES ENOUGH TO SERVE 8

Peanuts were an important ingredient in African cooking, and from the early days of slavery, black cooks in the South have used them creatively in soups, sauces, and savory dishes as well as sweets. This delicious casserole—inspired by a recipe we found in an old Warm Springs, Georgia, cookbook—uses peanut butter as a seasoning for the baked-eggplant filling and roasted peanuts in the bread-crumb topping.

- 2 medium to large eggplants
- 4 tablespoons rendered bacon fat or unsalted butter
- 1 large onion, finely diced
- 3 large cloves garlic, finely chopped
- 1/4–1/2 teaspoon crushed red pepper (optional)
- 1 teaspoon salt
- 1/2 teaspoon freshly ground black pepper
- 3 tablespoons all-natural peanut butter
- 1/4 cup heavy cream
- 1 tablespoon unsalted butter for greasing the casserole

THE TOPPING

- 1 cup fresh bread crumbs
- 1/4 cup chopped dry-roasted peanuts
- 1 tablespoon finely snipped parsley
- 1 tablespoon finely snipped chives
- 1/2 teaspoon salt
- 1/2 teaspoon freshly ground black pepper
- 3 tablespoons unsalted butter, melted

Preheat the oven to 425°F.

Prick the eggplants in several places and put them on a foil-lined baking sheet, and bake in the preheated oven for 1 hour, or until the skin of the eggplants is shriveled and the flesh is soft to the touch. Remove from the oven, and cool until you are able to handle them. Peel the eggplants, and chop the flesh into 1/3-inch pieces.

Heat the bacon fat or butter in a large, heavy-bottomed skillet. Add the finely diced onion, and stir well to coat with the hot fat. Cook, stirring often, over medium heat until the onion becomes translucent, about 10 minutes. Stir in the garlic, optional crushed red pepper, salt, and freshly ground black pepper, and cook for 5 minutes longer. Add the chopped eggplant, and continue cooking for 5 minutes. Stir in the peanut butter until well blended, followed by the heavy cream. Simmer gently for 3–5 minutes. Taste carefully for seasoning, adding more salt and pepper if needed. Set aside and let cool while you prepare the crumb topping.

To make the topping: Put the bread crumbs, chopped peanuts, parsley, chives, salt, and freshly ground pepper in a mixing bowl, and toss well to mix. Pour the melted butter over, and toss again to distribute it evenly.

Butter a shallow casserole or pie plate that will just hold the eggplant. Spoon the eggplant mixture into the buttered dish, and spread the topping evenly over the surface. Bake in the oven until the bread crumbs are golden brown and the eggplant is bubbly at the sides, about 20 minutes.

Serve hot or at room temperature.

Butter Beans in Cream with Country Ham and Chives

MAKES ENOUGH TO SERVE 6

- 3 cups fresh shelled butter beans
- Salt
- 1 cup heavy cream
- 2 tablespoons finely minced country ham
- 1 tablespoon very finely snipped chives
- 1 tablespoon unsalted butter
- ¼ teaspoon freshly ground black pepper

In the South, butter beans are a popular variety of fresh shelled bean—sort of like fresh limas, but in my opinion better! If you can't get authentic butter beans, baby limas can be used in this delicious preparation. In Southern fashion, the country ham and chives are used as seasonings here, like salt and pepper.

Put the butter beans in a large saucepan, and cover with water. Add 1 teaspoon of salt to the pot, and bring to a boil. Skim the surface until clear. Cook, partially covered, at a simmer for 30–40 minutes, until the beans are very tender but not mushy.

Drain the butter beans completely, and return to the saucepan. Add the heavy cream, ham, chives, butter, salt, and pepper, stirring well to blend. Bring to a simmer and remove from heat. Taste carefully for seasoning, and add more salt if needed. Serve hot.

Turnip Greens with Cornmeal Dumplings

MAKES ENOUGH TO SERVE 4–6 AS A SUPPER DISH, 8 AS A SIDE DISH

THE TURNIP GREENS

About 2–3 pounds turnip greens

8 cups Smoked Pork Stock (page 39)

Salt and freshly ground black pepper to taste

THE CORNMEAL DUMPLINGS

1 cup fine-ground white cornmeal

3/4 teaspoon salt

1/2 teaspoon freshly ground black pepper

1/4 cup finely chopped onion

2 tablespoons thinly sliced scallion

1 egg, lightly beaten

1/2–3/4 cup hot stock from cooking the greens

In the Deep South, turnip and mustard (which are slightly milder) are considered the top-shelf greens for cooking. In the Peacock house, turnip greens reigned supreme, and we ate them all year round except in the summer, when the leaves were bitter. My mother invariably served turnip greens with Fried Hot-Water Cornbread (page 214), which I loved. But I also like to make these cornmeal dumplings right in the "pot likker" and serve greens and dumplings together. Two things to remember about turnip greens: The leaves can hide lots of dirt, so they need repeated washing. And they cook down dramatically, so be sure you buy (and wash) several big bunches.

Pick over the turnip greens carefully, removing their stems at the base of the leaf and discarding any damaged or discolored leaves. Carefully wash the greens in two separate changes of water, following the directions in box on page 155, and drain.

Meanwhile, put the pork stock in a large, heavy pot and bring to a rolling boil. Add the turnip greens and bring them to a boil, using a large spoon to push them down into the boiling stock. Cook uncovered for 10–15 minutes, until just tender. Now taste the greens carefully for seasoning, and add salt or pepper if needed.

With a large slotted spoon or strainer, transfer the greens to a warm serving dish; reserve the cooking liquid, and keep it at a simmer.

While the turnip greens are cooking, set about making the cornmeal dumplings. Put the cornmeal, salt, and pepper into a mixing bowl, and stir well. Add the finely chopped onion, the scallion, and the egg. Stir briefly to blend, and add in 1/2 cup of the hot stock from cooking the greens. Mix well, and add more stock if needed, until the dough is the consistency of mashed potatoes.

Measure out the dumpling dough by heaping tablespoonfuls, and shape each spoonful into a disk approximately 2 inches in diameter and 1/4 inch thick. Drop the dumplings into the simmering pork stock, and cook at a low simmer, partially covered, for 10–12 minutes, until they are cooked through. Remove the dumplings from the stock, and serve on top of the warm greens.

Pumpkin Roasted with Rosemary and Walnuts

MAKES ENOUGH TO SERVE 4–6 AS A SUPPER DISH, 6–8 AS A SIDE DISH

- 1 medium cooking pumpkin (about 4 pounds), peeled, seeded, and cut into 1-inch cubes (about 6 cups)
- 1 teaspoon kosher salt
- ½ teaspoon freshly ground black pepper
- 4 tablespoons pure olive oil
- 4 large cloves garlic, thinly sliced lengthwise
- 1¼ cups large walnut pieces
- ¼ cup rosemary leaves

Small cooking (or "sugar") pumpkins are an excellent vegetable for savory dishes as well as for pie filling. Roasting brings out pumpkin's sweetness, and this dish is a good accompaniment to pork, duck, or lamb—though it could serve as a satisfying vegetarian entrée too.

Preheat the oven to 400°F.

Put the pumpkin on a lipped nonstick baking sheet. Sprinkle the salt and pepper on, and drizzle the oil over. Toss the pumpkin well to coat with the seasonings and oil, and spread in a single layer on the baking sheet. Put into the preheated oven, and bake for about 20 minutes, or until the pumpkin just begins to color on the edges and become tender. Give the pan a light shake to make sure the pumpkin isn't sticking. If it is, just use a flat spatula to separate the pieces gently from the pan.

Sprinkle the garlic, walnut pieces, and rosemary over the pumpkin, and toss gently to mix evenly and coat everything with the oil. Roast for 10 minutes longer, then remove from the oven and transfer to a serving platter. Taste carefully for seasoning, and sprinkle on a little salt and pepper if needed. Serve hot, warm, or at room temperature.

Cornmeal Soufflé

MAKES ENOUGH TO SERVE 4

This Cornmeal Soufflé is a refined version of spoonbread. It's rather delicate, because it has whipped egg whites folded in, but it's not as fragile as a classic soufflé. We usually serve it with foods that have a sauce or a gravy.

- 2 cups milk
- 1/3 cup stone-ground white cornmeal
- 3 tablespoons plus 1 teaspoon unsalted butter
- 1 1/4 teaspoons salt
- 3 eggs, separated

Preheat the oven to 425°F.

Put the milk in a heavy saucepan, and heat to just below the boil. Slowly whisk in the cornmeal and bring to a boil. Cook, stirring or whisking constantly, for 5 minutes. Remove from heat, and pour into a mixing bowl. Stir in 3 tablespoons of the butter and the salt. Let cool for 15 minutes, then beat in the three egg yolks. Butter a 4-cup soufflé or baking dish with remaining teaspoon of butter.

Beat the egg whites just until they form soft mounds (see whipping egg whites, below). Stir a third of the beaten whites into the cornmeal mixture to lighten it. Carefully fold in the remaining whites, and gently turn the batter into the buttered baking dish. Bake for 25–30 minutes, until risen and golden brown. Serve immediately.

A NOTE ON BEATING EGG WHITES

You will notice that when we give instructions for beating egg whites for the recipes in this book, we call for soft mounds rather than the conventional stiff peaks. We feel that egg whites whipped to this degree yield better results. Egg whites can only be extended so far, and when they reach their full capacity, the next step is to begin to break down, become dry, and deflate. When whipped to glossy mounds, they incorporate more easily into batters and produce superior results. Although egg whites may be beaten with an electric mixer, we prefer either a copper or stainless-steel bowl and a large balloon whisk to beat the whites by hand. Regardless of the choice of equipment, the most important things are that the bowl be immaculately clean and that there be no trace of yolk in the separated whites.

Salmon Croquettes

MAKES 8 CROQUETTES, ENOUGH TO SERVE 4

It's worth preparing salmon *just* to make these. So, if you happen to be baking or grilling salmon for dinner one evening, cook up a little extra and you can make a batch of these croquettes for supper (or breakfast or lunch) the next day or so. This recipe gives simple instructions for poaching the salmon needed, but any cooked leftover salmon (so long as it's not overcooked) will do.

The lightness of the croquettes makes them unique, but they also demand some careful handling. Be sure to chill the croquette mixture well before shaping. For an easy and neat croquette, I press the mixture gently into a round biscuit- or cookie-cutter set on a tray, then lift off the cutter and continue making the rest the same way. I chill the cakes again, right on the tray, until they're firm, then use a spatula to remove them from the tray and slide them carefully into the frying pan one by one. Turn them gently, using a spatula and spoon or fork as needed for support.

I like croquettes served with Old-Fashioned Creamy Grits (pages 170–171) and sautéed spinach or chard. But they're also very good in summer accompanied by coleslaw and slices of ripe tomato. For a more traditional plate, enjoy them with English peas and mashed potatoes.

THE SALMON

- 1 quart water
- ½ cup white wine
- 1 tablespoon plus 1 teaspoon salt
- 2 tablespoons plus 1 teaspoon Old Bay seasoning
- 1 pound fillet of salmon (see Note)
- 1 medium yellow onion, diced (about ¾ cup)
- ¼ cup thinly sliced green onion
- Juice of 1 lemon
- 1 egg, lightly beaten
- 3 tablespoons unsalted butter, melted
- 1½ cups fresh bread crumbs
- Vegetable oil for frying

Bring the water, wine, 1 tablespoon salt, and 2 tablespoons Old Bay seasoning to a simmer in a medium-sized skillet. When it comes to a simmer, place the salmon in the skillet, skin side down, turn off the heat, cover, and let sit for 10 minutes in the hot liquid. After 10 minutes, remove the salmon, discarding the liquid.

Peel the skin off the salmon. Using your fingers, separate the salmon into large pieces and drop them into a mixing bowl, checking for bones as you go. (The salmon may not be completely cooked through at this point, but that's okay, because it will get fully cooked when you fry the croquettes.) Mix in the yellow and green onions, 1 teaspoon salt, 1 teaspoon Old Bay, and lemon juice, then the lightly beaten egg, the melted butter, and the bread crumbs. Chill the mixture for ½ hour (or overnight, if it suits your schedule).

When the mixture has chilled, scoop up about ⅓-cup handfuls and use your hands to form small cakes about ½ inch high and 2½ inches in diameter. Try not to press the cakes down; just form them lightly into shape (for a quick and easy way, see the introduction to the recipe). You should have eight cakes. After they've been formed, place them back in the refrigerator.

Heat about 1 inch of vegetable oil in a large nonstick skillet (don't crowd the pan—you may have to cook them in two batches). Gently ease the salmon croquettes into the hot oil. Fry for about 4 minutes on one side, then gently flip them over and cook about 2 minutes on the other side. Drain well and serve.

NOTE You can use leftover cooked salmon and skip the first step.

Macaroni and Cheese

MAKES ENOUGH TO SERVE 10

- 1¾ cups (8 ounces) elbow macaroni
- Salt
- 1¼ cups (5 ounces) extra-sharp cheddar cheese cut into ½-inch cubes
- 2 tablespoons plus 1 teaspoon all-purpose flour
- 1½ teaspoons salt
- 1½ teaspoons dry mustard
- ¼ teaspoon freshly ground black pepper
- ⅛ teaspoon cayenne pepper
- ¼ teaspoon freshly grated nutmeg
- ⅔ cup sour cream
- 2 eggs, lightly beaten
- ⅓ cup grated onion
- 1½ cups half-and-half
- 1½ cups heavy cream
- 1 teaspoon Worcestershire sauce
- 1⅔ cups (6 ounces) grated extra-sharp cheddar cheese

Everyone has childhood memories of macaroni and cheese. I remember that I developed my taste for really good, really sharp-flavored macaroni and cheese as a child. My mother would take me to the butcher shop (which we called "the cold storage") to buy a wedge of sharp cheddar, freshly cut from a huge wheel of cheese with red wax rind, which we called "mouse cheese." At home, my mother and I would both nibble on little pieces of cheese while she prepared the macaroni and custard and I would grate more for sprinkling over the top.

Today it's hard to find cheese that is sharp enough, so I add dry mustard and sour cream to heighten the flavor. I also cut the cheese in small cubes to mix into the casserole, which gives an interesting texture to the finished dish. This macaroni and cheese is creamier and richer than most: it will seem very loose when you take it from the oven but will thicken nicely after a brief rest. It makes a generous amount, but you can reduce the ingredients by half and bake in a 9-by-9-inch pan.

Cook the macaroni in a large pot of boiling salted water until just tender. Drain well, and transfer to a buttered 9-by-13-by-2-inch baking dish. Mix in the cubed cheddar cheese.

Preheat the oven to 350°F.

Put the flour, 1½ teaspoons salt, dry mustard, black pepper, cayenne pepper, and nutmeg in a large mixing bowl, and stir to blend. Add the sour cream, followed by the eggs, and stir with a wire whisk until well blended and homogenous. Whisk in the onion, half-and-half, heavy cream, and Worcestershire sauce until blended. Pour this custard over the macaroni and cubed cheese, and stir to blend. Sprinkle the grated cheese evenly over the surface of the custard. Bake in the preheated oven until the custard is set around the edges of the baking dish but still a bit loose in the center, about 30 minutes.

Remove from the oven, and cool for 10 minutes to allow the custard to thicken.

Catfish Stew

MAKES ENOUGH TO SERVE 6

1 tablespoon unsalted butter

3 tablespoons bacon fat (box, page 51)

1 large onion, finely diced

1 shallot, finely diced

3 cloves garlic, minced

1 teaspoon dried thyme

1 teaspoon salt

1 medium carrot, peeled and thinly sliced

8 small new potatoes, sliced ⅓ inch thick

2 small ripe tomatoes, peeled, seeded, and chopped (1 cup)

½ cup dry white wine

8 cups water

2 pounds catfish fillet, cut into 1½-inch pieces

Salt and freshly ground black pepper

3 tablespoons finely snipped parsley

4 green onions or scallions, white and 2 inches of green, very thinly sliced

Catfish is a Southern favorite, particularly fresh-caught for summer fish fries (page 92). Today it is farm-raised and widely available all year round, with firm white flesh that can be prepared many ways. Here we use it in a delicate, light stew—almost a soup—that's delicious and quite beautiful, too.

Heat the butter and bacon fat in a heavy saucepan until foaming. Add the diced onion and shallot, and cook, stirring often, over medium heat for 5 minutes. Toss the garlic, thyme, and salt into the pan, and cook 5 minutes longer. Add the sliced carrot and potatoes, and cook, stirring often, for 5 minutes. Add the chopped tomatoes, white wine, and water, and bring to a simmer. Cook at a simmer, skimming the surface occasionally, until the potatoes and carrot are tender, about 15 minutes.

While the soup is simmering, season the catfish pieces liberally with salt and freshly ground pepper. When the potatoes are tender, add the seasoned catfish, parsley, and scallions to the pot. Cook, partially covered, at a very low simmer for 5 minutes. Taste carefully for seasoning, adding more salt and freshly ground pepper as needed.

Breakfast Shrimp for Supper

MAKES ENOUGH TO SERVE 4

Quickly sautéed shrimp over rice is a very old, traditional breakfast in the Carolina Low Country. But it would also make a nice quick-and-easy luncheon or supper dish, rounded out with a salad and maybe cornbread.

- 4 tablespoons (1/2 stick) unsalted butter
- 2 small onions, chopped (about 1 1/4 cups)
- 4 tablespoons thinly sliced green onion or scallion
- 1 clove garlic, finely minced
- 3/4 teaspoon salt
- 1/2 teaspoon freshly ground black pepper
- 1 pound large shrimp, peeled and deveined (see Note)
- 1/2 cup water

Heat the butter in a heavy skillet until hot and foaming. Add the onion, scallion, garlic, salt, and freshly ground black pepper. Stir well, and cook over medium heat for 5 minutes. Add the shrimp and cook for 1 minute, stirring often. Pour in the water, and simmer gently for 2–3 minutes, just until the shrimp are cooked through. Taste carefully for seasoning, adding more salt and freshly ground black pepper as needed. Serve hot over plain rice.

NOTE If using frozen shrimp, thaw them slowly in the refrigerator. After thawing, they benefit from a 5-minute soak in lightly salted ice water with a squeeze of lemon juice.

Trout Roe with Scrambled Eggs

MAKES ENOUGH TO SERVE 4

These rich scrambled eggs make a special springtime breakfast, especially if you're at a cabin in the woods on a successful trout-fishing trip. But if you can't catch trout loaded with roe, the roe is sometimes available in season from good fish markets—or you can use another kind of fresh fish roe. For a memorable breakfast or supper, accompany the eggs with hot Corn Griddle Cakes (page 217) and bacon.

THE TROUT ROE

- 4 tablespoons (1/2 stick) unsalted butter
- 8 trout roe
- 1/2 teaspoon salt
- 1/4 teaspoon freshly ground black pepper
- 1 rounded teaspoon minced garlic
- 1 tablespoon chopped parsley
- 1 tablespoon freshly squeezed lemon juice

THE SCRAMBLED EGGS

- 8 large eggs
- 6 tablespoons heavy cream
- 4 tablespoons (1/2 stick) unsalted butter
- Salt and freshly ground black pepper to taste

Heat 4 tablespoons butter in a small nonreactive frying pan until it is hot and foaming. Add the trout roe, and cook gently over medium heat for about 3 minutes, or until the roe begins to turn tan in color. Carefully turn the roe, and sprinkle the salt, pepper, minced garlic, and parsley over it. Cook 2–3 minutes longer, taking care not to brown the garlic, then sprinkle on the lemon juice, cook 1 minute longer, and remove from heat. Set in a warm place while you scramble the eggs.

To scramble the eggs: Break the eggs into a mixing bowl, and pour the heavy cream over. Beat lightly with a fork or whisk just until the heavy cream is blended into the eggs.

Heat the butter in a large nonreactive skillet, over medium heat, until hot and foaming. Pour the beaten eggs and cream into the skillet, and reduce the heat to low, stirring gently with a wooden spoon. Cook slowly, stirring gently every 20 seconds or so, until the eggs begin to form large "curds." When the eggs are nearly done but still wet, gently stir in the trout roe, and continue cooking until the eggs are cooked but still shiny and silky in appearance. Season with salt and pepper to taste. Serve at once.

Asparagus and Scallion Pie

MAKES ENOUGH FOR 6–8 SERVINGS

- Salt
- 1 pound thin asparagus, trimmed (yields 10 ounces)
- 3 bunches scallions (preferably small)
- 3 tablespoons unsalted butter
- 3 tablespoons all-purpose flour
- 1 cup milk
- 1 cup heavy cream
- Freshly ground black pepper
- Freshly grated nutmeg
- Basic Pie Dough (pages 242–243), double the recipe

Miss Lewis made this pie in Brooklyn in the 1980s, when she was chef at Gage & Tollner. On special occasions she would sometimes make it for more than five hundred people, and she would cut the pie herself, using kitchen scissors to slice neatly through the pastry and long vegetable spears.

This pie is simple and flavorful: asparagus and scallions with a light cream sauce baked between top and bottom crusts. You can prepare it a few hours ahead, refrigerate it, and bake it in the oven just before you want to eat. It's a fine appetizer, and with a salad makes a satisfying meal.

Preheat oven to 425°F.

Fill a large skillet with water, add 1 teaspoon salt per quart, and bring to a boil. Drop the asparagus in and blanch for 30 seconds, then remove them to a generously salted ice-water bath and chill 5 minutes. Place the scallions in the simmering water and blanch them as well, about 30 seconds, and chill in the water bath with the asparagus. Drain both and pat dry.

Make a cream sauce: Melt the butter in a saucepan, add the flour, and cook 2–3 minutes over low heat, stirring. Off heat, add the milk, a little at a time, followed by the cream, and whisk together, keeping it smooth as you go. Bring to a simmer, and cook, stirring, about 2 minutes. Add ½ teaspoon salt, a couple grinds of black pepper, and three gratings of nutmeg. Set aside to cool.

Roll out the pastry dough and line the bottom of a 9-inch pie pan (preferably Pyrex—we like to see things cooking) with a layer of dough. Arrange the scallions and asparagus in the dough-lined pan. Pour the cream sauce over the scallions and asparagus, moisten the rim of dough with a little water, and place another layer of dough over all. Tap the dough down lightly over the vegetables, and then trim the edge, leaving about ½ inch all around. Fold that over the rim of the pie pan, and crimp or press with the tines of a fork all around the edge. Cut a half-dozen slits in the top layer of dough for steam to escape.

Bake for 15 minutes in the preheated oven, until the pastry begins to puff and color, then turn the heat down to 375°F and bake for about 15 more minutes. Remove from the oven, and let cool for a few minutes. Slice with a serrated knife or, as Miss Lewis used to do it at Gage & Tollner, use sharp scissors to cut the pie, plunging the scissors into the center of the pie and cutting to the edge, snipping with the scissors to cut through both the top and bottom layers of pastry dough and the vegetables.

Edna Lewis during her Gage & Tollner days

Stuffed Peppers

MAKES ENOUGH TO SERVE 2–4

- 1 tablespoon unsalted butter
- ½ cup rice
- 1 teaspoon salt
- 1 cup water
- ¼ cup olive oil
- Freshly ground black pepper
- 2 medium onions, chopped (2½ cups)
- 2 bay leaves
- 1 tablespoon chopped garlic
- 4 stalks celery, chopped (2 cups)
- 1 large carrot, chopped (1 cup)
- 28 ounces canned whole peeled tomatoes (preferably San Marzano)
- 4 bell peppers, green, red, yellow, or a mix
- ½ pound ground beef
- ¼ cup torn mint leaves

In the summer heat of Alabama, many varieties of fresh peppers thrive in abundance. They appear everywhere as part of the landscape and, of course, are on every table. When I was growing up, even people who didn't have space for a vegetable garden would put a few pepper plants in their flower beds, so they could have fresh-picked peppers on the table at lunch, supper, and dinner. Most often, peppers were served uncooked—hot ones as well as the sweet banana and bell varieties—to be eaten as a condiment with the meal. On occasion, though, my mother would make stuffed bell peppers similar to these, with ground beef, rice, and tomato sauce, and we thought them exotic.

Stuffed peppers make a great dish for a party buffet and are a nice contribution to a covered-dish supper. You can expand this recipe as much as you want and prepare it ahead of time, to be baked when you're ready. At home, I serve these with garlic bread and salad.

Melt the butter in a small, heavy saucepan, pour in the rice, and sauté over medium-low heat, stirring, until the grains are coated and glistening, about 2 minutes. Add ½ teaspoon of the salt and the water, cover tightly, and cook over low heat for 20 minutes.

Meanwhile, heat all but 1 tablespoon of the olive oil in a pot over medium-high heat. Add the remaining salt, a generous sprinkling of freshly ground black pepper, the chopped onions, bay leaves, and garlic, and cook for 2–3 minutes, then add the celery and carrots and cook 2–3 minutes more. Remove the tomatoes from their can, crush them with your fingers directly into the pot, and add ¼ cup of the tomato juices, reserving the rest. Simmer, uncovered, on low heat for about 20 minutes.

Preheat the oven to 350°F.

Use a sharp knife to cut around the base of the stem on each pepper and set the stems aside. With a spoon, scrape out the ribs and seeds from inside each pepper and discard. Now, blanch the peppers and reserved stems in a large pot of salted boiling water for two minutes. Drain the peppers and allow them to cool while you finish the stuffing.

Heat the remaining teaspoon of olive oil in a large saucepan, and add the ground beef. Cook until browned, breaking the meat up, then drain and add 2 cups of the tomato sauce to the beef. Fluff up the rice, and stir it into the beef. Mix in the mint leaves and adjust the seasoning.

Stuff the peppers with the rice-and-meat filling, and stand them upright in a casserole dish that will hold them snugly. Top each pepper with one of the reserved stems, then cover the baking dish with parchment and a double thickness of aluminum foil, shiny side down. Seal tightly and put into the preheated oven and bake for 45 minutes. Then uncover and cook for 10 minutes longer. Serve the peppers hot from the oven and pass the remaining tomato sauce.

Chanterelles on Toast

MAKES ENOUGH TO SERVE 4

- 1 pound chanterelle mushrooms
- 4 slices good bread, suitable for toasting
- Butter for the toast
- 4 ounces St.-André or other triple-crème cheese
- 3 tablespoons unsalted butter
- Salt and freshly ground black pepper
- ¼ cup finely minced onion
- 1 shallot, finely minced
- 3 cloves garlic, finely minced
- 2 tablespoons very thinly sliced chives
- 12 drops lemon juice

One rainy spring day, while foraging in the Georgia woodland, I came upon a glorious patch of golden chanterelles, which inspired this dish. It's a fast sauté of the mushrooms served over buttered toast—with a slice of St.-André or another triple-crème cheese in between. Rich and earthy, it's a wonderful lunch, brunch, or light supper dish and, in small portions, an excellent first course. If you can get them, fresh chanterelles or morels (both of which grow wild in parts of the South) are superb prepared this way, but a mix of cultivated "wild" mushroom types like oyster, shiitake, and hedgehog (and a few common mushrooms too) will also be delicious.

Clean the chanterelles. Make sure they are really clean. I find it easiest to use a clean, dry pastry brush to brush away any bits of pine straw or earth. Whatever you do, don't run the mushrooms under water—it will spoil their flavor. Once the mushrooms are clean, tear or cut them lengthwise into pieces about ½ inch wide, and set aside.

Just before you sauté the mushrooms, toast the bread, butter it, and slice the cheese into four portions. Put one portion of the cheese on top of each slice of toast, and set aside.

To cook the mushrooms: Put the 3 tablespoons butter into a hot sauté pan, and heat until hot and bubbling. Immediately add the mushrooms to the pan in a single layer. Toss the mushrooms about the pan quickly, but allow them to brown a little. Sprinkle generously with salt and a few grindings of black pepper, then add the onion, shallot, garlic, and chives. Stir well for about 1 minute, taking care not to burn the onion and garlic. Sprinkle a few drops of lemon juice over the mushrooms, and spoon them onto the toast and cheese. Serve immediately.

THREE GOOD POULTRY HASHES

(Turkey Hash with Chestnuts; Squab or Quail Hash; Chicken Hash)

Doing research on Southern foodways a few years ago, Miss Lewis came upon a menu from a railroad dining car, circa 1920, listing a dish called "Turkey Hash with Corn Griddle Cakes." In those days, Southern trains offered food of legendary deliciousness—they would pick up fresh vegetables and supplies all along the route—and Miss Lewis became enchanted with the idea of poultry hash, though we had no recipe or description. So she started cooking up her own, not just with turkey, but with chopped cooked chicken, quail, and duck. I got caught up in this, too, and now believe that a good hash is one of the best things that can ever happen to leftover poultry.

Here are three hashes we've developed or discovered. They call for a specific kind of meat—turkey, quail or squab, and chicken, respectively—but in fact you can successfully use any kind of cooked poultry in each recipe. The Turkey Hash is saucy, light-colored, and creamy, with added sweetness and body from fresh-cooked chestnuts. The Squab or Quail Hash—which I learned about at a hunting plantation in northern Florida, where it was a specialty passed down from generations of cooks—is almost soupy, rich and dark from a brown *roux* and poultry gravy. The Chicken Hash is closest to the common diner style of meat hash, a blend of chicken meat, onions, and potatoes, barely moistened with cream, and fried slowly until it's glazed and turns almost crusty.

All of these are good any time of day, for breakfast, lunch, or supper. Serve the saucier Turkey or Quail Hash over Corn Griddle Cakes (page 217), as they did on the trains, or on biscuits, toast, or any of our cornbreads.

Turkey Hash with Chestnuts

MAKES ENOUGH TO SERVE 4

- 3 tablespoons unsalted butter
- ½ cup finely chopped onion
- ⅓ cup finely diced celery, preferably with tender leaves included
- ¾ teaspoon salt
- ¼ teaspoon freshly ground black pepper
- ½ teaspoon dried thyme (Spice Islands brand preferred)
- 1 small bay leaf
- 2 tablespoons all-purpose flour
- ¼ cup Chicken Stock (page 33), giblet gravy, or milk
- 1 cup half-and-half
- 1½ cups chopped cooked turkey
- ¾ cup chestnuts, either leftover or fresh (see Note)
- 1 tablespoon cognac or brandy (optional)

Heat the butter in a 12-to-14-inch sauté pan until melted and foaming. Add the onion, celery, salt, pepper, thyme, and bay leaf. Stir well to coat the vegetables, and cook over medium heat for 5 minutes, stirring often, until the vegetables are wilted and somewhat tender but not colored. Sprinkle the flour over, and stir well. Cook for 1 minute, stirring constantly, then, off heat, slowly stir in the chicken stock (or other liquid), followed by the half-and-half. Return the pan to the heat, and bring to a gentle simmer. Simmer for 1 minute, and taste for seasoning; you will most likely need more salt, unless you added gravy or stock that was highly seasoned. Add the turkey and chestnuts, and simmer until heated through. Taste again for seasoning. Add the optional booze, and cook 1 minute longer to cook off the alcohol.

Serve hot, spooned over toast, thin cornbread, or (best of all) Corn Griddle Cakes.

NOTE If you are using fresh chestnuts, peel (box, page 51) and cook them in a small amount of salted simmering water about 5–10 minutes (no need to chop the chestnuts, since they tend to break up on their own).

Squab or Quail Hash

MAKES ENOUGH FOR 2 SERVINGS

- 2 tablespoons unsalted butter
- 2 tablespoons all-purpose flour
- 1 cup Chicken Stock (page 33)
- 1 small onion, chopped (1 cup)
- 1 stalk celery, chopped (½ cup)
- ½ teaspoon dried thyme
- ½ teaspoon chopped garlic
- 1 firmly packed cup finely chopped squab or quail
- Salt and freshly ground black pepper
- ½ cup leftover gravy, if possible, or Chicken Stock

Melt the butter in a medium-sized, heavy skillet. Stir in the flour and cook, stirring, over medium-high heat until the butter and flour are deeply browned. Off heat, pour in the stock and whisk until smooth, then return the pan to medium heat and add the onion, celery, and thyme. Cook 5–6 minutes, until softened, then add the garlic and cook another minute. Stir in the squab, season with salt and pepper to taste, and add the gravy or some more stock. Stir and heat through; if it seems too thick, add a little more stock. The sauce should have the consistency of a thick soup.

Serve over toast, Corn Griddle Cakes, or biscuits.

Chicken Hash

MAKES ENOUGH FOR 2 SERVINGS

- 1 large all-purpose potato, peeled and cut into ½-inch cubes (1 cup)
- Salt and freshly ground black pepper
- 2 tablespoons unsalted butter
- 1 small onion, chopped (½ cup)
- ½ teaspoon finely chopped garlic
- 1 stalk celery, preferably with tender young leaves, chopped (½ cup)
- 1 cup cooked chicken, cut into small pieces
- ½ cup Chicken Stock (page 33), heated
- 2 tablespoons heavy cream

Put the cubed potato into a saucepan and cover with water. Season with ½ teaspoon salt and bring to a simmer. Cook just until potatoes are tender, about 10 minutes. Drain and reserve.

Heat the butter in a heavy skillet until melted and foaming. Add the onion and sprinkle lightly with salt. Cook, stirring often, until the onion begins to turn translucent—about 5 minutes. Add the garlic and celery, and sprinkle again with a little salt and a few grindings of black pepper. Stir well to coat the vegetables with the hot butter and seasonings, and cook 5 minutes longer. Add the reserved potato, the chicken, chicken stock, and cream.

Cook over moderate heat until the liquid is absorbed and the bottom is glazed. Turn with a spatula, and brown the other side.

Red Rice

MAKES ENOUGH TO SERVE 4

- 3 tablespoons bacon fat
- ½ cup chopped onion
- ¾ teaspoon dried thyme
- ½ cup chopped green bell pepper
- 1 small hot green chili, seeded and minced
- ½ teaspoon crushed red chili flakes (optional, to taste)
- 2 teaspoons chopped garlic
- 1 teaspoon salt
- ½ teaspoon freshly ground black pepper
- 1 tablespoon tomato paste
- 1¼ cups drained canned tomatoes (preferably San Marzanos)
- 1¼ cups Chicken Stock (page 33) or water
- 1 cup long-grain rice

One of Miss Lewis's discoveries during her sojourn in Charleston (as chef at Middleton Place) is this tomato-and-rice dish, an old specialty of that historic rice-growing region. I think of it as a "Low Country jambalaya," a versatile one-pot supper, chock full of meat or seafood morsels. Without all the additions, it's a delicious side dish.

Basic to red rice are tomatoes, peppers both sweet and hot, and (in my opinion) bacon fat; beyond these, add cooked meats or poultry or seafood of any kind. Bits of cooked ham and spicy sausage are traditional; leftover fried chicken is terrific too. Cooked fish can be flaked in just before serving; add lightly sautéed shrimp and scallops to finish cooking in the rice, which we do with oysters in our Red Rice Stuffing for Duck (pages 106–107). Use a shrimp or fish stock as a cooking liquid if you're adding seafood; for a basic red rice with meat or poultry, use a combination of Chicken Stock and Smoked Pork Stock (pages 33, 39).

Heat the bacon fat in a skillet and add the onion. Sauté until translucent, about 10 minutes. Add the thyme, bell pepper, fresh chili, and crushed red-pepper flakes. Cook until the vegetables are well cooked but not colored, about 10 minutes. Stir in the garlic, salt and pepper, tomato paste, and tomatoes, and cook about 5 minutes longer. Add the stock or water and simmer, partially covered, stirring frequently, about 15 minutes. Taste carefully for seasoning, and stir in the rice. Cover tightly and cook over very low heat for about 20 minutes, until the rice is tender.

Let rest, covered, for 5 minutes, then fluff gently with a fork before serving.

VII PRAISE THE LARD AND PASS THE BISCUITS

Yeast Breads, Cornbreads, Pancakes, and Biscuits

One of the first stories that Miss Lewis told me was about a man from the North who traveled south to experience the delights of Southern cooking, buttermilk biscuits in particular. When he returned, his friends asked him, "How was everything? How were the biscuits?"

"I don't know," he replied, sadly. "Every time someone would start to bring biscuits to the table, they'd stop and say, 'I'm sorry but they're not hot enough' . . . and they'd disappear."

This tale illustrates the pride, even fanaticism, with which Southern cooks regard traditional breads. In this chapter, you'll find exemplary biscuit recipes—to be served hot, of course—and our versions of other essential Southern breads: yeast loaves and rolls, muffins, and a variety of cornbreads. There are recipes for pancakes too, and some fritters (you'll also find some of those in the supper chapter), as well as an assortment of crackers that are as Southern as the term itself.

The distinctiveness of these regional Southern breads derives in large measure from the grains that were traditionally available: soft Southern wheat flour and fine-ground whole-grain cornmeal (preferably white). For the most authentic breads, rolls, cornbreads, and biscuits, it is worth getting these ingredients—see the discussions on wheat flour and cornmeal in this chapter, and mail-order sources in the back of the book. We also urge you to make, and bake with, your own baking powder, following the formula that Miss Lewis has been using for years: the improved flavor of quick breads and biscuits will be evident.

Southerners have bread on the table at every meal. Specific breads invariably accompany certain dishes: cornbread with greens, for example, or biscuits with fried chicken (and we set out jams and preserves). For occasions such as holidays, birthdays, or entertaining, particularly entertaining a non-Southerner, we like to offer a bread basket filled with yeast rolls, biscuits, and corn muffins. For us there's no greater gesture of respect for guests than to serve them home-baked breads and treasured preserves, foods into which you have put lots of time and care.

THE WHITE FLOURS USED (AND HOW THEY ARE MEASURED)

The baking recipes (in this and later chapters) call for three different kinds of white "all-purpose" flour. The different protein level in each flour is responsible for the different textures in the finished breads and cakes.

- For yeast breads and rolls, we use *bleached* all-purpose flour. Gold Medal, our preferred brand, and bleached flours from other national companies, are consistently milled to have a moderate protein content (about 10 percent). This provides enough gluten structure for a high rise and a texture that is light and feathery—as Southern white bread should be—rather than chewy.
- For biscuits (and cakes in Chapter IX) we use White Lily, a Southern brand of "all-purpose" flour with relatively low protein content (8 or 9 percent). Milled from soft winter wheat and given much sifting, bleaching, and processing, White Lily and similar flours have little gluten formation and so produce light and flaky biscuits and tender cakes. White Lily can be found at specialty markets around the country or mail-ordered (page 317). We use it exclusively for biscuits, although you can get reasonable results using bleached all-purpose. (For cakes, low-protein cake flours are acceptable substitutes for White Lily.)
- We use *unbleached* all-purpose flour (such as Hecker's, Gold Medal, or King Arthur) for our basic pastry dough (Chapter VIII). Milled from hard spring wheat, these flours have a higher protein level (about 12 percent) and strong gluten structure, which allow us to work in the fat needed for extra flakiness.

To measure flour: Use the "dip and sweep" method—stir up the flour in the bag a bit so it is not tightly packed, dip your measure into the flour, and scoop up an overflowing cupful, then sweep off the excess with a flat knife or spatula blade so the top of the cup is level. The one exception in this book is the Hot Crusty Buttermilk Biscuits recipe; there the flour is sifted before measuring.

White Loaf Bread

MAKES 2 LOAVES

- 1 package (1/4 ounce) active dry yeast (about 2 teaspoons)
- 1/4 cup warm water
- 2 cups whole milk
- 1 tablespoon unsalted butter or lard
- 2 tablespoons granulated sugar
- 5½–6¼ cups all-purpose flour
- 1 tablespoon salt

In my family, plain white bread wasn't just for sandwiches. A loaf was set next to my father's plate at every meal; he ate with a fork in one hand and a slice of bread in the other. When I started to cook from books, at about the age of 12, white bread was one of the first things I attempted to bake. And one summer, before going off to music camp, I baked and froze twenty loaves of bread for my family to eat—and I really felt I had accomplished something.

This recipe is an example of the style of bread I first learned to make: a recipe I've been working with, off and on, since junior-high school. And it is the bread we use now for chicken-salad and egg-salad sandwiches, and for Toast Cups (box, page 59). It makes great French toast too.

Dissolve the yeast in the warm water. Warm the milk with the butter or lard to dissolve. Pour into a large mixing bowl and add the sugar. Stir well, and cool to lukewarm.

Stir the yeast into the cooled milk mixture, then add 2 cups of the flour and beat well. Blend in the salt, and stir in by cupfuls enough of the remaining flour to make a moderately soft dough (at this point, it is better to add too little flour than too much).

Turn the dough out onto a lightly floured surface, and knead for 8–10 minutes, until the dough is smooth and satiny and springs back to the touch. If the dough is too wet and sticky to knead, dust lightly with flour, but avoid using more flour than is necessary. Shape into a ball, and put in a bowl, lightly greased with the butter or lard, turning the dough once to grease the surface lightly. Place a piece of plastic wrap directly over the surface of the dough, and then tightly cover the bowl with more plastic wrap. Set in a warm place, and let rise until doubled, about 1–1½ hours.

Turn the dough out, and gently deflate. Divide the dough in half, cover, and let rest for 10 minutes. Use a rolling pin to roll each half into a 7-by-13-inch rectangle on a very lightly floured surface. Beginning with the narrow end, roll up each piece like a jelly roll, gently sealing the dough with your fingers after each turn. Press down with the side of your hand to seal both ends of the loaves, and tuck the ends underneath the loaf. Put the formed loaves into two greased 9-by-5-by-3-inch loaf pans, cover them lightly, and let rise until a little more than doubled and almost even with the top of the pans, about 1½ hours.

Preheat the oven to 400°F.

Bake the loaves in the preheated oven for 40 minutes, until done (if they begin to brown too quickly, cover loosely with foil). To test for doneness, carefully turn the loaves out onto a clean kitchen towel and tap the bottoms with your fingers. Fully baked loaves have a hollow sound when rapped.

Remove from the oven, and unmold onto cooling racks to cool completely.

REALLY GOOD SANDWICHES ON WHITE BREAD

Sandwiches are a staple of Southern life. The white loaf here is the perfect bread for all kinds of sandwiches—and other recipes in this book make great fillings. You can make most of the following sandwiches in ordinary lunchbox size or in dainty tea party portions:

- Fried Soft-Shell Crab (page 83), topped with Coleslaw (page 61).
- Chicken Salad (page 58), on toast or plain slices.
- Pimento and Cheese (page 5), on plain slices or tea toast rounds (below), or spread on plain toast and baked in a hot oven until bubbly.
- Toast rounds for tea sandwiches: Cut 3-inch rounds from bread slices with a cookie or biscuit cutter; spread soft salted butter lightly on both sides, and toast in a 425°F oven until golden, turning once (5–10 minutes).
- Watercress-and-tomato tea sandwiches: Top cooled toast rounds with a spoonful of homemade Mayonnaise (page 57), a slice of fresh tomato seasoned with salt and pepper, and a sprig of watercress. Leave open, or top with another toast round.
- Shrimp-paste tea sandwiches: Spread Shrimp Paste (page 4) on toasted tea rounds. Leave open, or top with a toast round.
- Spring-Vidalia-onion tea sandwiches: Spread soft butter generously on untoasted rounds of white bread, and cover with paper-thin slices of spring Vidals.
- Spicy eggplant nibbles: Great for cocktails. Spread cool Spicy Eggplant Relish (page 6) on toasted tea rounds. Leave open, or top with a toast round.

Yeast Rolls from Potato Starter

MAKES APPROXIMATELY 4½ DOZEN ROLLS

THE STARTER

- 4 medium-sized all-purpose potatoes
- 5 cups purified water
- 3 tablespoons granulated sugar
- 1 package (¼ ounce) active dry yeast (about 2 teaspoons)
- 6 tablespoons all-purpose flour

- 1 cup milk, scalded and cooled completely
- 2 eggs, lightly beaten
- 7 cups all-purpose flour
- 1 tablespoon salt
- 5 tablespoons lard, melted and cooled
- 4 tablespoons (½ stick) unsalted butter, melted and cooled
- Additional unsalted butter for brushing the tops of the rolls as they bake

Miss Lewis's mother used to make these rolls in Freetown. In the evening, she'd mix the starter in a big stoneware crock, wrap it in a quilt, and set it by the hearth, to develop flavor overnight. She'd make the dough the next day, and sometimes give that a night to rise too. The result was the ultimate Southern dinner roll: fluffy, tender, and moist inside, a thin, crisp golden crust, and superb flavor from the starter.

We make these rolls today, especially for guests and on occasions when a special bread is called for. But though the procedure is essentially the same as it was in Freetown, with modern strains of yeast the rolls take much less time. I usually mix the starter in the morning, let it develop for 2–4 hours, then finish the dough and bake the rolls that same afternoon. The dough can also be refrigerated after the first rise, and held for a day or more before baking.

These special rolls deserve extra attention: don't let the dough overproof—especially during its second rise—or it may develop an unpleasant, strongly fermented flavor. Brush the rolls lavishly with butter near the end of baking (this rich baptism is certainly Miss Lewis's addition). For fancy dinners, I often shape the dough into cloverleaf rolls (see page 206), both for appearance and because I love pulling them apart as I eat them. In any shape, the rolls should be served hot, so if they've been baked earlier in the day reheat them in a 375°F oven for 5 minutes.

Leftover rolls are delicious for breakfast split, generously buttered, run under the broiler, and served with homemade jelly or fig preserves. (The recipe makes a lot, but they go quickly—the dough can also be divided and baked in smaller batches.)

To make the starter: Wash the potatoes, and boil them, covered, in the bottled water for 30 minutes or longer, until they are very soft and mushy. Remove the potatoes from the pot, reserving the cooking water, and allow them to cool slightly before peeling. Rub the peeled potatoes through a fine-meshed sieve, or press through a ricer. Measure out 1 cup of the mashed potatoes into a large mixing bowl. Whisk 1 cup of the reserved cooking water into the mashed potatoes until smooth. Let cool to tepid before stirring in the sugar, yeast, and flour. Cover the bowl loosely, and set it in a cool, draft-free area to develop for 4 hours or overnight. When it is ready, the potato starter will be light and foamy with an aromatic yeasty smell.

Make the dough: Add the scalded and cooled milk, the beaten eggs, and 2 cups of the flour to the starter, and stir until well blended. Add the salt, 2 tablespoons of the melted lard, 1 tablespoon of the melted butter, and 2 more cups of the flour, and stir until you have a smooth batter. Stir in the remaining flour 1 cup at a time until it has all been incorporated, and continue stirring vigorously until the dough becomes smooth and resilient and pulls back as you stir it. This will take about 8 minutes of continuous stirring.

When the batter is properly mixed, transfer it to a large, deep mixing bowl that has been lightly greased with some of the melted lard. Turn the dough in the greased bowl so that its surface is lightly greased all around. Cover the bowl tightly with plastic wrap, and set in a cool, draft-free place to rise—and double in volume—usually about 1½ hours. When the dough has doubled, gently press it down and turn it in the bowl one or two times before covering it again and leaving it to rise until doubled a second time. The second rising should take less time than the first, and it is important that the dough does not overrise. Dough that overrises has an unpleasant, overly fermented flavor.

Preheat the oven to 425°F.

When the dough has doubled again, mix together the remaining melted lard and butter and lightly grease two 9-inch cake pans. Using greased fingers, pinch off a piece of dough slightly smaller than a golf ball. Fold the piece of dough in half, then, using cupped hands, ease the edges of the dough under and form a round ball approximately 1¼ inches in diameter. Pinch the seam together on the bottom. Place the roll, seam side down, in one of the cake pans, and repeat the process, making sure that each roll is well coated with the lard-butter mixture and that the rolls just touch each other in the pan. When all of the dough is used up and both pans are filled, set them in a draft-free place, uncovered, for 1 hour or longer, until the rolls have risen even with the top of the cake pans.

Bake in the preheated oven for 30 minutes, then remove from the oven and brush liberally with soft unsalted butter before returning to the oven to bake for 10 minutes longer. Remove from the oven, and allow the rolls to cool in the pans for 5 minutes. Turn them out and serve.

Variation: Cloverleaf Rolls

MAKES 2½ DOZEN ROLLS

1 recipe Yeast Rolls from Potato Starter (preceding recipe)
4 tablespoons (½ stick) unsalted butter, melted
Muffin tins for 2½ dozen muffins

Prepare rolls exactly as in recipe up to the point of shaping the rolls. To make cloverleaf rolls, pinch dough off in pieces large enough to make balls 1 inch in diameter. Coat the balls of dough well with the melted butter, and put 3 balls in each greased muffin tin. Let the rolls rise, uncovered, at room temperature until they are doubled in size and crest the top of the muffin tins. Bake in a preheated 425°F oven for 15 minutes. Remove from the oven, and brush liberally with the softened butter. Return to the oven, and bake 4–6 minutes longer, until the rolls are golden brown. Remove the rolls from the muffin tins and serve hot.

NOTE Rolls baked earlier the same day can be reheated before serving in a 375°F oven for 5 minutes.

SCALDED MILK

In old Southern kitchens and cookbooks, milk for yeast breads was always "scalded"—that is, heated to a point just below the simmer—in order to destroy enzymes in unpasteurized milk that interfere with rising. That's not a problem today, but in these recipes I still advise warming the milk so as not to slow down the yeast growth.

Sally Lunn

MAKES 1 SALLY LUNN, ENOUGH TO SERVE 12–16

- 1 package (1/4 ounce) active dry yeast
- 2 cups milk, heated just to the boiling point and cooled to lukewarm
- 6 tablespoons (3/4 stick) unsalted butter, softened
- 4 large eggs
- 1/2 cup granulated sugar
- 6 cups unbleached all-purpose flour
- 1 1/2 teaspoons salt
- 1 1/2 tablespoons unsalted butter for buttering the tube pan

This sweet yeast bread supposedly originated in Bath, England (where Sally Lunn herself sold them), at the end of the eighteenth century. And it quickly became well known in Virginia and other parts of the South, judging by the many recipes Miss Lewis and I have found in old Southern cookbooks. Sally Lunn is a country cousin to brioche, simpler to make and almost as buttery. We bake it in a tube pan—very generously buttered—for a ring-shaped loaf with a golden, very crusty crust. It is most enjoyable for breakfast or tea (though it tastes good at dinner too), served with butter and an array of preserves. Fresh slices are also a delectable base for strawberry shortcake. The bread doesn't keep well, but even day-old Sally Lunn makes terrific toast, French toast, or bread-and-butter pudding.

The variation that follows is filled with bits of candied citrus and glazed with apricot preserves and makes a very nice cake for coffee or tea.

Dissolve the yeast in ½ cup of the lukewarm milk in a large mixing bowl. Put the butter in the remaining milk, and stir to melt. Beat the eggs and sugar together, then stir in the milk and melted butter. Add this to the dissolved

Bethel Church, the site of Freetown reunions, Unionville, Virginia, 1977

yeast, and mix well. Stir in the flour, 1 cup at a time, adding the salt on the second addition. Stir vigorously with a heavy wooden spoon until all of the flour is incorporated, then continue stirring for an additional 4 minutes to develop the texture of the bread. Scrape down the sides of the bowl, cover with plastic wrap, and let rise until doubled—about 1–1½ hours. Stir down the dough, which should be very silky and loose.

Butter a standard-size tube pan with the 1½ tablespoons unsalted butter. (The amount of butter is important, because it helps create a very golden and crusty crust.) Spoon the dough evenly into the buttered tube pan. Cover and let rise until almost doubled, about 1 hour.

Preheat the oven to 350°F.

Bake on the bottom rack of the preheated oven for 40–50 minutes, until a cake tester tests clean. Take care not to overbake, and cover the top loosely with foil, shiny side up, if it begins to brown too deeply before bread is done. Unmold immediately onto a cooling rack and cool completely.

Variation: Sally Lunn the Coffee Cake

Make exactly as the original except: Reduce the amount of granulated sugar to 2 tablespoons, and add ½ cup full-flavored honey and 1 teaspoon vanilla extract. After the first rise, stir in 1½ cups finely chopped candied orange peel or Candied Kumquats (page 15). Bake as above.

Make a glaze with 1 cup apricot preserves heated and strained and simmered with 3 tablespoons brandy or orange-flavored liqueur. Brush the glaze generously over the top and sides of the still-warm Sally Lunn.

CORNMEAL FOR CORNBREADS

Every Southerner has his favorite cornmeal. It's a personal matter.

In general, the choices are between white and yellow corn, and the kind of grind you want. Fortunately, Miss Lewis and I both maintain a strong preference for white cornmeal, which we grew up on. And we prefer to use fine (or very fine) stone-ground meal in all these recipes. Stone-ground meal is less processed, has no additives and more flavor. The advantage of a fine grind is that the grain can absorb more liquid, which results in a creamier, more custardy texture.

You can get the exact extra-fine grind cornmeal we use—by mail order (page 317) from Pollards, an excellent mill in my hometown of Hartford, Alabama. They grind both white and yellow cornmeal, to satisfy both camps, in several different grades.

You can also get high-quality stone-ground cornmeal at natural-food stores and some supermarkets, though none will likely be as fine-ground as Pollards. These will work fine in our recipes, as will conventionally processed national-brand cornmeals. However, different cornmeals—especially coarse meals—require different amounts of liquid to form a dough or batter of the consistency we describe in each recipe. So you may have to adjust the amount. Also, different grinds of meal will produce different textures in the finished bread—more crumbly with coarser meals, creamier with finer grinds.

Freshly ground cornmeal spoils quickly if not refrigerated in sealed jars or heavy-duty zip-locked bags. You can tell if it has turned simply by smelling it.

Our Favorite Sour Milk Cornbread

MAKES ENOUGH TO SERVE 6–8

- 1½ cups fine-ground white cornmeal (see page 209 about grinds)
- 1 teaspoon salt
- 1 teaspoon Homemade Baking Powder (page 230)
- 1¾ cups soured milk or buttermilk
- 2 eggs, lightly beaten
- 2 tablespoons unsalted butter

Sour-milk cornbread is one of those quintessential foods of the South for which there are hundreds of recipes (and infinite variations). Although we'd never claim to have the "definitive" version, Miss Lewis and I worked together on this recipe until we got just what we wanted: an all-cornmeal bread that's light, moist, and rich, full of corn flavor, with the tanginess of sour milk or buttermilk. Like all Southern cornbreads, it has no sugar—that's a Yankee thing.

Traditionally, milk that had started to culture was used in cornbread and other baked goods, both for its pleasant sharp taste and for a leavening boost (its acids react with baking soda to generate carbon dioxide). Since modern pasteurized milk doesn't sour nicely—it just goes bad—we use commercial buttermilk here instead. Sometimes—if we have no buttermilk—we make a quick "sour milk" by curdling sweet milk with vinegar and lemon juice (see box).

This is a genuine all-purpose cornbread, delicious as a savory bread or even as a dessert, slathered with butter and honey. My mother and grandmother only made this kind of leavened cornbread (which they called "egg bread") for cornbread stuffing, and it does make superb stuffing. It's also delicious in a time-honored Southern snack: cornbread crumbled into a bowl with cold milk or buttermilk poured over. Many Southerners—especially of an older generation—would call that a perfect light supper on a hot summer day, after a big midday meal.

Preheat the oven to 450°F.

Mix the cornmeal, salt, and baking powder together in a bowl. Stir the milk into the beaten eggs, and pour over the dry ingredients in batches, stirring vigorously to make a smooth glossy batter.

Cut the butter into pieces and put it in a 10-inch cast-iron skillet or baking pan. Put the skillet in the preheated oven, and heat until the butter is melted and foaming. Remove from the oven, and swirl the butter all around the skillet to coat the bottom and sides thoroughly. Pour the remaining melted butter into the cornbread batter, and stir well until the butter is absorbed into the batter. Turn the batter into the heated skillet, and put in the oven to bake for 30–40 minutes, until cornbread is golden brown and crusty on top and pulls away from the sides of the skillet.

Remove the skillet from the oven, and turn the cornbread out onto a plate. Allow to cool for 5 minutes before cutting into wedges. Serve the cornbread while it is hot.

A QUICK SOUR MILK

It only takes about 10 minutes to make this tangy substitute for buttermilk. Stir into 1¾ cups sweet milk 2 teaspoons lemon juice and 2 teaspoons cider vinegar. Let sit until curdled.

Cornbread Vegetable Bake

MAKES ONE 9-INCH ROUND OF BREAD, ENOUGH TO SERVE 8

- 1 recipe Sour Milk Cornbread batter (preceding recipe)
- 1 cup corn kernels, freshly cut from the cob
- 1 cup thinly sliced okra (about 4 ounces)
- 1 medium onion, finely chopped (1 cup)
- ½ teaspoon salt
- ½ teaspoon freshly ground black pepper

The addition of fresh vegetables transforms sour-milk cornbread into a substantial dish for a summer lunch or supper. The moisture of the vegetables also gives the bread a creamier-than-usual texture, almost like a frittata. This vegetable bake will take a few minutes longer in the oven than plain cornbread—but don't let it dry out.

Preheat the oven to 450°F.

Prepare the sour-milk cornbread batter following the preceding recipe. Put the corn, okra, and onion on a piece of wax paper, and sprinkle with the salt and freshly ground black pepper. Stir the vegetables into the cornbread batter, then pour it into the baking pan or skillet, prepared as described. Bake in the middle of the oven for 40–50 minutes, until golden brown on top. Remove from the oven, and immediately invert onto a plate or cooling rack. Allow the bread to cool for 5 minutes before cutting into wedges and serving.

Dorothy Peacock's Skillet Cornbread

MAKES ONE 10-INCH HOE CAKE, ENOUGH TO SERVE 4–6

- 1¾ cups fine-ground white cornmeal (see page 209 about grinds)
- 1¼ teaspoons salt
- 1–2 cups boiling water
- 2 tablespoons lard or unsalted butter

This is what we knew as cornbread in the Peacock household: a thin disk-shaped cornmeal cake, cooked, as in the preceding recipe, in a cast-iron skillet, but on top of the stove, so it is crusty on the outside and creamy on the inside. We had it at least once or twice a week.

There are, in fact, many traditional names and countless variations for this basic type of cornbread, such as "corn pone," "corn dodgers," "hoe cake," and "johnnycake" (or "journey cake"). The dough is a simple mush of cornmeal, salt, and boiling water. Miss Lewis calls them "ashcakes," and she remembers making them in the hearth, placing thick rounds of dough directly into hot ashes and covering them with wood coals to bake.

Boiling water is the only "leavening" in my mother's skillet cornbread (and her deep-fried breads; see next recipe). Mixed with cornmeal, the hot water penetrates and swells the grains quickly; then, when heated, the escaping steam creates a slight rising effect. A thick cast-iron frying pan is best for producing a crispy brown crust, but you can use a heavy nonstick pan.

I love to serve this cornbread with greens to sop up the "pot likker." But Miss Lewis prefers it for breakfast.

Mix together the cornmeal and salt, and slowly stir in 1 cup of the boiling water, mixing vigorously to dissolve any lumps that form. Blend in enough of the remaining water to give the mixture the texture of mashed potatoes. Set aside, and allow to cool for 5 minutes so that it will be easier to handle.

Meanwhile, use half of the lard or butter to grease generously a 10-inch preferably cast-iron skillet. Turn the cooled cornmeal batter, which will have thickened somewhat as it sat, into the greased skillet. Wet your hands with cold water, and pat the batter into a flat, evenly thick pancake filling the entire bottom of the skillet. Cook over medium-low heat, checking often to see that it isn't burning on the bottom. When the cake is very firm and the bottom is crisp and brown, in about 15 minutes, carefully turn it out onto a lightly greased plate, and swirl the remaining lard or butter into the skillet. Gently slide the hoe cake back into the skillet to brown and crisp the other side; this usually takes 5–10 minutes. When it is browned, slide out onto a cooling rack and allow to cool for 5 minutes before cutting into wedges and serving.

Dorothy Peacock's Deep-Fried Cornbread or Fried Hot-Water Cornbread

MAKES ABOUT 20

- 1½ cups stone-ground white cornmeal (see page 209 about grinds)
- ¾ teaspoon salt
- ¾ cup or more boiling water
- Cooking oil for deep-frying

My mother made these bite-sized breads from the same simple "pone"—cornmeal and boiling water—as her skillet cornbread (preceding recipe). Dropped by the teaspoon into hot fat, the batter expands slightly as it cooks, becomes extremely crispy outside and creamy inside. We frequently had a big platter of these on the table in summer, alongside bowls of fresh peas and tomatoes.

I've never had these anywhere but Hartford, Alabama, at home and at friends'. Nor had Miss Lewis ever tasted them before we met. But we both love them.

Put the cornmeal and salt in a mixing bowl, and stir to blend. Pour ¾ cup boiling water over and stir until well blended. The mixture should have the consistency of mashed potatoes; if it is too thick, stir in more boiling water.

Heat the oil to 340°F. Carefully spoon the batter by rounded teaspoonfuls into the hot oil. Cook for 3 minutes or longer, turning once, until golden. Drain on crumpled paper towels, and serve hot.

Fresh Corn Fritters

MAKES ABOUT 30 FRITTERS

- 2 cups stone-ground white cornmeal
- 1 tablespoon all-purpose flour
- 1 teaspoon baking soda
- 1 teaspoon Homemade Baking Powder (page 230)
- 1 teaspoon salt
- 1 egg, separated, plus 2 egg whites
- 1 small onion, grated (1⁄3 cup)
- 1½–2 cups buttermilk
- 1 cup fresh corn kernels, cut from the cob
- Oil for deep-frying (box, page 216)

These airy fritters, studded with sweet corn kernels, make a wonderful appetizer, bread, supper, or even a vegetable side dish. The leavened cornmeal base is similar to traditional Hush Puppies (page 218) but lightened by whipped egg whites. The batter can be the base for all sorts of vegetable fritters, using grated carrots or zucchini, or slivered okra, in place of the fresh corn. (For tips on deep-frying, see page 216.)

Put the cornmeal, flour, baking soda, homemade baking powder, and salt into a large mixing bowl, and mix well to blend. Add the egg yolk, the grated onion, and 1½ cups of the buttermilk. Stir until the dough is thoroughly blended and has the consistency of loose mashed potatoes; if it is too stiff, add more buttermilk. Stir in the corn kernels.

Whip the 3 egg whites in a clean bowl until they mount, then quickly and carefully fold them into the reserved batter. Heat the fat to 340°F, then drop rounded tablespoonfuls of the batter into fat and fry until golden brown. Remove with a slotted spoon or strainer to a draining rack or crumpled paper towels (page 216). Serve hot.

TIPS ON DEEP-FRYING CORNBREADS

Follow these tips for deep-fried cornbreads and fritters that are crusty outside, fully cooked inside, and not greasy.

- Use a heavy, deep saucepan with sides at least 8 inches high.
- Fill it to a depth of 6 inches with peanut oil or other vegetable oil with a high smoking point.
- Heat the oil slowly to a temperature of 340°F as measured on a deep-frying thermometer.
- Test-fry one cornbread or fritter until brown all over. Drain and break open: if the inside is at all raw, the oil is too hot; lower the heat.
- Cook only 5 or 6 fritters at a time, or fewer if the pan is crowded. Turn when bottom is nicely browned (though they will often turn over themselves). Dunk fritter tops under the oil occasionally too, and fry until golden on all sides.
- Drain on a wire rack or on a nest of crumpled paper towels (since they will get soggy sitting on flat towels or brown paper).
- After the oil has cooled completely, strain it and store it in closed containers in a cool place. You can use it again three or four times.

TIPS FOR GRIDDLE AND PAN CAKES

- A standard flat griddle is fine if you have one, but we just use a well-seasoned cast-iron pan. A heavy-duty nonstick will also work.
- Heat the griddle or pan slowly—at least 4 or 5 minutes over low heat—before testing batter.
- Grease the pan lightly before adding batter by wiping the surface with a bit of butter on paper towel. Repeat greasing only if necessary.
- Test a teaspoon of batter to see if it bubbles up in under a minute. Adjust heat as necessary.

Corn Griddle Cakes

MAKES ABOUT 16 GRIDDLE CAKES

- 1 cup white cornmeal
- ½ teaspoon salt
- 2 teaspoons Homemade Baking Powder (page 230)
- 2 eggs
- ⅔–1 cup milk, at room temperature
- 1 tablespoon melted butter

Miss Lewis grew up on these thin and tender cornmeal cakes. Years later, she paired them with Sourdough Pancakes (page 225) as a special on the Gage & Tollner menu. We make them at home for breakfast—or "breakfast for supper"—served with cane syrup, honey, and lots of butter, and as a special bread for one of the hashes on pages 194–196, and for Trout Roe with Scrambled Eggs (page 187), with which their sweet corny flavor goes so well. The cakes cook quickly—barely a minute in the pan—and the batter must be thin. If it becomes thick on standing, stir in a few tablespoons of milk.

Put the cornmeal, salt, and baking powder in a bowl and mix. In a separate bowl, beat the eggs lightly and stir in the milk. Stir the eggs and milk into the cornmeal mixture and blend thoroughly. Add the melted butter and blend.

Spoon about 2 tablespoons of the batter onto a hot, greased griddle or skillet. Cook until bubbles appear on the top, then turn and cook for about 10 seconds longer. Transfer cooked griddle cakes to a warm platter, and cover loosely with foil until all of the cakes are cooked. Serve immediately.

Hush Puppies

MAKES ABOUT 30 HUSH PUPPIES

- Oil for frying
- 2 cups stone-ground white cornmeal
- 2 tablespoons all-purpose flour
- 1 teaspoon baking soda
- 1 teaspoon Homemade Baking Powder (page 230)
- 1 heaping teaspoon kosher salt
- ½ cup grated onion
- ¼ cup thinly sliced green onion
- 1 egg yolk
- 1½–2 cups buttermilk
- 3 egg whites

Hush puppies, an essential component of fried-fish plates (page 92), are made from a cornmeal batter similar to the fritters, including eggs and baking powder, except they have no beaten egg whites. There are many explanations for the name "hush puppies"—the most common referring to the scraps of fried corn dough thrown to hungry hounds to hush them.

Start slowly heating at least 3 inches of cooking oil until it reaches 340°F. Meanwhile, put the cornmeal, flour, baking soda, baking powder, and salt into a mixing bowl, and whisk to blend. Add the grated and sliced onions, egg yolk, and 1½ cups of the buttermilk. Stir vigorously until the batter is well blended and the consistency of loose mashed potatoes. If it is too stiff, add more buttermilk. (The finer the grind of the cornmeal, the more liquid you will need.)

Whip the egg whites in an immaculate bowl until they begin to mound (not stiff peaks). Quickly fold the beaten whites into the batter. Drop by rounded tablespoonfuls into the heated oil. Puppies usually roll over on their bellies when they are done, but you may need to turn them to be sure they cook evenly. Fry until golden brown all over, then remove with a slotted spoon, and drain well on a rack or crumpled paper towels.

Cornmeal Muffins

MAKES 1 DOZEN CORNMEAL MUFFINS

- 1¾ cups stone-ground white cornmeal
- ⅓ cup all-purpose flour
- 1 tablespoon plus 1½ teaspoons Homemade Baking Powder (page 230)
- 1½ teaspoons salt
- 5 tablespoons unsalted butter
- 2 eggs
- 2½ cups milk
- Lard or unsalted butter for greasing muffin tins

Southern cornmeal muffins are simple but they look a bit fancy, so we like to make them for special occasions. Like our Sour Milk Cornbread, these muffins are golden and crusty outside, rich and moist on the inside. But the flavor's somewhat different, because they have lots more butter, a small amount of white flour, and sweet milk rather than sour—without the tang of the cultured milk, you can really taste the corn.

Preheat the oven to 425°F.

Put the cornmeal, flour, baking powder, and salt in a large mixing bowl, and mix until well blended. Use your fingers or a pastry blender to work the butter finely into the cornmeal mixture.

In a separate bowl, beat the eggs lightly, then stir in the milk. Pour the eggs and milk over the dry ingredients, and stir just until the batter is smooth and free of lumps.

Generously grease twelve muffin tins with lard or butter, and fill each cup with ½ cup of the muffin batter. Bake in the preheated oven for 15–20 minutes, until golden brown and crusty. Cool on a cooling rack for 2 minutes before turning out and serving. (If some of the muffins are stubborn about releasing, it may be necessary to run the blade of a knife between the muffins and the muffin tin.)

Cornmeal Crisps

MAKES ENOUGH TO SERVE 8–10

Paper-thin and crunchy, these crisps make a delicious nibble and are good cocktail snacks or as an accompaniment to soups and salads.

- 1 cup stone-ground white cornmeal
- 1 teaspoon salt
- 3 tablespoons unsalted butter, divided
- 1½–2¼ cups boiling water

Stir together the cornmeal and salt in a stainless-steel mixing bowl, and add 2 tablespoons of the butter cut into small pieces. Slowly stir in enough boiling water so that the mixture resembles very wet mashed potatoes. Beat vigorously until the butter is melted and absorbed and the batter is smooth. Allow to cool slightly.

Preheat the oven to 375°F.

Use the remaining tablespoon of butter to grease two 15-by-10-by-1-inch baking sheets. Put even amounts of the batter on the two baking sheets, and use a rubber spatula to spread it as evenly and thinly as possible (dipping the spatula in water helps with this). Bake in the preheated oven for 20–35 minutes, until crisp and golden brown. Cool on the baking sheets, and break into large irregular pieces for serving. Stored in an airtight container, the crisps keep well for several days.

Angel Biscuits

MAKES ABOUT 2½ DOZEN BISCUITS

- 1 package (¼ ounce) active dry yeast
- ¼ cup warm water
- 2 cups buttermilk, at room temperature
- 5 cups all-purpose flour
- ¼ cup granulated sugar
- 1 tablespoon Homemade Baking Powder (page 230)
- 1 teaspoon baking soda
- 1 tablespoon salt
- 1 cup lard, chilled
- Melted butter for brushing the biscuits

Angel biscuits are a twentieth-century hybrid—a cross between a yeast roll and a baking-powder biscuit—which became quite popular across the South. Though they don't have the fine texture of classic biscuits, their yeasty flavor and crumb are quite appealing. The name, some cooks assert, denotes their heavenly lightness. But I think they're angelic because the two leavenings protect the home baker from failure: even if your regular biscuits turn out hard as rocks, these will rise reliably. Another virtue is that the dough can be made ahead and refrigerated for 3–5 days. This is a great convenience when baking up a large batch for a party, which is when I usually make them. It also allows you to cut off a bit of dough to make a few fresh biscuits whenever you want them during the week.

Dissolve the yeast in the warm water, and let it stand for 5 minutes. Stir in the room-temperature buttermilk. Put the flour, sugar, homemade baking powder, baking soda, and salt in a large mixing bowl, and stir with a whisk to blend thoroughly. Using your fingers, quickly work the chilled lard into the dry ingredients, incorporating until about half of the mixture resembles coarse meal while half of the lard remains the size of large peas and marbles. Stir in the yeast and buttermilk, and mix just until well blended.

Turn the dough out onto a lightly floured surface, and knead lightly six or seven times. Roll out to a thickness of ½ inch and, using a 2½–3-inch biscuit cutter, stamp out biscuits. Place the biscuits on a lightly greased baking sheet, leaving about ⅓ inch in between.

Cover lightly with plastic wrap, and let rise in a warm place for 45 minutes. Bake in a preheated 450°F oven for 10–12 minutes, until golden brown. Brush the tops with melted butter and serve.

CANE SYRUP

Southerners love sweetness. We always have and I suspect we always will. It is part of our culinary, and perhaps our genetic, makeup. Southern cookbook coffers are filled with recipes for all manner of sweets. Look in any Southern church or community cookbook and more often than not the first and largest chapters are devoted to baked goods and confections—cakes, cookies, pies, ice creams, candies, and other sugary treats.

My father tells me that during the 1940s, when he was a boy growing up in the boonies of Alabama, his family was too poor to buy sugar. He said that during the war years, "gasoline and sugar were rationed and you had to have a voucher to buy either, but it didn't matter to our family because our mule-drawn wagons didn't use gas and we didn't have any money for sugar." So my father and his family, like most rural families in the South, relied on syrup made from sugar cane to satisfy their sweet tooth.

Each year my dad's family would grow a big field of sugar cane and let it cure into the fall to mature and develop its sweetness. Then they would harvest the cane, cutting it as close to the ground as possible, because that was where the sweetest sugar reserves were stored. They then readied it for grinding by stripping off the sharp leaves from the stalks. This had to be done carefully because the leaves had stiff, sharp edges that cut easily. The stubs left after the cutting were left intact in the field and covered over with earth to protect them from the cold of winter, with the hope that they would sprout a new crop of cane in the spring. Additionally, my grandfather would select the finest-looking stalks of cane and cover them with fodder to winter over until the spring, when he would unearth them and cut them on either side of their bamboo-like joints, which he would plant in the cane field to improve and augment his crop.

With the harvest completed, arrangements were made with a local family who had a cane mill. My dad and his father would load their mule-drawn wagon with the stripped cane early each morning and head over to the mill, where they would spend the entire day processing the cane into syrup. First they would grind the sugar cane in a mill (powered by the same mule that had driven them that morning) to extract all of the juice. Then, the spent cane discarded, they boiled the dark juice in enormous, wood-fired iron cauldrons, skimming off the foam and impurities so the finished syrup would be clear and have a pure flavor, and cooking it down until it was of a desired consistency—my grandmother liked her syrup thin and pourable, my grandfather preferred a more viscous product. When the syrup was ready they would pack it into one-gallon metal syrup buckets and deliver them home to store and use until sugar-cane season the following year. It took about six hours to boil a pot of cane juice into syrup, and my dad tells me that for a week or more they would cook two pots a day to make enough syrup to last them through the year. My father's family's par was one hundred buckets of syrup. They paid the miller for the use of his mill with a percentage of their syrup, and any surplus they could use for bartering and to share with other families in their community. They used the syrup in cooking and baking, and my grandmother would make a special iced tea that was flavored with crystallized cane syrup, but it was especially popular at meal time when they sopped it up with hot biscuits and cornbread and lavish amounts of freshly churned butter.

The flavor of cane syrup is unique and fortunately you don't have to grow and grind your own to try it today. Enjoy it as you would any other syrup over all sorts of cakes from the griddle, and of course with well-buttered hot biscuits and cornbread.

Popovers

MAKES 12 POPOVERS

- 2 cups sifted unbleached all-purpose flour
- 1 teaspoon salt
- 3 eggs
- 2 cups milk
- Unsalted butter

Popovers were once a very popular item in the Southern bread basket but are rarely seen these days. They are simple to make, however. The only trick is keeping the oven door shut while they are baking; don't peek or you will wind up with soggy, fallen popovers. These are good at any meal, but we like them best for breakfast or lunch. Popover batter needs to rest for an hour or more, and for convenience you can mix it up the night before baking.

Preheat the oven to 375°F.

Put the flour and salt in a mixing bowl and mix well. Beat the eggs lightly with a fork. Pour the milk into the eggs, mix well, then pour slowly into the flour, stirring constantly. Cover lightly, and let rest for 1 hour or longer before baking. Generously grease twelve muffin cups or Pyrex custard cups with the unsalted butter. Taking care not to burn the butter, heat the muffin tins or custard cups in the oven. Remove from the oven after 2 minutes, and quickly pour ⅓ cup batter into each cup. Bake in the preheated oven for 25 minutes without opening the oven door—otherwise the popovers will collapse and be ruined. Serve hot from the oven.

Sourdough Pancakes

MAKES ABOUT 18 PANCAKES

These thin, crêpelike pancakes have a distinctive taste and texture because of the sourdough starter. It's nice to serve them on the same plate with Corn Griddle Cakes (page 217) and various syrups and preserves. Make the starter in the evening, and mix up the batter the next morning—it can be stored for a day in the refrigerator before using.

THE STARTER

- 1½ cups unbleached all-purpose flour
- 1½ teaspoons active dry yeast
- 1 cup bottled water or well water, heated to lukewarm

- 1 cup milk, at room temperature
- 1 egg, lightly beaten
- ½ teaspoon salt
- 1 teaspoon granulated sugar
- 1 teaspoon baking soda
- 2 teaspoons melted butter
- Lard or butter for greasing the griddle

Make the starter: Put the flour and yeast in a medium-sized mixing bowl. Slowly stir in the lukewarm water, mixing until well blended. Cover lightly, and leave out in the kitchen overnight—8–10 hours.

Mix the milk, beaten egg, salt, sugar, baking soda, and melted butter together thoroughly, then stir into the starter just until well blended. Heat the griddle or frying pan, and brush lightly with grease. Spoon the batter by ¼ cups onto the hot surface, and cook until the pancakes are dotted over with little bubbles, about 1–2 minutes. Carefully flip the pancakes over and cook 1 minute longer. Transfer to a heated platter, and keep warm while you cook the rest of the pancakes.

Serve hot with fresh butter and preserves or syrups of your choice.

Buttermilk Pancakes

MAKES ABOUT 14 PANCAKES, ENOUGH TO SERVE 3 OR 4

Effortless to make, these are the best buttermilk pancakes we have ever eaten.

- ¾ cup unbleached all-purpose flour
- ½ teaspoon salt
- 1 teaspoon baking soda
- 1 cup buttermilk
- 1 egg
- 3 tablespoons unsalted butter, melted
- Unsalted butter for greasing the skillet

Put the flour, salt, and baking soda in a mixing bowl, and whisk briefly to blend. In a separate mixing bowl, whisk the buttermilk into the egg and add the melted butter. Dump the dry ingredients into the wet and whisk briefly, until the batter is well blended and there are no large lumps.

Heat a skillet or griddle over medium heat, and grease very lightly with a little butter. Spoon out about 2 tablespoons of batter for each pancake, and cook until bubbles appear on top. Flip the pancakes, and cook 30 seconds longer.

Serve hot with lots of butter and heated syrup.

ABOUT BENI SEEDS

Beni seeds were brought to the New World from Africa with the slave trade (*beni* is the Nigerian word for "sesame seed"). Jefferson grew beni seeds at Monticello, primarily for its oil, which he thought could free America from its dependence on imported European olive oil. The term "beni seeds" is still common in the Low Country, and it is a commonly used ingredient in both sweet and savory preparations.

Beni Wafers

MAKES ABOUT 50 WAFERS

- 1 cup beni seeds (sesame seeds)
- 3 cups unbleached all-purpose flour
- 1½ teaspoons single-acting Homemade Baking Powder (page 230)
- 1 teaspoon salt
- ⅔ cup lard, chilled
- ⅔ cup milk, chilled
- Additional salt for sprinkling

Toasted beni (or sesame) seeds make these rich wafers delicious, hot from the oven or anytime after. They keep well and are convenient to have on hand to serve with cocktails, soups, or stews. We like to use them for canapés, spread with Shrimp Paste (page 4), or as sandwiches enclosing thin slices of country ham or spring-Vidalia onions.

Preheat the oven to 425°F.

Put the beni seeds in a large, shallow baking dish, and toast them in the preheated oven. After 5 minutes, check them and stir well to ensure even browning. The beni seeds have a tendency to brown faster around the edges of the baking dish, so it is important to check and shake or stir them often. Continue toasting until they are the color of butterscotch—about 10–15 minutes. Remove them from the oven and allow to cool completely.

Meanwhile, sift the flour, baking powder, and salt into a large bowl. Add the chilled lard, and work it into the flour with your fingertips until it is the texture of coarse meal. Stir in the cooled beni seeds and the milk, and mix just until blended. Turn the dough onto a lightly floured surface, and knead quickly eight to ten times, until the dough forms a cohesive ball. Flatten the dough into a disk, and roll it out as thinly as possible or until it is the thickness of a dime. Prick the rolled dough all over with the tines of a dinner fork, and, using a 2-inch biscuit cutter, stamp out rounds as close together as possible, and transfer them to an ungreased baking sheet.

Bake in the preheated oven for 12–15 minutes, until the wafers are a deep golden brown. Remove from the oven, sprinkle with salt, and serve hot. Cooled biscuits may be stored in an airtight container for a week or longer, then reheated before serving or served at room temperature.

NOTE You can freeze the uncooked wafers wrapped tightly and bake frozen.

Crispy Thin Biscuits

MAKES ABOUT 1½ DOZEN THIN BISCUITS

1½ cups unbleached all-purpose flour
½ teaspoon salt
2 tablespoons unsalted butter, chilled
½ cup cold water

Thin, crisp, and rich-tasting—more like wafers than biscuits, really—these golden rounds are good by themselves or with cheese, pâté, or warm baked Spicy Eggplant Relish (page 6). You can make them large or small, puffy or flat. We like them puffy, but if you object, pierce the dough with a fork before baking. They keep well if stored in a tightly covered container.

Preheat the oven to 375°F.

Put the flour and salt in a bowl, and stir well to blend. Work the butter thoroughly into the flour, then stir in the cold water. Mix until the dough is well blended and forms a cohesive mass. Turn out onto a lightly floured surface, and knead two or three times, then roll out as thinly as you can, at least as thin as a dime. Stamp out rounds with a 3-inch cutter, and bake on ungreased baking sheets in the preheated oven for 12–15 minutes, until crisp and lightly golden brown. Serve hot or at room temperature.

Cheese Straws

MAKES ABOUT 4 DOZEN PIECES

- 1⅔ cups unbleached all-purpose flour
- 1 teaspoon salt
- 1 teaspoon dry mustard
- ¼ teaspoon cayenne pepper, or more to taste
- ½ cup (1 stick) unsalted butter, cut into pieces
- 8 ounces extra-sharp cheddar cheese, grated
- 2 tablespoons water

Everyone in the South seems to love cheese straws—the thin, crisp pastry sticks with the tang of cayenne and sharp cheddar—and they are always served at cocktail parties and church socials alike. They are almost mandatory at weddings: I remember receptions where the only fare was a silver compote of cheese straws, another of mints, and the wedding cake.

Usually cheese-straw dough is piped from a cookie press and snipped into short lengths. Miss Lewis uses the simple technique of rolling out the dough and slicing off the "straws." Cheese straws improve as the flavors mellow, so make them a day before serving, if possible. A tin of cheese straws makes an excellent hostess gift.

Preheat the oven to 425°F.

Sift together the flour, salt, dry mustard, and cayenne pepper. Put the butter and grated cheese in a mixing bowl, and mix for several minutes, until thoroughly blended. Gradually add the dry ingredients to the butter and cheese, and mix until completely incorporated. Add the water, and mix for 1 minute longer.

Turn the dough onto a lightly floured surface, and knead five or six times. Roll the dough out ¼ inch thick, and cut into strips ¼ inch wide and 4–6 inches in length. Place the strips on ungreased cookie sheets ½ inch apart, and bake in the preheated oven for 12–16 minutes, until golden brown and crisp. Cool completely, and store in airtight containers.

Homemade Baking Powder

MAKES ABOUT ½ CUP

¼ cup cream of tartar
2 tablespoons baking soda

Distressed by the chemical additives and aftertaste of commercial "double-acting" powders, Miss Lewis years ago started making her own baking powder—a traditional mixture of cream of tartar and baking soda. When I first used her formula (from her books, before we met), I couldn't really taste any difference. Soon, though, I realized that muffins and quick breads made with aluminum-sulfate–based powders left a metallic "tingle" on my tongue. Today, I make up a batch of this powder every week for use at the restaurant and bring a jar home for Miss Lewis. We recommend it for all the recipes here. If necessary, you can substitute commercial baking powder in equal amounts.

Sift all of the ingredients together 3 times, and transfer to a clean, tight-sealing jar. Store at room temperature, away from sunlight, for up to 6 weeks.

GOOD LARD

I grew up in peanut-oil country, where we didn't use lard. But I quickly learned how important lard was to Miss Lewis, and to fine Southern cooking, about a year into our friendship, when we started exchanging gifts of food. She would give me things I'd never tried: frozen gooseberries, damson plums, and sugared raspberries from Freetown—and half-gallon Mason jars of lard, rendered by her sister Jenny. As I baked and cooked with this pure, white fat, I soon started making my own. And I became almost fanatical, developing a rendering process that took 3 days to remove every impurity. When Jenny told me that my lard was the finest she'd ever used, I was thrilled (but I realize not everyone is going to indulge in this laborious process).

Rendered from the white leaf or kidney fat of the pig, lard is a very dense fat with a high smoking point. This makes it excellent for frying (see Southern Pan-Fried Chicken, page 104), and in baked goods like biscuits and pastry, where flakiness is prized.

Only buy lard that is fresh and well stored. It should be refrigerated and purchased at a store where there's a steady turnover of it: don't buy packages that are dusty or old! If you have any doubt about the freshness of lard, open the package and sniff. There should be only a faint smell of pork and not a hint of rancidity.

Hot Crusty Buttermilk Biscuits

MAKES ABOUT FIFTEEN 2½-INCH BISCUITS

- 5 cups sifted White Lily flour (measured after sifting)
- 1 tablespoon plus ½ teaspoon Homemade Baking Powder (preceding recipe)
- 1 tablespoon kosher salt
- ½ cup (¼ pound) packed lard, chilled
- 1¼ cups buttermilk
- 3 tablespoons unsalted butter, melted

Here are the secrets to a great biscuit: soft Southern flour such as White Lily (page 201); Homemade Baking Powder (preceding recipe); good, fresh, very cold lard; good, fresh, very cold buttermilk—and a very hot oven. Work the fat into the flour with your fingers; stir together and knead the dough as little as possible; don't twist the biscuit cutter when stamping out biscuits; and, finally, place them on the baking sheet as close together as you can without touching.

Preheat oven to 500°F.

Put the flour, homemade baking powder, and salt in a mixing bowl, and whisk well to blend thoroughly. Add the lard, and, working quickly, coat it in flour and rub between your fingertips until approximately half the lard is finely blended and the other half remains in large pieces, about ½ inch in size. Pour in the buttermilk, and stir quickly just until the dough is blended and begins to mass.

Turn the dough immediately out onto a floured surface, and with floured hands knead briskly eight to ten times, until it becomes cohesive.

Gently flatten the dough with your hands into a disk of even thinness; then, using a floured rolling pin, roll it out to a uniform thickness of ½ inch. With a dinner fork dipped in flour, pierce the dough completely through at ½-inch intervals. Lightly flour a 2½- or 3-inch biscuit cutter and stamp out rounds, *without twisting* the cutter in the dough. Cut the biscuits from the dough as close together as you can, for maximum yield. Transfer them to a parchment-lined baking sheet, placing them so that they just barely kiss. Don't reroll the scraps. Just arrange them around the edge of the sheet, and bake them—cook's treat.

Put the baking sheet immediately on the center rack of the preheated oven. Bake 10–12 minutes, checking after 6 minutes or so, and turning the pan if needed for even baking. When the biscuits are golden brown, remove from the oven and brush the tops with the melted butter.

VIII IT DOESN'T HAVE TO BE FANCY

Pies, Custards, Cobblers, and Puddings

On a June morning in 1990, I went to the train station on Peachtree Street in Atlanta to pick up Miss Lewis, who was arriving from New York to prepare desserts for a gala dinner celebrating Southern chefs—herself among them. It was only our second encounter, and, nervously pacing the platform, I finally spied her at the far end. She was nearly seventy-five at the time, tall and regal—and dragging behind her a huge cardboard box with a rope. She explained that there would be no time to make pastry for her desserts in Atlanta, nor was it a task she could entrust to a stranger. So she had brought what she needed in the box: 100 pounds of pie dough, packed in ice.

Most of the next day, I helped roll out the dough for the pies and big cobblers she planned to bake. Miss Lewis was eager to get wild blackberries, but the farmers' market had only cultivated ones, so, early the following morning, I went into the woods near my home and picked all the wild blackberries I could find. There were only a handful, but she was happy to have them. In the end, we worked together to bake a dozen peach-and-rhubarb cobblers, thirty pecan-and-damson-plum pies—and one blackberry pie.

Coming from a family where cakes were the specialty (and pies were not), I learned a lot from that visit about good Southern pastry. I noticed that Miss Lewis didn't make her pies too sweet, and I appreciated for the first time the special quality that lard lent to pastry crusts: a crisp flakiness that shattered beautifully, far better than butter or shortening doughs. But as a young chef, prone to make showy dishes when cooking for public occasions or even just for friends, I learned from Miss Lewis's desserts something more fundamental about cooking: that is, a great dessert—a great dish—doesn't have to be fancy. It can be as simple and homey as blackberry pie, if it is made with integrity and if every part of it, both pastry and filling, is the best of its kind. That's the sort of traditional pies and custards and other desserts you'll find in this chapter.

Virginia-Style Blackberry Cobbler with Nutmeg-Brandy Sauce

MAKES ENOUGH TO SERVE 8

Miss Lewis's fruit cobblers are made in a baking dish lined with a bottom crust of pastry and a top crust—sometimes a woven lattice—from the same dough. After you've trimmed the top and bottom crusts, toss all the little pieces of dough trimmings with the berries. They bake into delicious little bits, much like the dumplings in *my* berry "cobbler," which follows. You can make this kind of cobbler with almost all summer fruits, including rhubarb and peaches.

THE PASTRY

- 3 cups unbleached all-purpose flour
- 1½ teaspoons kosher salt
- 1 teaspoon granulated sugar
- 1 cup (2 sticks) unsalted butter, cut into ½-inch pieces and frozen 10 minutes
- 2 tablespoons lard, cut into ½-inch pieces and frozen 10 minutes
- 8–12 tablespoons ice water

THE FILLING

- 8 cups fresh blackberries
- ¾ cup granulated sugar
- 1 tablespoon all-purpose flour
- ¼ teaspoon salt
- ½ teaspoon freshly grated nutmeg
- 4 tablespoons (½ stick) unsalted butter, thinly sliced
- ½ cup crushed Cardamom-Scented Sugar Cubes (box, page 243)

Using the above proportions, prepare the pastry following the directions on pages 242–243. Divide the dough in half, wrap in wax paper or plastic wrap, and refrigerate for at least 1 hour before rolling out.

Preheat the oven to 425°F.

Roll out half of the dough ⅛ inch thick, and with it line a 2-quart, 2-inch-deep baking dish. Trim the edges as needed, leaving ½ inch of pastry hanging over the rim of the dish. Cut any trimmings of pastry into 1-inch pieces and reserve.

Fill the pastry-lined dish with the blackberries. Mix together the sugar, flour, salt, and nutmeg in a small bowl, and sprinkle over the berries. Tuck any pieces of reserved dough in among the blackberries. Dot 3 tablespoons of the thinly sliced butter over the top. Refrigerate while you roll out the top dough.

Roll out the other half of the dough large enough to cover the top of the cobbler—it should be ⅛ inch thick. Trim the dough as needed, and add the trimmings in small pieces to the berries. Moisten the rim of the dough in the baking dish with a little cold water, and lay the top dough over. Gently press the edges together to seal, then fold the edge over inside the rim of the baking dish. With a sharp knife, cut a few 1-inch slits in the top dough to allow steam to escape. Sprinkle the crushed sugar cubes over the top, and dot with the remaining butter. Bake in the preheated oven for 20 minutes. Reduce heat to 375°F and bake for 30–45 minutes longer, until the crust is a deep golden brown and the filling begins to bubble through the slits. Cool the cobbler on a rack until it is warm, and serve with whipped cream or ice cream.

Variation: Peach Cobbler

Use 8 cups peeled, sliced peaches, firm but ripe, and increase the 1 tablespoon flour to 2 tablespoons.

Nutmeg-Brandy Sauce

MAKES ABOUT 1¼ CUPS

Miss Lewis always serves this unusual sauce with her Peach Cobbler.

- ⅔ cup granulated sugar
- ⅛ teaspoon salt
- 2 teaspoons cornstarch
- ½ teaspoon freshly grated nutmeg
- 1 cup boiling water
- 2-inch piece orange peel, dried or fresh
- 3 tablespoons brandy

Mix the sugar, salt, cornstarch, and nutmeg together in a small saucepan. Pour the boiling water over, and stir to dissolve the sugar and cornstarch. Add the orange peel, and simmer gently for 10 minutes. Add the brandy, and simmer for 2 minutes longer. Remove from the heat, and keep covered and warm until ready to use. Remove the orange peel before serving.

Peacock Family Alabama-Style Blackberry Cobbler

MAKES ENOUGH TO SERVE 8

This is what we called "blackberry cobbler" in Alabama—rounds of biscuit dough covered with the cooked juice of the berries, baked together in the oven. Buried in the fruit juices, the biscuits cook up like dumplings. When I was a child, my mother would use canned biscuits, but now I make these delicious cream biscuits from scratch. Sprinkling the biscuits with crushed sugar cubes gives them a nice crunchy top, an idea I borrowed from Miss Lewis. The biscuits or dumplings are served warm, swimming in their sauce, which only gets better as the vanilla ice cream melts and the flavors mingle.

THE BLACKBERRY SAUCE

6 cups fresh blackberries
2½ cups water
½ teaspoon salt
¾–1 cup granulated sugar

THE DUMPLINGS

2 cups all-purpose flour
2 teaspoons Homemade Baking Powder (page 230)
2 tablespoons granulated sugar
½ teaspoon salt
4 tablespoons unsalted butter, chilled
¾ cup half-and-half

2 tablespoons unsalted butter, cut into small pieces
6 tablespoons crushed sugar cubes
Vanilla Sugar for garnish

To make the sauce: Put the blackberries and water into a nonreactive saucepan. Crush the berries gently with the back of a wooden spoon, and bring to a low simmer. Cook, partially covered, for 25 minutes, stirring occasionally. Strain the berries through a fine-meshed sieve, pressing gently on the solids until all of the juice is extracted. Discard the solids, and add the salt to the juice along with ¾ cup of the sugar. Taste for sweetness—the juice should be rather sweet, so add more sugar if needed. Reserve the sweetened juice and allow it to cool. (You can do this step 1 or more days ahead.)

Preheat the oven to 425°F.

Make the dumplings: Sift together the flour, baking powder, sugar, and salt into a mixing bowl. Using your fingers or two dinner forks, quickly work the chilled butter into the flour mixture until it is the texture of oatmeal. Pour the half-and-half over, and stir just until the dough comes together. Turn it onto a lightly floured surface, and knead briefly, six to eight turns, with floured hands.

Pat or roll the dough into a disk ½ inch thick. With a biscuit or cookie cutter, stamp out eight rounds 2½–3 inches in diameter.

Arrange the cut dumplings in a buttered 2-quart baking dish, and pour the cooled blackberry sauce over them. (The juice should cover the dumplings, but do not be concerned if the dumplings float.) Bake in the preheated oven for 20 minutes. Remove the baking dish from the oven, and carefully baste the dumplings, then dot the tops with the small pieces of butter and sprinkle the crushed sugar cubes over. Return to the oven, and continue baking for an additional 10–15 minutes, until the dumplings are golden brown.

Serve the dumplings warm with some of the blackberry sauce spooned over and a large scoop of homemade Vanilla Ice Cream (page 292).

WHAT'S A COBBLER?

In the South, the term "cobbler" is applied to a host of baked fruit desserts. To Miss Lewis, "cobbler" meant a kind of deep-dish pie with fruit baked between a bottom and top layer of pastry, as in her Virginia-Style Blackberry Cobbler. To other Southern bakers, a cobbler might only have a top pastry crust. In Alabama, we called anything a cobbler that had fruit covered by a baked topping. My mother made a biscuit dough that cooked like dumplings in the bubbling fruit and formed a topping, as in the recipe for Peacock Family Blackberry Cobbler that follows Miss Lewis's.

One of the more distinctive cobblers of my childhood in Hartford came from Doc's, a modest barbecue stand where we often got takeout Sunday dinners of barbecue or fried chicken. We'd phone in our order in the morning, before church, and pick up our dinner after services. Dessert was always "peach cobbler": canned peaches covered with a box of Duncan Hines Yellow Cake mix—dry—with melted butter poured on top of that, then put in the oven; the cake topping formed while the dish was baking. It was a bit overly sweet, but we always thought it a treat.

Basic Pie Dough

MAKES ENOUGH PASTRY FOR ONE 9-INCH PIE

- 1½ cups unbleached all-purpose flour
- 1 teaspoon kosher salt
- ½ teaspoon granulated sugar
- 8 tablespoons (1 stick) unsalted butter, cut into 8 pieces and frozen for 10 minutes
- 2 tablespoons lard, cut into 2 pieces and frozen for 10 minutes
- 4–6 tablespoons ice water

Here's the pastry dough we use as a crust for our favorite pies, including the Lemon Chess, Bourbon-Pecan, and Egg Custard Pie in this chapter. For the best texture, it's important to make this dough by hand, following the instructions for blending the fats and water with the flour. There are several steps, but each one is, in fact, quite simple. Note that the recipe calls for *unbleached* all-purpose flour, not the bleached all-purpose that we use in our bread recipes. The higher protein content of unbleached flour provides more gluten structure to incorporate the butter and lard into the dough.

Put the flour, salt, and sugar on a large cutting board, and mix them with your fingers to blend. Put the frozen butter and lard on top of the flour mixture, and use a large kitchen knife or pastry cutter to cut the fats quickly into the flour until the mixture resembles coarse meal with some butter and lard pieces still as large as ½ inch in diameter. Ideally, half of the fat should be cut finely into the flour and the other half left in larger chunks.

Working quickly, gather the flour-fat mixture into a mound and, using your fingers, draw a trench lengthwise through the center. Sprinkle 1 tablespoon of the ice water down the length of the trench, and with your spread, upturned fingers fluff the flour so that it absorbs the water. Redraw the trench and continue incorporating the ice water by tablespoons in the same manner. After you have incorporated 4 tablespoons of the water, the dough should begin to clump together into large pieces. If there are any unmassed areas, sprinkle them lightly with droplets of water, and mix as before.

Gather the dough into a mass with a pastry scraper, and, again working quickly, with the heel of your hand smear a hunk of dough roughly the size of an egg by pushing it away

An old lard strainer

from you. Continue with pieces of dough until the entire mass has been processed this way (you'll do about six smears in all). When finished, gather all the dough together with a pastry scraper and repeat the process. Regather the dough, quickly shape it into a flat disk, and wrap it in a double thickness of plastic wrap, pressing firmly with the palm of your hand to flatten the wrapped dough further and bind it. Refrigerate for at least 2 hours or overnight before rolling and using.

Roll out the chilled dough into a circle 1½ inches larger than your pie pan. Line the pan with the dough, and trim it to leave a ½-inch overhang of pastry around the pan. Fold this under, forming a thick edge on the rim of the pan.

CARDAMOM-SCENTED SUGAR CUBES

MAKES 12 OUNCES OF CARDAMOM-SCENTED SUGAR CUBES

I got the idea for these scented cubes when, without realizing it, I spilled some cardamom pods into a container of pistachio nuts and a few weeks later discovered that the nuts were permeated with the cardamom flavor. I like to crush these sugar cubes and sprinkle them over the pastry of rhubarb pies and cobblers or over sugar cookies before baking. Because sugar cubes have a lower moisture content than granulated sugar does, they will not dissolve when sprinkled over baked goods before going in the oven, and result in a crunchy texture that is delightful. Cardamom-scented sugar cubes are also good to serve with tea, because they impart a delicate flavor.

30 whole green cardamom pods
12 ounces sugar cubes

Use a rolling pin to crush the cardamom pods in their husks. Layer the crushed cardamom pods and sugar cubes in a 1-quart glass jar. Seal the jar tightly, and store in a cool, dark place for 2 weeks before using.

To use the sugar cubes, remove as many cubes as needed from the jar and brush off any bits of cardamom pod.

Bourbon-Pecan Pie

MAKES ONE 9-INCH PIE, ENOUGH TO SERVE 8

- 3 eggs, lightly beaten
- 1 cup granulated sugar
- ½ cup light corn syrup
- ½ cup dark corn syrup
- ⅓ cup unsalted butter, melted
- 2 tablespoons bourbon
- 1 teaspoon vanilla extract
- ¼ teaspoon salt
- 1 unbaked 9-inch pastry pie shell (preceding recipe)
- 1¼ cups coarsely chopped pecans

Pecans—a type of hickory nut—grew wild in Louisiana and other parts of the South and, once cultivated, became a prized crop across the region. Today, pecan pie is as identified with the South as fried chicken. Our version is a little less sweet than most, and the bourbon adds a subtle depth of flavor. This is as delicious as a dessert can be, especially (in my opinion) served warm with a scoop of vanilla ice cream.

Preheat the oven to 375°F.

Mix together the eggs, sugar, corn syrups, butter, bourbon, vanilla, and salt until well blended.

Using a fork, prick the sides and bottom of the pie shell at ½-inch intervals. Spread the pecans on the bottom of the pastry, and pour the egg-syrup mixture over them. Bake in the preheated oven for 30–40 minutes, until just set but still slightly loose in the center. The pie will finish setting as it cools.

Remove from the oven, and cool on a cooling rack before serving.

Egg Custard Pie

MAKES ONE 9-INCH PIE, ENOUGH TO SERVE 8

- 3 eggs
- ¼ cup granulated sugar
- ¼ teaspoon salt
- 2¼ cups milk
- 1 teaspoon vanilla extract
- ⅛ teaspoon freshly grated nutmeg
- 1 unbaked 9-inch pie crust (pages 242–243)

An almost forgotten Southern classic, this pie used to appear regularly on the Sunday dinner table, sometimes baked in custard cups, as in the recipe on page 255. It can be gilded with whipped cream, but traditionally it is served chilled and unadorned.

Preheat the oven to 450°F.

Beat the eggs lightly in a mixing bowl. Whisk in the sugar and salt just until blended, followed by the milk, vanilla, and grated nutmeg; don't overmix.

Pour the filling through a fine strainer directly into the unbaked pie crust, and bake in the preheated oven for 10 minutes. Reduce the temperature to 350°F, and continue baking for 25–30 minutes, until the filling appears set around the edges but slightly loose in the very center. Remove immediately to a rack, and cool completely before serving. Once cooled, the pie should be refrigerated if not served right away.

Lemon Chess Pie

MAKES ONE 9-INCH PIE, ENOUGH TO SERVE 8

- 4 eggs, at room temperature
- 1½ cups granulated sugar
- 1 tablespoon white cornmeal
- 1 tablespoon unbleached all-purpose flour
- ½ teaspoon salt
- ⅓ cup (5 tablespoons) unsalted butter, melted and cooled to room temperature
- ½ cup buttermilk, at room temperature
- ⅓ cup freshly squeezed lemon juice, at room temperature
- 1 tablespoon finely grated lemon zest
- 1 teaspoon vanilla extract
- 1 unbaked 9-inch pie crust (pages 242–243)
- Whipped cream

Chess pie is a very old Southern pie, made from the basic ingredients any farm cook would have on hand—eggs, sugar, butter, cream, a bit of flour or cornmeal for thickening. Versions abound today: some are flavored with chocolate, others use brown sugar. Ours has the tang of lemon and buttermilk; serve it with slightly sweetened whipped cream.

Preheat the oven to 350°F.

Put the eggs in a large mixing bowl, and whisk briefly to blend. One at a time, whisk in the following, blending until each ingredient has been incorporated before proceeding to the next: the sugar, cornmeal, flour, salt, melted butter, buttermilk, lemon juice, lemon zest, and vanilla.

Pour the filling into the unbaked pie crust, and bake in the middle of the preheated oven for 30–40 minutes, until the pie is golden brown on top and almost set. The center of the pie should remain slightly loose; it will set as it cools. Remove to a cooling rack, and cool completely before serving.

Serve at room temperature with lightly sweetened whipped cream.

NOTE It is important that all ingredients for the pie be at room temperature. Otherwise blending may be difficult, and any cold ingredients, especially buttermilk or lemon juice, will cause the butter to resolidify and separate from the mixture.

Country-Style Rhubarb Tart with Rich Custard Sauce

MAKES ENOUGH TO SERVE 8

- 1 recipe Basic Pie Dough (pages 242–243)
- 6 cups rhubarb sliced on the bias 1/2 inch thick
- 1/3–2/3 cup granulated sugar
- 2 tablespoons all-purpose flour
- 1/2 teaspoon kosher salt
- 1/2 teaspoon freshly grated nutmeg
- 3 tablespoons unsalted butter, cut into small pieces and chilled
- 1/2 cup crushed plain or Cardamom-Scented Sugar Cubes (box, page 243)

For Miss Lewis, rhubarb was a welcome herald of spring in Virginia, where it was called "pie plant" because that's what rhubarb was used for, primarily. But rhubarb, which needs a cold winter to grow, was unknown in Alabama—I knew of it only from the TV show *The Waltons.* The first time I actually tasted rhubarb was many years later, on a trip with Miss Lewis to northern California. Lindsey Shere, the original pastry chef at Chez Panisse, prepared for us a rustic tart like this one.

The free-form European-style tart—so popular these days—has a parallel in American baking. One of the many kinds of Southern cobblers is made in much the same way, from a single large sheet of rolled-out pastry. I think of it as cobbler-in-a-hurry: the sheet is draped into a deep dish and filled with fruit, and then the wide flaps of pastry are just folded on top, leaving most of the center open. Our tart is flatter, with proportionately less fruit than a cobbler.

Preheat the oven to 425°F.

On a lightly floured surface, roll the pastry out into a piece roughly 14 by 16 inches. Fold the rolled pastry in half, and use a clean, dry pastry brush to brush off any flour from the bottom. Fold in half again so that the pastry is folded into quarters, and brush the remaining two sides to remove all excess flour. Transfer and unfold the pastry onto a baking sheet lined with either parchment paper or a Silpat (box, page 251), and put into the refrigerator or freezer to chill while you ready the other ingredients for assembly. (Pastry for the tart can be rolled out the day before and stored, carefully wrapped, in either the refrigerator or freezer.)

Taste the sliced rhubarb for tartness, and judge how much sugar you will need to sweeten to your liking. (We love the sharp flavor of good rhubarb and lean in the direction of less sugar, but tastes, like rhubarb, can vary widely, and how much sugar to add is a personal choice. Just be sure to remember that there will be crushed sugar cubes on the pastry, which will contribute intense sweetness, and remember to consider the added sweetness of any accompaniment—such as ice cream, Rich Custard Sauce, or sweetened whipped cream.)

Put the sugar, flour, kosher salt, and freshly grated nutmeg into a small mixing bowl, and stir well to blend. Sprinkle a third of the sugar mixture over the rolled-out pastry, starting in the center and extending out to within 2 inches of the edge. Arrange half of the rhubarb over the sugar, then sprinkle half of the remaining sugar over the rhubarb. Layer with the remaining rhubarb, and finish by sprinkling the rest of the sugar mixture over the top. Scatter 2 tablespoons of the butter pieces over the rhubarb, and gently fold the edges of the pastry up over the filling. Place the remaining bits of butter on the pastry, followed by the crushed sugar cubes.

Bake in the middle of the preheated oven for 10 minutes, or until the pastry just begins to brown. Turn the oven down to 375°F and bake for 25–30 minutes longer, until the filling in the tart bubbles in the center. Remove from the oven, and allow to cool for 5 minutes. After the tart has cooled briefly, slide the tart and the Silpat or parchment off the baking sheet onto a cooling rack. Use a long, flat spatula to separate the tart gently from the Silpat or parchment, and carefully, slightly elevating the cooling rack at one end, slip the Silpat or parchment out from under the tart.

Serve warm or at room temperature with ice cream or Rich Custard Sauce (recipe follows) spooned over.

Rich Custard Sauce

MAKES ABOUT 2½ CUPS

- 1 cup milk
- 1 vanilla bean, twisted to bruise and release the essence, but not split
- 4 egg yolks
- ¼ cup plus 2 tablespoons granulated sugar
- 1 cup heavy cream
- 2 teaspoons vanilla extract
- ¼ teaspoon salt

Heat the milk and vanilla bean in a medium-sized nonreactive saucepan to just below the boiling point. Remove from the heat, and allow to sit, covered, for 10 minutes to allow the vanilla bean to infuse the milk.

While the milk is steeping, whisk together the egg yolks and sugar. Remove the vanilla bean, and slowly whisk the hot milk into the sugar-and-egg-yolk mixture. Transfer back to the saucepan, and return the pan to the stove. Cook over medium heat, stirring constantly, until the custard coats the back of a spoon. At no time should the custard reach a simmer or boil. Remove from the heat, and stir in the cup of heavy cream. Pour through a fine-mesh strainer, and stir in the vanilla and salt.

Cool and refrigerate.

Banana Pudding

MAKES ENOUGH TO SERVE 8

Not the banana pudding you make from a package or find in a cafeteria, this is a layered dessert of rich custard, angel-food cake, and fresh banana slices topped with a dramatic meringue. Long a popular dessert in the South, it is clearly in the English trifle tradition. My Grandmaw Peacock would make it, my father tells me, with whatever she had on hand—leftover cake, toasted white bread, or even stale biscuits. Today it is most commonly made with store-bought vanilla wafers. But I love it made with toasted cubes of homemade Angel Food Cake (page 269), so it's worth the extra effort (and angel-food cake is good with so many things). The addition of cream after the custard's been cooked and strained gives the pudding a glossy, silky texture and the delicious taste of fresh cream.

THE CUSTARD

2 cups whole milk
2 cups heavy cream
1 vanilla bean
12 egg yolks
¾ cup granulated sugar
⅓ cup all-purpose flour
¼ teaspoon salt
3 teaspoons vanilla extract

4 cups Angel Food Cake (page 269) cut into 1-inch cubes and lightly toasted, or vanilla wafers
4 large ripe bananas, peeled and sliced ½ inch thick (about 5 cups)

THE MERINGUE

8 egg whites, at room temperature
½ teaspoon vanilla extract
¾ cup plus 2 tablespoons granulated sugar

Put the milk, 1 cup of the heavy cream, and the vanilla bean into a nonreactive saucepan. (Do not split the vanilla bean, just twist and bend it a bit to bruise and release its oils.) Heat slowly until the milk and cream are just below a simmer, then cover and remove from the heat and allow to steep 20 minutes.

Meanwhile, put the egg yolks in a bowl and whisk in the sugar, followed by the flour and the salt, mixing until there are no lumps and everything is completely smooth. Remove the vanilla bean from the steeped milk and cream, and slowly whisk into the egg yolks. Return the mixture to the saucepan, and cook, whisking constantly, over moderately high heat until the custard thickens and begins to bubble. Be sure to whisk all over the bottom of the pan as well as along the bottom edges. Cook for 1 minute after the custard begins to boil, then remove from the heat. At this point, it should be very thick. Strain through a fine-meshed sieve into a mixing bowl, and immediately whisk in the remaining 1 cup of heavy cream and the vanilla extract.

Preheat the oven to 400°F.

To assemble: Spoon a thin layer of the custard onto the bottom of an 8-cup ovenproof baking dish. Top with a layer of cubed angel-food cake and sliced banana. Spoon more custard over and continue layering, ending with custard spooned over the top.

Make the meringue: Put the egg whites into a spotlessly clean bowl (see whipping egg whites, page 181). Beat the whites slowly until they become frothy. Add the vanilla, and continue beating until the egg whites just begin to form soft mounds. While still beating, begin sprinkling in the sugar ¼ cup at a time, beating only until each addition is incorporated before proceeding to the next. When all of the sugar is incorporated, beat the egg whites until they are moist and very glossy and hold peaks that are firm but still bend when lifted on the end of a whisk.

Immediately spoon the beaten egg whites over the surface of the assembled custard and, using a spoon or spatula, spread the whites to the edge to make sure you get a good seal between the meringue and the sides of the baking dish. Work quickly to make decorative swirls and patterns in the meringue, and put the dish immediately into the preheated oven to bake for about 5 minutes, until golden brown. (Be sure to check after 2 minutes to see how the meringue is browning, and turn the dish from time to time, if needed, to ensure even browning.) Serve the banana pudding warm or at room temperature.

A NOTE ABOUT SILPATS

Neither Miss Lewis nor I am very big on kitchen gadgets. Too often they are just gimmicks that perform poorly, serve a limited function, and take up precious room in the kitchen. One very notable exception, however, is an increasingly popular baking tool called a Silpat.

Silpats are baking-pan–sized liners made of silicon that are absolutely nonstick and able to withstand temperatures of over 1,000°F. They are excellent used for the baking of cookies, cheese straws, biscuits, country-style tarts, etc. But they are also wonderful when used for roasting vegetables or whole fish.

They are reusable (just rinse them off) and make cleanup much easier. They also greatly reduce the need for parchment or wax paper. We keep two sets on hand: one for baking, and one for roasting. You'll find they are now widely available at kitchen shops.

Warm Tender Cakes with Guava Syrup and Cream

MAKES EIGHT 3-INCH CAKES, ENOUGH TO SERVE 8

- 2 cups sifted all-purpose flour
- 1 tablespoon Homemade Baking Powder (page 230)
- 1 teaspoon salt
- 1/4 cup granulated sugar
- 1/4 cup (1/2 stick) cold, unsalted butter, cut in 1/2-inch pieces
- 1/2–3/4 cup heavy cream
- 1/2 cup crushed Cardamom-Scented Sugar Cubes (box, page 243)
- 1 cup Guava Syrup (recipe follows)
- Additional heavy cream for serving with the cakes

This lovely dessert is the happy result of a kitchen mistake. Early in our friendship, Miss Lewis and I spent a week cooking together in Atlanta, culminating in a tasting party for friends. She'd spied guavas in the market and cooked them into a favorite fragrant "jelly"—more of a syrup, because the fruit lacks pectin. I made rich cream biscuits, intending to use them as dessert shortcakes, and piled them in a basket.

As dessert time neared, I looked for the basket of biscuits, only to find it had been passed around during dinner. So I whipped up another batch and, without letting them cool, served the split biscuits with unwhipped, unsweetened cream and Miss Lewis's guava syrup. The combination was scrumptious, and no one knew of our moments of consternation. Moreover, I discovered that when the biscuits are eaten warm they are remarkably different from when they are cool—distinct enough to merit the name "warm tender cakes."

Enjoy these biscuits all ways—as shortcakes filled with fresh berries and cream (page 304), or just served plain with tea. They're extremely convenient to prepare, because you can mix the dough, roll and cut the cakes, and refrigerate them right on the baking sheet for up to 3 hours before you bake them.

The guava syrup, with its delicate floral-honey scent, is also quite versatile—wonderful spooned on toast; or drizzled over ice cream or a bowl of fresh strawberries.

Preheat the oven to 450°F.

Put the flour, baking powder, salt, and sugar in a mixing bowl, and stir well with a wire whisk to mix. Using your fingers or two forks, quickly work the butter into the flour until it is roughly the texture of oatmeal with some larger lumps remaining. Make a well in the center of the flour mixture, and pour in 1/2 cup of the heavy cream. Stir just until blended, adding a little more cream if the dough is too crumbly and dry.

Turn the dough out onto a lightly floured surface, and knead briefly but assertively, five or six strokes. Roll out the dough to a thickness of ½ inch. With a floured dinner fork, prick the surface of the dough all over at roughly 1-inch intervals, taking care that the fork goes all the way through the dough. Stamp out rounds of the dough using a 3-inch biscuit cutter, plunging it straight down through the dough, not twisting the cutter. Place the cakes close together on a parchment- or Silpat-lined baking sheet, and sprinkle the crushed sugar cubes over the top. Bake in the middle of the preheated oven for 8–12 minutes, until the cakes are a light golden brown. (Because ovens so often bake unevenly, you may need to rotate the baking sheet halfway through baking to ensure evenly browned and baked cakes.) Remove from the oven, and allow to cool briefly on a wire rack.

To serve, split the warm cakes, and drizzle the guava syrup and a little cream over them. Pass additional syrup and cream to indulge as desired.

Guava Syrup

MAKES ABOUT 2½ CUPS

- 2 fresh guavas
- 3½ cups filtered or bottled water
- 2 cups granulated sugar
- ½ teaspoon kosher salt

Wash the guavas, and cut them in half lengthwise. Slice each half as thin as you can, and put into a nonreactive saucepan. Pour the water over them and bring to a boil, then reduce to a simmer, and cook for 30 minutes. Strain the cooked guavas, pressing gently against them to extract as much liquid as you can. Pour the strained liquid back into the saucepan, and discard the guava pulp.

Stir the sugar and salt into the guava water and bring to a boil. Cook at a boil, skimming often, until it is slightly thickened and large, dime-sized bubbles appear on the surface. Remove from heat and cool. Strain into a clean jar, and store in the refrigerator.

Chocolate Fritters

MAKES ENOUGH TO SERVE 4

- 1¼ cups all-purpose flour, sifted
- ½ teaspoon salt
- 2 teaspoons Homemade Baking Powder (page 230)
- 1 tablespoon granulated sugar
- 1 egg, lightly beaten
- 1 tablespoon unsalted butter, melted
- ⅔ cup milk
- Fresh oil for deep-frying (page 216)
- 4 ounces semisweet chocolate, cut into ½-inch chunks and refrigerated
- Confectioners' sugar for sprinkling
- ¼ teaspoon ground Ceylon cinnamon
- 1 cup sweetened whipped cream

With a crisp exterior and molten chocolate interior, you could serve these morsels as a dramatic ending to an important dinner, or a special treat for breakfast in bed with a steaming hot bowl of coffee. Almost any kind of chocolate will make a good fritter—our preference is for semisweet, but you could use bittersweet or even milk chocolate. The trick is to make sure that the chocolate pieces are completely coated with the fritter batter so no chocolate leaks into the oil. This batter makes a very crisp fritter, and you could dunk and fry pieces of apple, banana, or other fruit instead of (or in addition to!) the chocolate.

Sift the flour, salt, homemade baking powder, and sugar together into a mixing bowl. Add the egg, melted butter, and milk, and mix until smooth.

Slowly heat 3 inches oil to 340°F.

Dip the chocolate into the fritter batter, taking care to coat each piece completely. Fry a few fritters at a time in the hot oil until golden brown all over, about 1 or 2 minutes. Drain each batch well on a draining rack or crumpled paper towels, then transfer to a warm serving platter and sprinkle generously with the confectioners' sugar and cinnamon. Serve immediately with the whipped cream.

Egg Custard Baked in Custard Cups

MAKES 8 CUSTARDS

- 6 eggs
- 3/4 cup granulated sugar
- 1/4 teaspoon salt
- 4 1/2 cups milk
- 1/4 teaspoon freshly grated nutmeg
- 1/2 teaspoon vanilla extract

This classic Southern dessert is rarely made these days, which is unfortunate, because it is a refreshing and simple—almost austere—and delicious dessert. When I was growing up, Gertrude Moore, who cooked for our family, made this egg custard regularly. Its sweet nutmeg flavor is one of the most wonderful and powerful taste memories of my life.

The basic recipe is for custard in cups, which can be served warm, at room temperature, or chilled. Though some people garnish it with whipped cream, I like it best the old-fashioned way, completely unadorned.

Preheat the oven to 350°F.

Put the eggs in a mixing bowl, and stir with a wooden spoon just until mixed. Add the sugar, salt, and milk, and mix until well blended. Strain through a fine-meshed sieve, and stir in the grated nutmeg and vanilla. Divide evenly among eight 6-ounce custard cups. Put the cups in a deep baking pan, and fill the pan halfway up the cups with hot water.

Bake in the preheated oven for 20–30 minutes, just until custards are set. Remove from the hot-water bath and cool. Serve warm, at room temperature, or chilled.

Gooseberries Baked in Custard

SERVES 8

- 1 cup fresh gooseberries, washed and trimmed
- Unsalted butter for greasing the pan
- 4 eggs, separated
- 1 cup granulated sugar
- ½ teaspoon salt
- 2 tablespoons unsalted butter, melted
- 1 tablespoon all-purpose flour
- 1 teaspoon vanilla extract
- 1 cup milk, at room temperature
- Confectioners' sugar for dusting the baked custard
- Soft whipped cream as a garnish (page 257)

Here's a custard dessert that is decidedly different from the more traditional Egg Custard in this chapter. The beaten egg whites give this custard a light, almost fluffy texture. It's richer and sweeter than Egg Custard, making it a perfect complement to the tartness of unsugared gooseberries. The small amount of flour binds the fruit and juice and keeps the finished pudding from separating. Other fresh fruit can be baked in this custard—rhubarb, raspberries, even sliced peaches—for simple fruit desserts all through the summer.

We found this unusual custard recipe in a 1912 Southern cookbook. It was called Jefferson Davis Custard, honoring the Confederate politician. Though he's no hero of ours, the custard is delicious.

Preheat the oven to 350°F.

Spread the gooseberries around the bottom of a buttered 9-inch baking dish or pie plate. Put the egg yolks with the sugar in a mixing bowl, and use a wire whisk to blend them. Add the following, blending each one thoroughly before proceeding to the next: the salt, melted butter, flour, vanilla, and room-temperature milk.

In a separate mixing bowl, whip the egg whites until they form soft mounds. Quickly whisk the egg-yolk–milk mixture into the whipped egg whites. Pour this custard gently over the gooseberries. Bake in the preheated oven for 25–35 minutes, just until the custard is set. Remove from the oven and cool. Just before serving, sprinkle with a light dusting of confectioners' sugar, and serve warm with a dollop of softly whipped cream.

WHIPPED CREAM

Softly whipped cream is an essential element in berry shortcake and many other desserts. In my opinion, whipping by hand—just before serving—is the quickest and best method. Use a good balloon-type whisk, with thin flexible wires, and the whipping is quickly accomplished.

Here's our standard whipped-cream formula: for every cup of heavy cream, add 1 tablespoon sugar and ½ teaspoon vanilla extract. This amount (when whipped) makes enough for four servings of shortcake or six servings of gingerbread, coffee jelly, or anything else you wish to garnish. Multiply the recipe as needed.

Dump all the ingredients into a cold mixing bowl. Whip in a circular motion, using only your wrist; if you use your whole arm, you'll get tired sooner. To get the right whisking action, hold a tea towel or a newspaper against your side with your upper arm—this will force you to move your wrist.

Whip only until the cream thickens to a soft consistency that barely mounds and holds its shape—it should not form peaks. (If you prefer to use an electric mixer, whisk with the machine until the cream just starts to thicken, then finish by hand.)

Serve right away. If you do whip the cream ahead of time, keep it in the refrigerator for no more than a couple of hours. If it has started to weep, or separate, gently fold the liquid (on the bottom) into the thicker cream for a few moments with a spatula, then whisk briefly until smooth. Or, if you've overbeaten the cream and it gets too firm or grainy, pour in a few tablespoons of cream and gently incorporate to bring it back to softness.

Coffee Jelly

SERVES 6

In the Old South (and in England and Europe today), a "jelly" meant a chilled gelatin dessert, not something to spread on toast. But despite its antique name, this unusual and refreshing summer treat was born of my love for very strong iced coffee. Barely jelled, but intensely flavored and slightly sweetened, the dark "jelly" trembles in its glass—or demitasse cup—and melts in the mouth. Soft whipped cream offers the perfect relief to the slightly bitter coffee.

1 envelope (1 tablespoon) unflavored gelatin
¼ cup cold water
¾ cup granulated sugar
⅛ teaspoon salt
4 cups double-strength coffee

FOR THE TOPPING

1 cup heavy whipping cream
½ teaspoon vanilla extract
1 tablespoon granulated sugar
Ground Ceylon cinnamon

Stir the gelatin into the cold water, and let it sit for 5 minutes to soften.

Stir the sugar and salt into the hot coffee until the sugar is completely dissolved. Add the softened gelatin, and mix well until the gelatin is completely dissolved. Divide between six small dessert bowls or coffee cups, cover, and chill for several hours or overnight.

To serve, whip the heavy cream with the vanilla and sugar to soft peaks, and spoon over each jelly. Sprinkle a little ground cinnamon on top, and serve.

Edna Lewis carving her ham, along with other dishes she prepared for a Revival Day Sunday dinner

IX CAKEWALK WINNERS, AS GOOD AS GINNY HAYSTALK'S

Cakes, Cookies, and Confections

A century ago, people all around the country knew about a popular dance called the "cakewalk." An entertainment originated by slaves on Southern plantations, it crossed from black society to white during the 1890s and first decades of the twentieth century, spread by contests, minstrel shows, musical plays, sheet music, advertisements, and early movies. Although I've never seen the dance, films, photos and written accounts depict it as a promenade of elegantly dressed couples, tipping top hats and twirling canes, affecting low bows and high kicks—a stylized parody of the ballroom mannerisms of the slave-owning white aristocracy. From its earliest days, the dance was staged as a competition (often by the white plantation-owners themselves) with a cake awarded to the best dancer—a custom that gave the dance its name and made the phrase "That takes the cake!" a part of the American idiom.

I knew none of this, however, when I was doing another cakewalk—the Hartford, Alabama, version—as a grade-schooler in the early 1970s. (Indeed, I suspect that few in our white community had any inkling of its origins.) To me, it was just a thrilling chance to win one of the best cakes in Hartford, all for myself.

Our cakewalk was the featured attraction of the big autumn fund-raising fairs (for the High School Band Boosters or the JayCees) that were held in the vast National Guard Armory. There might be apple bobbing and bingo, balloon shaving, and dunking machines too, but the cakewalk was the big draw. People would crowd around the prize table, which displayed dozens of gorgeous cakes contributed by the ladies of the town (like my mother). And people would pay to compete—or "walk"—to win each cake as it was announced over the public-address system, something like "Next prize, a beautiful twelve-layer lemon-cheese cake made by Velma Hardy."

Each "walk" was a suspenseful variation of "musical chairs." The line of contestants would strut round a circle of numbered chairs, taking whichever seat was before them when the music stopped. Then a number was drawn from a raffle basket, and the lucky soul in the corresponding chair "took the cake." I remember walking and walking but cannot remember ever winning.

Most of the cakes in this chapter are ones that would have been prizes at the cakewalk, elaborate layered ones like Lane Cake, Orange Marmalade, and Lemon-Cheese Cake, and everyday, homey ones like Pineapple Upside-Down Cake and Pound Cake. In fact, there are few cakes as much loved in the South as a simple pound cake. My mother baked one every week, and in Miss Lewis's home, pound cake was always on hand to offer to a visitor. To this day, the version made by her aunt Ginny Haystalk, the legendary cook of Freetown, is Miss Lewis's benchmark for a baker's accomplishment. When a cake is really good—whether it's mine, hers, or a recipe we've worked on together—she'll say happily, "This tastes like Ginny Haystalk cake."

Edna Lewis with her sister, Virginia Ellis, and her brother, Lue Stanley Ellis, having a Sunday breakfast

Pound Cake with Lemon-Butter Glaze

MAKES 1 CAKE, ENOUGH TO SERVE 10–12

- 1 cup (2 sticks) cold unsalted butter
- 1⅔ cups granulated sugar
- ¼ teaspoon salt
- 5 large eggs, at room temperature
- 2¼ cups sifted cake flour
- 1 tablespoon vanilla extract
- 1 teaspoon freshly squeezed lemon juice

LEMON-BUTTER GLAZE

- ⅓ cup freshly squeezed lemon juice
- ½ cup granulated sugar
- 1 tablespoon unsalted butter
- ⅛ teaspoon salt

Pound cake is one of the oldest and most common cakes found in the South. Many cooks routinely make one a week: it keeps well the full 7 days, and there's always some on hand for an unexpected guest, to pack in a lunchbox, or take to a picnic. One cook we know keeps a brood of chickens to have a constant supply of fresh eggs for her pound cakes.

Though one of the simplest cakes to make, pound cake is also a standard by which many a good cook is measured. Care must be taken to blend thoroughly the sugar, eggs, butter, and flour without overmixing. In our recipe, the cake starts in a cold oven, and the temperature is raised several times during baking. This method heats the cake batter slowly, so a crust doesn't form before it is fully risen. The cake is delicious without the lemon-butter glaze, but I love the pleasantly sharp flavor it adds.

To make the cake: Butter and flour the bottom and sides of a 9-inch tube pan. Put the 1 cup butter into the bowl of an electric mixer and mix on medium-low speed for 5 minutes, until it becomes waxy and shiny. With the mixer running, slowly add the sugar and salt, and continue mixing, scraping down the sides and bottom of the bowl occasionally, until the sugar and butter become light and fluffy, about 5–7 minutes. Add the eggs one at a time and mix well after each addition, making sure that each egg is fully incorporated before adding the next. After you have incorporated the third egg, add 2 tablespoons of the flour, in order to keep the batter from separating. Add the remaining eggs, and then, on low speed, add the remaining sifted flour in four additions, taking care not to overmix. Once the flour has been incorporated, gently blend in the vanilla and lemon juice.

Spoon the batter into the buttered and floured tube pan, and gently drop the pan on the kitchen counter to deflate any large air bubbles. Put the cake into a *cold* oven and turn the temperature to 225°F. Cook for 20 minutes, then increase the temperature to 300°F and bake 20 minutes longer. Finally, increase the temperature to 325°F and continue cooking for 20–30 minutes longer, until a cake tester inserted in the middle of the cake comes out clean. Begin testing after 20 minutes at 325°F.

Remove the cake from the oven, and allow to cool on a cooling rack in the pan for 5 minutes. Run a long spatula or knife around the sides of the cake to loosen it from the pan, and turn the cake out onto the cooling rack. While the cake is cooling, make the glaze.

To make the lemon-butter glaze: Put the lemon juice, sugar, butter, and salt in a small nonreactive saucepan, and simmer over medium heat for 1 minute, stirring until the sugar is dissolved. Remove from the heat, and spoon the warm glaze over the cooled cake.

Stored in an airtight container, pound cake will keep for up to 1 week.

Orange Marmalade Layer Cake

MAKES ONE 9-INCH LAYER CAKE, ENOUGH TO SERVE 10–12

THE ORANGE SYRUP

1 cup freshly squeezed orange juice

¼ cup granulated sugar

THE CAKE

3 cups cake flour

½ teaspoon baking soda

½ teaspoon salt

1 cup (2 sticks) unsalted butter, at room temperature

2 cups granulated sugar

3 large eggs, at room temperature

1 cup buttermilk, at room temperature

1½ teaspoons vanilla extract

1 tablespoon grated orange zest

FOR THE FROSTING

¾ cup sour cream, chilled

¾ cup heavy cream, chilled

3 tablespoons granulated sugar

THE FILLING

1 cup orange marmalade

This lovely cake is moist, sweet, and tangy. Two buttermilk-cake layers are soaked with orange syrup, filled with marmalade, frosted on the sides with whipped sweet and sour cream, and topped with a glistening pool of marmalade. It is best made ahead (even the night before) and refrigerated, so the flavors blend.

Those familiar with writer Jan Karon's very popular Mitford Chronicles may recognize this cake. Several years ago I was commissioned by *Victoria* magazine to create a recipe for Esther's Orange Marmalade Cake, which is written about in several of the Mitford books. Since then it has appeared on a Hallmark card and is the subject of the best-selling book *Esther's Gift.*

Preheat the oven to 325°F.

Before or while baking the cake layers, make the orange syrup: Stir together the orange juice and sugar until the sugar is completely dissolved, and reserve for spooning over the baked layers.

To make the cake: Sift the flour, baking soda, and salt together onto a piece of wax paper. Beat the butter and sugar together until light and fluffy, then mix in the eggs one at a time, incorporating each egg completely before adding the next. Blend in one-third of the flour mixture, then half of the buttermilk; repeat, ending with the remaining third of flour. Make sure that each addition is fully blended before proceeding to the next. Stir in the vanilla and orange zest, and divide the batter between two round 9-by-2-inch cake pans that have been buttered and floured and lined with wax paper or parchment. Spread the batter evenly in the pans, and drop each pan sharply on the kitchen counter to remove any large air pockets from the cake batter. Bake in the preheated oven for approximately 45 minutes, until a cake tester inserted in the center of the layers comes out clean.

Remove the pans from the oven, and cool on a rack in their pans for 20 minutes. Pierce the layers all over about 1 inch apart with a toothpick or wooden skewer. Spoon over the reserved orange syrup, dividing evenly between the layers and allowing each addition to be absorbed before adding more. Allow the layers to cool *completely* in the pans.

To fill and frost the cake: While the layers are cooling, whisk together the sour cream, heavy cream, and sugar in a chilled mixing bowl. Whip until thick enough to spread, and refrigerate until needed. Once the layers are completely cooled, turn one of them out onto a cake plate, and carefully peel off the wax paper or parchment from the bottom. Heat the marmalade gently until it begins to liquefy. Spread two-thirds of the marmalade over the cake layer, spreading it all the way to the edges. Turn the remaining layer out directly on top of the first. Again remove the wax paper or parchment from the bottom, and spoon the remaining marmalade onto the center of the cake layer, leaving a 1-inch border around the edge. Frost the sides and the top border of the cake with the reserved frosting, leaving the marmalade exposed. Refrigerate for 2 hours or longer before serving. Can be made the night before.

Small Cakes

MAKES 24 CAKES

- 1 cup (2 sticks) unsalted butter, chilled and cut into large pieces
- 2 cups unbleached all-purpose flour
- 1/4 cup granulated sugar
- 1/2 teaspoon salt
- 1 1/2 teaspoons ground ginger
- Confectioners' sugar for dusting the baked cakes

These bite-sized cakes, baked in a small muffin tin, are a kind of ginger-flavored shortbread. They're great with ice cream or fresh fruit or on a plate of mixed cookies to serve with coffee or tea. This dough also makes a delicious crust for apple or peach or pecan pie. Press the dough into a pie plate, or roll it between pieces of wax or parchment paper. It can be cut into strips for a lattice top too.

Preheat the oven to 350°F, and butter twenty-four small muffin tins.

Put the butter, flour, sugar, salt, and ginger in the bowl of an electric mixer. Mix on low speed, scraping the sides and bottom of the bowl occasionally, until thoroughly blended, 5–7 minutes. Spoon equal amounts of the batter into the buttered muffin tins and press gently on top to flatten the cakes.

Bake for 15–20 minutes, until the cakes are very lightly browned. Remove from the oven, and allow the cakes to rest for 5 minutes before turning them onto a cooling rack to cool completely. Small cakes may be stored in an airtight tin for 1 week or longer. Dust lightly with confectioners' sugar before serving.

NOTE When you have extra egg yolks, they can be used to make the Banana Pudding and/or a rich custard or ice cream.

Angel Food Cake

MAKES ONE 10-INCH CAKE, ENOUGH TO SERVE 10–12

- 1 cup cake flour, sifted
- 1½ cups granulated sugar, divided
- 12 egg whites, at room temperature
- ½ teaspoon cream of tartar
- ¼ teaspoon salt
- 1 tablespoon water
- 1½ teaspoons vanilla extract

A slice of airy angel food cake is a treat all by itself, but I make it mainly to use as a component in other desserts. Toasted cubes of cake are essential in the Banana Pudding recipe (pages 250–251), and make a nice garnish for fruit salad. Angel-food cake is also an excellent base for strawberry or peach shortcake.

The secret to a good angel food cake is properly beaten egg whites. Make sure that the whites are at room temperature and completely free of yolks; that your bowls and beaters are immaculately clean; and that you do not over-beat the egg whites. They should be very moist and glossy, and just firm enough to form soft peaks. It is important to cool the angel food cake upside down in its pan; otherwise, it will collapse and fall.

Preheat the oven to 375°F.

Sift the flour and ¾ cup of the sugar together twice onto wax paper or a plate, and set aside.

Put the egg whites into a large, clean mixing bowl, and beat them on low speed until they become frothy. Add the cream of tartar, salt, water, and vanilla, and gradually increase beating speed until the egg whites begin to mound softly. Sprinkle the remaining ¾ cup sugar over the whites ¼ cup at a time, and beat only until each addition is incorporated. Do not overbeat. The egg whites should be very moist and glossy, and just firm enough to form soft peaks.

Sift a quarter of the reserved flour and sugar over the beaten whites and gently fold in; repeat three times, proceeding with each successive addition only until all of it has been incorporated. Carefully and evenly spoon the batter into an ungreased 10-inch tube pan. Use a long spatula or butter knife to draw a deep line through the center of the batter the entire circumference of the pan (this will release any large pockets of air from the batter, which could result in large tunnels or holes in the finished cake).

Bake in the preheated oven for 35–40 minutes, until the cake is golden brown and springs back to the touch. Remove from the oven, and *invert* the cake to cool completely in the pan. When completely cooled, use a long straight-edged spatula to loosen the cake from the sides of the pan and turn out. Store tightly covered.

Lane Cake

MAKES ONE 3-LAYER CAKE, ENOUGH TO SERVE 12–16

THE CAKE

- 1 cup (2 sticks) unsalted butter, softened
- 2 cups granulated sugar
- 3½ cups cake flour
- 1 tablespoon Homemade Baking Powder (page 230)
- ¼ teaspoon salt
- 1 teaspoon vanilla extract
- 1 cup milk, at room temperature
- 8 egg whites, at room temperature

THE FILLING

- 12 egg yolks
- 1½ cups granulated sugar
- ¾ cup (1½ sticks) unsalted butter, melted
- 1½ cups finely chopped pecans
- 1½ cups finely chopped raisins
- 1½ cups freshly grated coconut (box, page 169)
- 1½ teaspoons vanilla extract
- ½ cup bourbon

This traditional southern-Alabama layer cake was the one I liked for my birthday cake when I was growing up, though my mother made the filling with grape juice instead of bourbon. Created by Emma Rylander Lane, from Clayton, Alabama, who published the recipe in 1898, it has since become popular all over the South. It is a favorite holiday cake, with a creamy egg-yolk–based filling with coconuts, dried fruit, and nuts. In some versions the cake is frosted with a cooked white icing, but I prefer to coat the sides with more of the delicious filling, made here with bourbon. Lane cake has excellent keeping ability too.

Preheat the oven to 325°F.

To make the cake: Beat the butter in the large bowl of an electric mixer until creamy. On medium speed, slowly add the sugar and beat until the sugar and butter are light and fluffy. (Stop occasionally to scrape down the sides and beaters to ensure even mixing.)

Sift together the flour, baking powder, and salt. Add the vanilla to the milk. On low speed, add the flour to the butter-sugar mixture in 3 batches, alternating with the milk. Mix only until each addition is well blended before proceeding to the next, stopping once or twice, again, to scrape the sides of the bowl and beaters.

In a separate bowl, beat the egg whites just until they form soft peaks. Stir a third of the beaten egg whites into the cake batter to lighten, then carefully fold in the remaining egg whites. Turn the batter into three 9-inch buttered and floured parchment-lined cake pans, bang each cake pan gently on the counter to remove any large air pockets from the batter, and bake in the preheated oven for 20–25 minutes, until the cake centers spring back lightly when gently tapped with the fingertips. Remove immediately to cooling racks, and allow to rest 5 minutes before turning out of the pans onto the racks to cool completely. *Cool the layers completely* before peeling off the parchment bottoms and proceeding with filling and frosting the cake.

To make the filling: Stir together the egg yolks and sugar in a large nonreactive saucepan until well blended. Stir in the melted butter and cook, stirring constantly, over moderate heat until mixture thickens enough to coat the back of a spoon thickly. Take care that it does not simmer or boil. When thickened, stir in the pecans, raisins, and coconut, and continue cooking for 1 minute before adding the vanilla extract and bourbon. Stir briefly over heat, then remove from the stove and allow to cool slightly before filling and frosting the cake layers.

To assemble the cake: Spread approximately 1 cup of filling between all the cake layers. Frost the top and sides of the cake with remaining filling. Allow to cool completely before cutting.

NOTE Lane cake improves in flavor as it ages and mellows. Covered and uncut, this cake can be made 1 week before serving. It's not necessary to refrigerate.

Very Good Chocolate Cake

MAKES ONE 9-INCH CAKE, ENOUGH TO SERVE 12–16

This is an ideal two-layer chocolate cake. Rich, moist, and chocolaty, it can be stirred together by hand, no mixer necessary. As with some other Deep South cake recipes, vegetable oil, especially peanut oil, is used in place of butter or other solid shortening. This is so moist it doesn't travel well; store in a cool, dark area, but do not refrigerate.

THE CAKE

2 cups granulated sugar
1½ cups cake flour
½ teaspoon salt
¾ teaspoon baking soda
1 cup hot double-strength brewed coffee
4 ounces unsweetened chocolate, finely chopped
2 eggs, at room temperature
½ cup vegetable oil
½ cup sour cream, at room temperature
1½ teaspoons vanilla extract

THE FROSTING

1 cup heavy cream
8 tablespoons (1 stick) unsalted butter, cut into ½-inch pieces
⅓ cup granulated sugar
¼ teaspoon salt
1 pound semisweet chocolate, finely chopped
¼ cup hot double-strength brewed coffee
1 teaspoon vanilla extract

Preheat the oven to 325°F.

To make the cake: Sift together the sugar, flour, salt, and baking soda in a bowl. Pour the hot coffee over the finely chopped chocolate, and allow the chocolate to melt completely.

In a separate bowl, whisk together until well blended the eggs and vegetable oil, followed by the sour cream, vanilla, and coffee-chocolate mixture. Stir this liquid mixture into the dry ingredients by thirds, stirring well after each addition until completely blended. Divide the batter evenly between two buttered and floured parchment-lined 9-inch cake pans. Drop each cake pan once onto the counter from a height of 3 inches, to remove any large air pockets, which could cause holes or tunnels in the baked cake layers. Bake in the preheated oven for 30–40 minutes, until the cake springs back slightly when gently tapped in the center or a cake tester inserted in the center comes out clean. Remove immediately to cooling racks, and allow to rest for 5 minutes before turning out of the pans. To unmold, run a flat-edged knife or spatula between the cake layers and the sides of the pans. Turn the pans facedown onto the cooling rack, and carefully lift them off. Allow cakes to cool *completely* before peeling off the parchment bottoms and frosting.

To make the frosting: Heat the cream, butter, sugar, and salt in a heavy saucepan until the butter is melted. Add the chocolate, and cook over very low heat, stirring constantly, just until the chocolate is melted and the mixture is smooth. Remove from heat, and blend in the coffee and vanilla. Transfer the frosting to a bowl to cool, stirring occasionally, until it is of a spreading consistency—about 1 hour, depending on the temperature of the kitchen. (If your kitchen is very warm, move the frosting to a cooler area to cool and thicken, but *do not* refrigerate or chill over ice water. Chocolate and butter solidify at different temperatures, and harsh chilling could cause the frosting to separate and turn grainy.)

To assemble the cake: When the frosting is of a spreading consistency and the cake layers are completely cooled, put one cake layer on a serving platter, bottom side up, and frost the surface thickly. Top with the other layer, bottom side down, and frost the top and sides. For best results, allow the cake to sit for 2 or more hours before slicing. Store, covered, at room temperature.

NOTE For the richest, darkest frosting possible, resist the urge to whisk or beat to cool faster. Excessive stirring incorporates air, which will cool and set the frosting more quickly, but will also dilute its dark color and flavor. And, because it takes a little while to cool to the proper consistency, have all of the ingredients ready and make the frosting as soon as the cake layers are in the oven to bake.

Dark Molasses Gingerbread Cake with Soft Whipped Cream

MAKES ENOUGH TO SERVE 6–8

- 2 cups bleached all-purpose flour
- 1/4 teaspoon baking soda
- 2 teaspoons Homemade Baking Powder (page 230)
- 1/2 teaspoon ground cloves
- 1 tablespoon ground ginger
- 1 teaspoon ground Ceylon cinnamon
- 1/2 teaspoon salt
- 1/2 cup (1 stick) unsalted butter
- 1 cup boiling water
- 2 eggs, beaten
- 1 1/2 cups molasses

WHIPPED CREAM

- 1 cup heavy cream, chilled
- 2 teaspoons vanilla extract
- 2 tablespoons granulated sugar

This is the best gingerbread I've ever tasted. It's very dark and moist, with a puddinglike consistency. Try to wait a day before eating it: as good as it is fresh from the oven, it is even better when the spices and molasses have had the opportunity to mellow and meld.

Preheat the oven to 350°F.

Sift the flour, soda, and baking powder into a large mixing bowl. Using a wire whisk, blend in the spices and salt. Melt the butter in the boiling water, then whisk into the flour mixture. Add the eggs and molasses, and whisk until well blended.

Turn into a buttered and floured 8-by-8-by-2-inch baking pan, and bake in the preheated oven for 35–40 minutes, until done, or until a skewer plunged in the center comes out with no trace of raw batter.

Whip the cream with the vanilla and sugar until it forms soft peaks. Serve with the warm gingerbread.

NOTE If you only have unbleached flour, you could use it, but reduce the total amount of flour by 1/3 cup. Otherwise you are likely to end up with dry, coarse gingerbread.

Old-Fashioned Tea Cakes

MAKES APPROXIMATELY 5 DOZEN TEA CAKES

- ½ cup (1 stick) unsalted butter, softened
- 2 cups granulated sugar
- 2 eggs, lightly beaten
- ½ cup buttermilk, at room temperature
- 1 tablespoon finely grated lemon zest
- 4 cups unbleached all-purpose flour
- 4 teaspoons Homemade Baking Powder (page 230)
- 1½ teaspoons salt
- Granulated sugar for sprinkling

To Southerners of a certain age, tea cakes are as madeleines were to Proust. A single bite can magically usher in the faces and events of a time gone by. Though seemingly little more than a simple sugar cookie, tea cakes are beguiling. Easily made, and with ingredients found in most kitchen cupboards, they deserve a place in your pantry. Also, befitting their relationship to memory, they seem to improve in flavor the day after they are made.

Preheat the oven to 400°F.

Either by hand or with an electric mixer, mix together in a large mixing bowl the softened butter and sugar. When well blended, add the eggs one at a time, then slowly add the buttermilk and lemon zest. Sift together the flour and baking powder in a separate bowl, and stir in the salt. Add the flour mixture by cupfuls to the liquid ingredients, mixing well before each addition. If using an electric mixer, you will probably need to mix in the last of the flour by hand, because the dough will and should be quite stiff.

Divide the dough into four portions. Roll each portion on a lightly floured surface to a thickness of ⅛ inch. Use a biscuit or cookie cutter to cut out 2½-inch rounds. Place ½ inch apart on parchment-lined cookie sheets. Sprinkle the surface of each tea cake lightly with granulated sugar.

Bake on the middle rack of the preheated oven for 8–10 minutes, just until the edges begin to turn golden brown. Remove immediately to a cooling rack to cool. When completely cooled, store in a tightly sealed tin for up to 1 week.

Three-Layer Carrot Cake

MAKES ONE 3-LAYER CAKE, ENOUGH TO SERVE 12–16

THE CAKE LAYERS

- 2 cups all-purpose flour, sifted after measuring
- 1 teaspoon salt
- 2 teaspoons baking soda
- 1 tablespoon ground Ceylon cinnamon
- 1 tablespoon cocoa powder
- 1 cup light-brown sugar
- 1 cup granulated sugar
- 1¼ cups peanut oil
- 4 eggs
- 1 tablespoon vanilla extract
- 3 cups finely grated carrots
- 1½ cups not-too-finely chopped pecans
- Three 9-inch cake pans, lightly buttered and floured

THE FROSTING

- 12 tablespoons (1½ sticks) unsalted butter, chilled
- 24 ounces cream cheese, chilled
- 1½ cups sifted confectioners' sugar
- 1 teaspoon vanilla extract
- 1½ cups chopped pecans

Carrot cake is fairly ubiquitous, but this one is a bit above the rank and file. Peanut oil, common in the Deep South, is the shortening and makes for an exceptionally moist cake. The cocoa and the large amount of pecans—another crop of the region—give a greater depth of flavor and more texture too. It will look like there's a huge amount of frosting, but all of it will be used. No one has ever complained to me that there's too much frosting on their carrot cake. Like many cakes, this one seems to develop more flavor if made several hours, or a day, before serving.

Preheat the oven to 350°F.

Put the flour, salt, baking soda, cinnamon, and cocoa in a mixing bowl, and whisk together to blend. Put the sugars in a large mixing bowl, and whisk in the peanut oil. Then whisk in the eggs one at a time, followed by the vanilla. When fully blended, add the flour mixture all at once, and mix just until smooth. Stir in the grated carrots and the pecans. Divide the batter evenly between the three cake pans. Drop each pan sharply onto the counter from a height of about 6 inches to remove any air pockets. Bake for 25 minutes in the preheated oven, or until the center of the layers springs back gently when touched. Remove from the oven, and place on cooling racks until completely cooled, then unmold.

To make the frosting: Cut the butter into 2-inch pieces, and put in the mixing bowl of an electric mixer. Mix on medium speed just until the butter begins to become malleable, about 3–4 minutes. Add the cream cheese in pieces, and mix until thoroughly blended. Slowly add the confectioners' sugar and vanilla, and mix until blended. Increase mixer speed slightly, and continue mixing for 2–3 minutes, until the frosting becomes light and fluffy. Remove from the mixer, and fold in the pecans.

To assemble the cake: Place one of the cake layers, bottom side up, on a cake plate or pedestal. Spoon approximately a quarter of the frosting onto the layer, and spread it over evenly. Place a second layer, bottom side down, on top of the first, and spread with an equal amount of frosting. Place the final layer, bottom side down, on top of the others, and frost the top and sides with the remaining frosting. Store in a cool but not refrigerated area until serving.

Fresh Apple Cake with Caramel Glaze

MAKES 1 CAKE, ENOUGH FOR 12 GENEROUS SERVINGS

This is a cake that I first served for breakfast on a hunting plantation in South Georgia. It's a great cake for potlucks, to take on picnics, or for packing in a lunch bag. Spicy and flavorful, with a moist, puddinglike texture, this is a truly easy cake—just stir together by hand.

THE CAKE

1 cup light-brown sugar, packed
1 cup granulated sugar
1½ cups vegetable oil
3 eggs
3 cups unbleached all-purpose flour
1 teaspoon baking soda
2 teaspoons ground Ceylon cinnamon
½ teaspoon freshly grated nutmeg
½ teaspoon salt
5 fresh apples (such as Winesap or Granny Smith), peeled and diced into ½-inch pieces
1¼ cups not-too-finely chopped pecans
2¼ teaspoons vanilla extract

THE GLAZE

4 tablespoons (½ stick) unsalted butter
¼ cup granulated sugar
¼ cup light-brown sugar
Pinch of salt
½ cup heavy cream

Preheat the oven to 325°F.

Put the sugars and vegetable oil in a mixing bowl, and beat until very well blended. Add the eggs one at a time, beating well after each addition. Sift together the flour, baking soda, cinnamon, nutmeg, and salt, and gradually add to the sugar and eggs, mixing just until well blended. Stir in the apples, pecans, and vanilla, and pour into a buttered and floured 9-by-13-inch baking pan.

Bake in the preheated oven until a skewer or toothpick inserted into the center of the cake comes out clean, about 1¼ hours (begin checking after 50 minutes). Remove from the oven, and allow to cool in the pan while you prepare the caramel glaze.

To make the glaze: Melt the butter in a saucepan, and add both the sugars and the salt. Stir until blended, and cook over medium-low heat for 2 minutes. Stir in the heavy cream, and boil for 2 minutes, stirring constantly. Remove from heat.

Use a skewer or toothpick to poke holes all over the top of the cake, and pour the warm glaze over the surface. Serve warm or at room temperature.

Lemon Cheese Layer Cake

MAKES ONE 3-LAYER CAKE, ENOUGH FOR 12–16 SERVINGS

In southern Alabama, everyone calls this beautiful special-occasion cake a "lemon cheese cake" because of the deep-yellow lemon curd that fills and frosts the layers. (There's no cheese in it at all.) For best flavor, bake and assemble the cake the day before, and store, covered, at room temperature.

THE CAKE

- 3¼ cups cake flour
- 1½ teaspoons cream of tartar
- ¾ teaspoon baking soda
- ¼ teaspoon salt
- 2 cups granulated sugar
- 1 cup (2 sticks) unsalted butter, at room temperature
- 8 egg whites
- 1 cup milk
- 2 teaspoons vanilla extract

THE LEMON FILLING

- 2¼ cups granulated sugar
- ¾ cup plus 1 tablespoon freshly squeezed lemon juice
- ¾ cup (1½ sticks) unsalted butter, melted
- 12 egg yolks
- 3 tablespoons finely grated lemon zest
- ½ teaspoon salt

Preheat the oven to 350°F.

Sift the flour, cream of tartar, baking soda, and salt onto a piece of wax paper or parchment. Beat the sugar and butter in a large mixing bowl, scraping the bottom and sides once or twice, until light and fluffy. Whisk the egg whites until blended but not foamy, then add to the butter in four batches, beating well after each addition. Add the sifted dry ingredients in three parts, alternating with the milk, and mixing only until well blended after each addition before proceeding to the next. Scrape the bottom and sides of the bowl again, and blend in the vanilla.

Divide the cake batter between three buttered parchment-lined baking pans. Drop each filled cake pan gently on the kitchen counter to remove any large air pockets. Bake in the preheated oven for about 20 minutes, until the cake layers spring back in the center when lightly tapped, or a cake tester inserted in the center comes out clean. Transfer the pans to cooling racks, and let rest for 5 minutes before turning the cake layers onto the racks to cool completely.

Make the filling: Put all of the filling ingredients into a nonreactive saucepan, and whisk well to blend. Set over moderate heat and cook, stirring constantly, until the filling thickens and a candy thermometer registers 170°F, about 10 minutes. *Do not* allow the filling to boil or come to a simmer. Transfer the cooked filling to a bowl, and cool to room temperature.

Place one layer on a platter or cake stand, and spread with ½ cup of the cooled lemon filling. Top with a second cake layer and ½ cup more of the lemon filling. Continue stacking and filling this way, using all of the remaining filling to spread over the top layer and sides of the cake.

NOTE Because the filling is somewhat translucent, the layers of the cake will be visible through the filling on the side. Also, because of the thin layers and generous amount of filling used, it is a good idea to use three or four wooden skewers, inserted through the layers, to prevent any sliding until the cake has fully set. This is especially a good idea if you are planning on traveling with the cake.

Pineapple Upside-Down Cake

MAKES ENOUGH TO SERVE 8

THE GLAZE

6 tablespoons (3/4 stick) unsalted butter, melted

1 1/2 cups dark-brown sugar

12 ounces canned pineapple rings packed in pineapple juice (reserve juice)

THE CAKE

1 1/2 cups cake flour, sifted

2 teaspoons Homemade Baking Powder (page 230)

1/4 teaspoon salt

1/2 cup granulated sugar

1 egg

1/2 cup whole milk

1 teaspoon vanilla extract

8 tablespoons (1 stick) unsalted butter, melted

Whipped cream or vanilla ice cream (optional)

Pineapple upside-down cake is one of those simple, familiar dishes that is nonetheless festive and special—the kind of dessert that disappears immediately at church and covered-dish suppers. I've tried making this with fresh pineapple, but to me it is the nostalgic taste of upside-down cake made with canned rings that I like. Traditionally, upside-down cake is baked in a black cast-iron skillet, but you can use a 9-inch round cake pan instead—just cook the brown-sugar syrup in a saucepan first, then pour into the cake pan.

Preheat oven to 400°F.

Put 6 tablespoons butter in an 8- or 9-inch cast-iron skillet (see Note), add the 1 1/2 cups dark-brown sugar, and stir until dissolved. Add 1/2 cup pineapple juice from the can, and bring to a simmer for 1 minute, then remove from heat.

Arrange the pineapple slices in a layer on the bottom of the pan, and break any remaining slices into pieces. Work the pieces into the empty spaces left by the whole slices, in and among and over them, until you've used all the pineapple.

Put the sifted flour, baking powder, salt, and sugar in a mixing bowl, and whisk to blend. In a separate bowl, beat the egg, then add the milk, vanilla, and melted butter, and mix well. Pour these liquid ingredients into the dry ingredients, and whisk assertively just until smooth.

Pour the cake batter into the cast-iron pan, over the pineapple. Bake in the preheated oven for about 25 minutes, or until a cake tester or skewer inserted in the center of the cake comes out clean.

Remove from the oven, then let the cake rest 5 minutes in the pan. Invert it onto a serving plate, and cut slices with a serrated knife. Serve with whipped cream or vanilla ice cream if desired.

NOTE Don't worry if you don't have an 8- or 9-inch cast-iron skillet; this works just as well in a cake pan.

Boiled Peanut Butter Cookies

MAKES ABOUT 32 COOKIES

- ½ cup crunchy peanut butter
- 3 cups quick-cooking oatmeal
- 1 teaspoon vanilla extract
- ½ cup (1 stick) unsalted butter
- ½ cup milk
- 2 cups granulated sugar
- ½ teaspoon salt
- ½ cup unsweetened cocoa powder

These are, hands down, my very favorite cookie from childhood. I first tasted them at our next-door neighbor's, though they quickly became my sister Janet's specialty and a family classic. Quick, easy, and cooked on top of the stove, they are really more confection than cookie. And be forewarned, they are powerfully addictive.

Mix together the peanut butter, oatmeal, and vanilla in a mixing bowl.

Heat the butter and milk in a heavy saucepan, over moderate heat, until the butter is melted. Whisk in the sugar, salt, and cocoa until smooth. Bring to a boil, and cook for 1½ minutes, stirring often to prevent scorching. Stir in the peanut-butter–oatmeal mixture, and continue cooking for 1 minute longer, stirring constantly.

Drop the cooked mixture by tablespoonfuls onto wax paper or aluminum foil. Allow to cool and become firm. Store in a tightly sealed container for up to 1 week.

Cats' Tongues

MAKES ABOUT 2½ DOZEN COOKIES

Miss Lewis made these extremely delicate ginger-flavored cookies when she lived in New York. She used to bake thousands of them each week to sell at Dean & DeLuca, they were so popular. Be sure to use ground ginger that is very fresh and aromatic. These cookies have a distinctive shape, and we think they look a lot more like cats' tongues than the French cookie of the same name.

- ⅔ cup all-purpose flour
- 1⅔ cups confectioners' sugar
- 1 teaspoon ground ginger
- ⅛ teaspoon salt
- 2 egg whites
- ½ cup heavy cream

Preheat the oven to 400°F.

Sift together in a bowl the flour, confectioners' sugar, ginger, and salt. Whip the egg whites in one bowl and the heavy cream in another, just until both are frothy. Pour the beaten egg whites over the sifted ingredients, and stir until well blended. Pour in the heavy cream, and stir just until blended.

Drop 1 level teaspoon of the batter onto a well-buttered cookie sheet. Draw the dull blade side of a butter knife downward through each teaspoon of batter until you form a cookie that is approximately 2½ inches long and tapered to a fine point on one end. Repeat with the remaining batter, allowing about 1½ inches between cookies.

Bake in the preheated oven for 5–8 minutes, until the edges of the cookies begin to brown. Remove from the oven, and allow to cool for 1–2 minutes, then lift the cookies from the cookie sheet with a thin spatula and place them on a wire rack to cool. (If the cookies cool too much and become difficult to remove, place the baking sheet back in the oven for about 1 minute to soften.)

Store the cooled cookies in an airtight container for up to 4 days.

Spritz Cookies

MAKES ABOUT 2½ DOZEN COOKIES

- 1 cup (2 sticks) unsalted butter, at room temperature
- ½ cup extra-fine granulated sugar
- 1 egg yolk, lightly beaten
- ½ teaspoon vanilla extract
- ½ teaspoon almond extract
- 1¾ cups all-purpose flour

These Spritz Cookies are so rich and delicate they must be chilled for a few hours after you have piped them onto a baking sheet. If baked immediately, they will flatten in the oven and lose their decorative shape. These are my favorite butter cookie.

By hand or with an electric mixer, cream the butter until it is light and satiny in appearance. Add the sugar gradually, and mix until the mixture becomes light and fluffy. Add the egg yolk, and mix until it is incorporated. Beat in the vanilla and almond extracts. Add the flour ¼ cup at a time, and mix only until blended.

Spoon the cookie dough into a cookie press, and on ungreased cookie sheets press out "S" and "O" shapes that are approximately 2 inches in length.

Put the cookie sheets with the formed cookies into the refrigerator or freezer for 3 hours or overnight. (This is essential so that the cookies will hold their shape when baked.)

Preheat the oven to 375°F.

When the cookies are chilled, bake them in the preheated oven for 10–12 minutes, until they begin to brown around the edges. Remove them from the oven, and allow them to cool for 2–3 minutes before transferring them with a thin spatula to a cooling rack. If the spritz cookies cool too much and begin to stick to the cookie sheets, put them back into the oven for 1 minute to soften.

Store the cooled cookies in airtight tins for up to 1 week.

Nut Butter Balls

MAKES ABOUT 4 DOZEN COOKIES

- 1 cup (2 sticks) unsalted butter, at room temperature
- 1/4 cup granulated sugar
- 1/8 teaspoon salt
- 1 teaspoon almond extract
- 1 teaspoon vanilla extract
- 2 cups unbleached all-purpose flour, sifted after measuring
- 1½ cups very finely chopped or grated pecans (about 6 ounces)
- 3 cups Vanilla Sugar (box, page 285)

In Virginia, Miss Lewis and her family would gather wild hickory nuts in the fall and make holiday cookies with the delicious morsels of nut meat. It's hard to find hickory nuts these days—and really hard to crack their tough shells—so we make these with pecans (a cultivated variety of hickory nuts) or walnuts. The flavor improves if you make the cookies a day or two ahead of serving. You'll need to make Vanilla Sugar (box, page 285) for coating the cookies in advance too, but you can use ordinary granulated or confectioners' sugar in a pinch.

Beat the butter and sugar together until light and fluffy. Add the salt and extracts, and mix until well blended. Beating on low speed, gradually add the flour, followed by the nuts, stopping to scrape the sides and bottom of the bowl. Continue beating on low speed for 3 minutes. Spoon the dough into a bowl, cover tightly, and chill in the refrigerator for several hours or overnight.

Preheat the oven to 375°F.

Shape the cookie dough into 1-inch balls, and place them on ungreased cookie sheets, ½ inch apart. Bake in the preheated oven for 12–15 minutes. The cookies are done when they have become firm to the touch and are lightly golden brown.

Remove from the oven, and allow to cool for 10 minutes before transferring them to a large piece of wax paper or parchment over which you have spread the vanilla sugar. Allow the cookies to sit on the paper and cool for an additional 5 minutes before rolling them in the sugar to coat. When the cookies are all coated and cooled completely, store them in an airtight container for up to 1½ weeks.

Chocolate Macaroons

MAKES ABOUT 3 DOZEN

These delicious, chewy cookies are great for parties; they are especially wonderful with ice cream. For a culinary event, we've even made little ice-cream sandwiches of chocolate macaroons with mint ice cream in the middle. Rolling the balls of dough in crushed sugar cubes before baking gives them an unusual texture—but do not overbake, because they quickly become hard and dry.

- 1½ ounces unsweetened chocolate, chopped
- 1½ ounces semisweet chocolate, chopped
- 1 cup blanched almond pieces
- 1 cup granulated sugar
- ¼ teaspoon salt
- ⅓ cup egg whites (about 3 egg whites)
- ½ teaspoon vanilla extract
- ¼ teaspoon almond extract
- 1 cup finely crushed sugar cubes

Put the chocolates in a small bowl, and melt over hot but not boiling water. When melted, stir until smooth and set aside.

Put the almonds and half of the granulated sugar in a food processor or blender, and process until the almonds are finely ground. Transfer them to a mixing bowl, and stir in the remaining granulated sugar, the salt, egg whites, melted chocolate, and extracts until thoroughly blended. If the cookie dough seems loose, let it sit for a few minutes at room temperature and it will soon firm up enough to be shaped into balls. (At this point, the cookie dough may be refrigerated for up to 3 days before you proceed with the recipe.)

Preheat the oven to 350°F.

To shape and bake the cookies, use a melon-baller or teaspoon to scoop up and shape the dough into rough 1-inch balls. Moisten the palms of your hands with cold water to prevent dough from sticking, and roll the balls of dough between your palms to make them perfectly round and smooth. Then roll each ball in the crushed sugar cubes until thoroughly coated. Place on parchment-lined cookie sheets, allowing 1 inch between cookies, and bake in the preheated oven for 10–12 minutes, until the cookies are set and crackled on top. *Do not overbake.* Allow the cookies to cool slightly before transferring them from the baking sheet to a cooling rack.

When the cookies are completely cooled, store them in an airtight container for up to 1 week.

Peanut Brittle

MAKES ABOUT 2 POUNDS OF BRITTLE

Peanut brittle—like many new products and ideas for using the peanut crop—came out of the South in the late nineteenth century. It is wonderful, especially at Christmas.

- 2 cups granulated sugar
- 1 cup light corn syrup
- 1 cup water
- 2 cups raw peanuts
- ½ teaspoon salt
- 2 tablespoons unsalted butter
- ¼ teaspoon baking soda
- 1 teaspoon vanilla extract

Put the sugar, corn syrup, and water in a large, heavy saucepan, and cook over moderate heat, stirring only until the sugar has dissolved. Continue to cook to soft-ball stage (238°F). Add the peanuts and salt and cook, stirring constantly, until mixture reaches the hard-crack stage (300°F). Remove from heat and stir in the butter, baking soda, and vanilla.

Pour into a generously buttered shallow 9-by-13-inch baking pan or rimmed cookie sheet. Cool completely. When hardened and completely cooled, break into irregular 2-inch pieces and store immediately in a tightly sealed airtight container.

VANILLA SUGAR

MAKES 4 CUPS VANILLA SUGAR

Vanilla sugar is useful to have for rolling cookies in and for using in recipes that benefit from an added layer of vanilla flavor. The vanilla beans can be used more than once for making vanilla sugar, and the same beans can also be used in other recipes that call for vanilla bean. Conversely, you can use vanilla beans that you have used once in other recipes, such as Banana Pudding or Vanilla Ice Cream to make vanilla sugar. Just rinse and dry the used beans carefully before storing them in granulated sugar.

- 2 vanilla beans
- 4 cups granulated sugar

Twist and bend the vanilla beans back and forth a bit to bruise them and help release their oils. Use a sharp paring knife to split them lengthwise. Put them into a 1-quart jar, and pour the sugar over. Store in a cool, dark place for 4 days or longer before using.

Marshmallows

MAKES ABOUT 100 MARSHMALLOWS

2 envelopes (2 tablespoons) unflavored gelatin
½ cup cold water

1 cup granulated sugar
1 cup light corn syrup
⅓ cup water
2 egg whites, at room temperature
⅛ teaspoon salt
½ teaspoon vanilla extract
Confectioners' sugar for dusting

Marshmallows are really fun to make at home, and so much better than store-bought. They can last for a month and make an unusual petit four for a tea party, a lovely gift, and a special treat to float in Hot Chocolate (page 21).

Sprinkle the gelatin into a small bowl, and mix with the ½ cup water to soften. Set aside.

Put the sugar, corn syrup, and ⅓ cup water in a large saucepan, and cook to the soft-ball stage (240°F), stirring only until the sugar dissolves. Remove from the heat, and stir in the softened gelatin. Allow to cool for 2 minutes. Beat the egg whites in the large bowl of an electric mixer on low speed until very frothy. Add the salt, and gradually increase mixer speed to high, beating the egg whites until they are stiff and shiny. With the mixer still running, begin adding the hot syrup in a slow, steady stream. Continue beating until all of the syrup is incorporated and the candy stands in soft peaks (this may take 10 minutes or longer). Mix in the vanilla, and pour the candy into a 9-by-13-inch baking pan lined with parchment paper that has been dusted with confectioners' sugar. Gently spread the candy into an even layer. In a safe place, allow to cool and set, uncovered, for several hours or overnight.

When ready, dust the top with confectioners' sugar, and turn onto another piece of parchment paper. Gently peel the parchment from the bottom of the candy and, using kitchen scissors dusted with confectioners' sugar, cut the marshmallows into 1-by-½-inch pieces. Roll each piece in confectioners' sugar to coat, and store between layers of parchment paper in a tightly sealed airtight container.

Marshmallows will keep, tightly covered, for 1 month or longer.

NOTE If the parchment sticks to the bottom of the candy when turning out, moisten the paper lightly with wet paper towels or a pastry brush and the parchment will release.

Spiced Pecans

MAKES 1 POUND

These delicious nuts—coated with sugar, salt, cinnamon, and nutmeg—are a Deep South specialty served at weddings, teas, and holiday gatherings. Other nuts—walnuts, almonds, or peanuts—can be prepared in the same way. They will keep for months but are best served warm, so reheat them briefly in a low oven.

- 4 cups granulated sugar
- 2½ teaspoons ground Ceylon cinnamon
- ½ teaspoon freshly grated nutmeg
- ½ teaspoon salt
- 2 quarts water
- 1 pound fresh pecan halves
- Wire basket for deep-frying
- Fresh oil for deep-frying

Mix together the sugar, cinnamon, nutmeg, and salt in a 9-by-13-inch baking pan or a large, shallow bowl, and set aside.

Bring the water to the boil, drop in the pecans, and boil for 2 minutes. Drain them thoroughly in a colander, and turn immediately into the sugar-cinnamon mixture. Use a large slotted spoon to toss the pecans about in the sugar, making sure they are well coated. Transfer the pecan halves to the wire frying basket and shake gently to remove any excess sugar.

Heat the oil to 340°F.

Carefully lower the pecans in the frying basket into the hot oil. Fry for 1½–2 minutes, until the pecans are lightly browned and the sugar has begun to caramelize. Lift the pecans from the oil, and drain well. Turn the fried pecan halves back into the sugar mixture, and toss well with a slotted spoon, taking care that they are well coated. Allow the pecan halves to cool in the sugar.

When cool, clean the frying basket and use it to gently shake off any excess sugar gently from the pecan halves. Store in airtight jars or tins in a cool, dark place for up to 3 months.

NOTE You can make a spicier version of these nuts by adding 1 teaspoon ground cumin, 2 teaspoons paprika, 1 teaspoon ground ginger, and ½ teaspoon cayenne pepper to the basic recipe mix. Extra-spicy nuts are great in a hearty salad with meat or cheese.

WHITE

Ice Cream, Ices, and Fruits

With a few exceptions—apples and chestnuts in autumn, citrusy Ambrosia and Tangerine Ice in winter—this chapter is dedicated to summer desserts.

The key to these fruit desserts—a prerequisite, in fact—is perfectly ripe sweet fruit, the kind you can only get in summer, likely grown as close to home as possible: don't expect to make an ice with imported raspberries in January. That's also why these desserts are so simple: when summer berries or peaches are at a peak of natural flavor, we don't do anything that interferes with it. And usually the preparation is simple and quick, so we can have a fruit dessert every day of summer.

Homemade ice cream, on the other hand, is usually *not* an everyday affair, or particularly quick. Yet both of us remember fondly hot afternoons churning vanilla ice cream (and sometimes peach or strawberry) in a hand-cranked wooden freezer. For Miss Lewis, homemade was the only ice cream they had in Freetown, and she recalls that there were always many hands eager to turn the crank. In my generation, we kept store-bought ice cream or ice milk in the kitchen freezer in Hartford, but still there were eight or ten times each summer when we'd make homemade, out in the yard or at the farm. And despite the unspeakable heat and humidity, or maybe because of it, the task never ceased to excite me. I remember feeling that my arms were about to fall off from cranking when my father would spell me for a couple of minutes—and then I'd start turning again until he assured me the ice cream was ready.

Today, homemade vanilla ice cream is still both Miss Lewis's and my favorite. And I am still turning the crank on a big wooden freezer, since I make ice cream at the restaurant almost every day through the summer and continue to believe that hand-turning produces the best texture. The ice cream, ice milk, and watermelon ice recipes in this chapter will also be delicious made in an electric freezer, if that's the kind you have. And for our Tangerine Ice, which Miss Lewis always likes on her birthday in April, you don't need a machine at all.

Homemade Vanilla Ice Cream

MAKES ABOUT 2 QUARTS, ENOUGH TO SERVE 8–10

- 2 cups milk
- ½ vanilla bean, split lengthwise
- 8 egg yolks
- ¾ cup granulated sugar
- 2 cups heavy whipping cream
- ¾ teaspoon salt
- 3 tablespoons vanilla extract

Only four recipes exist in Thomas Jefferson's handwriting—one of them is for vanilla ice cream. It has continued to be a favorite dessert for Southerners. The formula here is rich with egg yolks and cream, and both vanilla bean and vanilla extract for deeper flavor. The salt in the custard serves to heighten the flavor without adding a salty taste.

Heat the milk and vanilla bean in a medium-sized nonreactive saucepan until just below the boiling point. Remove from the heat and let sit, covered, for 20 minutes to allow the milk to become infused with the flavor of the vanilla.

Meanwhile, put the egg yolks in a mixing bowl, and whisk in the sugar to blend. Slowly whisk 1 cup of the hot milk into the egg-and-sugar mixture to temper the egg yolks, and then stir the tempered yolks into the remaining milk in the saucepan. Return the saucepan to the stove, and cook over moderate heat, stirring constantly with a wooden spoon, until most of the air bubbles that begin to cover the surface have dissipated and the custard thickens enough to coat the back of the spoon thickly. *Do not* ever allow the custard to simmer or boil.

Remove from heat, and stir in the heavy cream. Allow the custard to cool completely, and stir in the salt and vanilla and chill overnight. Next day, strain through a fine-meshed strainer to remove any bits of coagulated egg and the vanilla bean. Rinse and dry the vanilla bean, and reserve for future use. Freeze the custard in an ice-cream freezer, following the manufacturer's directions.

Two Chocolate Sauces

Nothing's better with vanilla ice cream than warm chocolate sauce, and here are two—both deliciously bitter—that we like. The first is the pure, barely sweetened sauce Miss Lewis developed to accompany her chocolate soufflé, a signature dessert at Café Nicholson. My Bitter Chocolate Sauce has more chocolate, even less sugar, and some sweet cream, milk, and butter in the base. Both sauces can be made ahead and reheated for serving.

Edna Lewis's Famous Chocolate Sauce

MAKES 1 CUP

- 1½ ounces unsweetened chocolate
- 1 cup cold water
- 2 tablespoons granulated sugar
- ½ teaspoon vanilla extract

Grate or finely chop the chocolate, and put in a saucepan with the water and sugar. Cook at a gentle simmer, stirring often, for 15–20 minutes. Remove from the stove, and stir in the vanilla. Serve warm.

Sauce may be made ahead up to 1 week and reheated before serving.

Scott's Bitter Chocolate Sauce

MAKES ABOUT 1¼ CUPS

- ½ cup milk
- ½ cup heavy cream
- 1 tablespoon unsalted butter
- 3 ounces unsweetened chocolate, finely chopped
- 1 tablespoon granulated sugar
- ⅛ teaspoon salt

Heat the milk and heavy cream to just below a simmer, and set aside.

Melt the butter and chocolate in a double boiler over just-simmering water. Add the sugar and salt, and stir well. Slowly stir in the heated milk and cream, and cook, stirring constantly, for 3 minutes. Remove from heat, and cool slightly before serving.

Serve the chocolate sauce warm or at room temperature.

NOTE Cooled and refrigerated, the chocolate sauce will keep for 3 weeks and can be reheated before serving.

Strawberry Ice Cream

MAKES ABOUT 1½ QUARTS, ENOUGH TO SERVE 6–8

- 1½ cups milk
- 6 egg yolks
- ½ cup granulated sugar
- 1 cup heavy cream
- 3 cups fresh ripe strawberries, washed, topped, and hulled
- ¼–½ cup granulated sugar for sweetening the berries
- 2 teaspoons vanilla extract
- ½ teaspoon salt

Really great strawberry ice cream—like this one—needs lots of berries for a true fruit flavor. And they should be very ripe. If your berries are not fully ripened, hull (remove) the hard white cores under the stem, and sweeten the crushed berries with extra sugar.

Heat the milk in a medium-sized nonreactive saucepan, to just below the boil.

Put the egg yolks in a small mixing bowl, and whisk in the ½ cup sugar to blend. Slowly whisk the hot milk into the egg-and-sugar mixture to temper the egg yolks. Pour the hot milk-and-egg mixture back into the saucepan, and cook over moderate heat, stirring constantly with a wooden spoon, until the air bubbles that cover the surface have dissipated and the custard thickens enough to coat the back of the spoon thickly. *Do not* ever allow the custard to simmer or boil. Remove from heat, and stir in the heavy cream. Strain through a fine-meshed sieve, and allow to cool completely.

Put the strawberries in a bowl, and sprinkle over them ¼ cup granulated sugar. Using two large forks or a potato masher, crush the strawberries to a pulp. Taste the mixture, and add more sugar if needed. The berries should be quite sweet but not cloying.

Stir the sugared and mashed berries into the cooled custard. Add the vanilla and salt, and stir well to blend. Chill until very cold, preferably overnight. Freeze in an ice-cream freezer, following manufacturer's directions.

Variation: Peach Ice Cream

To make peach ice cream, prepare exactly as for strawberry ice cream, only substitute an equal amount of sliced peaches for the strawberries. Sugar and crush the fruit the same as with the strawberries.

Ice Milk

MAKES A GENEROUS 1 QUART

- 1 quart milk
- ½ cup plus 2 tablespoons granulated sugar
- 3 egg yolks
- 1 tablespoon vanilla extract
- ¾ teaspoon salt

In Alabama, ice milk was the frozen dessert we ate all the time. Obviously less caloric than Vanilla Ice Cream, I find it more refreshing. And with an egg-yolk custard base, it is still quite rich-tasting.

In a heavy nonreactive saucepan, slowly heat the milk to just below the boil. Meanwhile, whisk the sugar into the egg yolks until well mixed and smooth. When the milk is hot, slowly whisk about 1 cup of it into the egg yolks and sugar to temper the yolks. Now whisk the egg mixture into the remaining heated milk. Cook over moderate heat, stirring continuously with a large wooden spoon or spatula, until the mixture is just below a simmer and has thickened slightly—it won't coat a spoon, but it will thicken.

Remove from the heat, and continue stirring briefly to help cool. Strain through a fine-mesh strainer, and allow to cool before adding the vanilla and salt. Chill thoroughly, preferably overnight. Freeze in an ice-cream freezer, following manufacturer's instructions.

Tangerine Ice

MAKES ABOUT 6 CUPS, ENOUGH TO SERVE 8 GENEROUSLY AS DESSERT OR 10–12 AS A PALATE CLEANSER OR A LIGHT ENDING TO A RICH MEAL

- 1¼ cups granulated sugar
- 1½ cups water
- Grated rind of 5 tangerines
- ½ teaspoon salt
- 5 cups freshly squeezed and strained tangerine juice

You can use this simple method for a refreshing ice with any kind of citrus fruit, but tangerines have a unique and deep flavor. Freezing the syrup until solid in a glass dish is easier than using an ice-cream freezer and results in a denser, more intensely flavored and colored dessert.

For Miss Lewis's 80th birthday celebration, I served this ice for dessert with Cats' Tongues (page 281) and a garnish of Candied Mint Leaves and Violets (box, page 303).

Put the sugar and water in a nonreactive saucepan. Stir just until the sugar is dissolved, and simmer for 10 minutes. Remove from the heat, and allow to cool completely. Add the grated rind, salt, and tangerine juice. Chill until cold, and pour into a 9-by-13-inch Pyrex dish. Cover with plastic wrap, placing the wrap directly on the surface of the tangerine syrup, and put into the freezer to freeze overnight.

To serve, scoop portions of the ice out into individual chilled bowls.

NOTE Because of pesticides, always try to find organic citrus, which has not been sprayed, especially if using the zest, which contains the essential oils that hold the most intense flavor. If citrus is waxed, as it often is, rinse the fruit briefly under warm water and wipe dry.

Watermelon Ice

MAKES APPROXIMATELY 2 QUARTS FROZEN ICE

The presence of cinnamon and cardamom gives this simple ice a delicate, flowery quality that is both elusive and enticing. Leftover watermelon rind can be made into preserves or pickles.

- About 5 pounds watermelon (to yield 3¾ cups watermelon juice and pulp, sieved)
- 3 cups water
- 1¾ cups plus 2 tablespoons granulated sugar
- 1 stick Ceylon cinnamon
- 10 green cardamom pods, crushed
- 2 tablespoons freshly squeezed lemon juice
- ¾ teaspoon kosher salt

Cut open the watermelon and scoop out flesh. Squish it with your hands to break it up, then press it through a sieve or food mill (you should have 3¾ cups).

In a heavy saucepan, stir together the water, sugar, cinnamon stick, and cardamom pods. Place over moderate heat, and simmer for 10 minutes. Remove from heat, and allow to cool completely. Strain the syrup to remove the spices. Add the cooled, strained syrup to the watermelon juice. Stir the lemon juice and salt into the watermelon-syrup mixture. Freeze in an ice-cream freezer, according to the manufacturer's instructions.

SLICED PEACHES IN MILK

"Peaches and cream" may be an expression used for something adorable, but to me there's no better way to eat a perfectly ripe peach than in a bowl with cold milk. There's something about milk—more than half-and-half or heavy cream—that brings out the best in the fruit. This was my favorite dessert as a child, and I've never improved on my mother's method: peel and slice a sweet ripe peach (or two) into a cereal bowl, sprinkle sugar over lightly, and pour ice-cold milk over to come about halfway up the peaches. That's it. You can let the sugar melt into the fruit for a couple of minutes before adding the milk, or even longer, so the slices give off more peach juice. But I like to pour in the milk and eat right away—I love the crunching of the grains of sugar.

Ambrosia

MAKES ENOUGH TO SERVE 12

- 12 large juice oranges, peeled, sectioned, and seeds removed
- Any juice given off while sectioning and seeding the oranges
- 2½ cups grated fresh coconut (box, page 169)
- 3 tablespoons granulated sugar, or more to taste
- 3 tablespoons cream sherry, or more to taste
- ¼ teaspoon salt

This fruit salad of oranges and fresh coconut is a traditional holiday dessert in the South and often served as a side dish at breakfast or brunch. Ours is an uncommonly pure version—you'll find many that include assorted ingredients such as Maraschino cherries, marshmallows, pecans, and even canned fruit cocktail.

Put the orange sections, juice, and grated coconut into a large mixing bowl. Sprinkle the sugar, sherry, and salt over, and mix well. Taste carefully for seasoning, adding more sugar or sherry if needed. Transfer to a crystal serving dish, and serve.

RHUBARB COMPOTE

I learned this technique for sweetening and softening rhubarb—without diluting its flavor or making it mushy—from our editor, Judith Jones, who has a rhubarb plant growing on her place in northern Vermont. Judith lets sugared rhubarb sit overnight to release its juices, but I give it just a couple hours and then cook the fruit and its liquid very briefly in a wide pan. Served warm or cold, this compote is a delicious accompaniment for all sorts of dishes in this book: over our vanilla ice cream, on pancakes, shortcakes, or gingerbread. Or just serve it in small bowls, plain or with a bit of whipped cream or rich custard sauce poured over. It's good with pound cake, too.

Glazed Strawberries

MAKES 24

- 24 large, unblemished strawberries, preferably with stems
- 2 cups granulated sugar
- ½ cup light corn syrup
- ½ cup water

These glistening berries make a lovely dessert all by themselves with a glass of dry champagne—or put them on a petit-four tray at a tea or lawn party, or use them to decorate a special-occasion cake. They should be made no more than 2 hours in advance, and be sure that the berries you use are dry and at room temperature.

Do not wash the strawberries, but use a dry tea towel to wipe them carefully. If they have been refrigerated, allow them to come to room temperature.

Meanwhile, put the sugar, corn syrup, and water in a saucepan and cook over moderate heat, stirring once or twice, only until the sugar dissolves. Raise the heat to high and continue to cook until the temperature reaches 300°F on a candy thermometer. Remove from heat, and allow to cool for 2 minutes.

Hold the strawberries by the stem or leaves and one at a time, *carefully,* dip each strawberry three-quarters of the way into the hot syrup. (It is helpful to hold the pan of syrup at an angle so that you have a deeper area to dip into.) After dipping, hold each berry over the syrup for a moment to allow any excess to drip off, and place on aluminum foil to cool and harden.

Serve within 2 hours.

Chestnuts in Heavy Syrup

MAKES 1 QUART

These rich chestnuts are excellent served over ice cream, sautéed with apples, or eaten by themselves as a sweetmeat. They're also delicious dipped in chocolate and served, after dessert, with coffee.

- 2 cups granulated sugar
- 1½ cups water
- ½ vanilla bean, split
- ¼ teaspoon salt
- 1 pound large chestnuts, peeled (box, page 51)
- 3 tablespoons rum

Put the sugar, water, vanilla bean, and salt in a 1-quart saucepan over high heat. Bring to a boil, stirring only until the sugar is dissolved. Simmer briskly for 10 minutes, and add the peeled chestnuts. Simmer gently for 15 minutes, and remove from heat. Cover, and let cool completely. Strain the chestnuts from the syrup, and transfer them to a sterilized 1-quart jar. Return the syrup to the saucepan, and boil for about 10 minutes, or until syrup becomes quite thick. Skim off any scum that rises to the surface. Stir in the rum, and pour the hot syrup over the chestnuts. Tightly screw on a sterilized jar lid, and invert the jar to cool. When completely cooled, store in a cool, dark place or in the refrigerator.

Apples Baked in Pastry with Clabber and Nutmeg Sauce

MAKES 8

- 8 tablespoons raw or light-brown sugar
- 1 tablespoon finely grated lemon zest
- ½ teaspoon ground Ceylon cinnamon
- ½ teaspoon freshly grated nutmeg
- ¼ teaspoon salt
- 2 recipes Basic Pie Dough (pages 242–243)
- 1 egg yolk
- 2 teaspoons water
- 8 large cooking apples, such as Granny Smith or Winesap, peeled, cored, and sprinkled with lemon juice
- 3 tablespoons brandy
- 3 tablespoons unsalted butter, cut into 8 pieces
- ⅓ cup heavy cream
- ½ cup crushed sugar cubes
- Nutmeg-Brandy Sauce (page 239) and clabber cream

This is a lovely autumn dessert when you can find many varieties of heirloom apples, such as Winesap and Stayman, that hold their shape when baked whole. Granny Smith apples work well too (and are usually available year-round). Serve with clabber cream, which is the old-fashioned term for crème fraîche or naturally soured cream. The simple nutmeg-brandy sauce given here is delicious with fruit cobblers too.

Put the sugar, lemon zest, cinnamon, nutmeg, and salt in a small bowl, and stir until evenly blended. Roll each portion of pastry into a 12-by-12-inch square that is slightly more than 1⁄16 inch thick. Quarter the square of dough so that you have four 6-by-6-inch squares. Refrigerate the rolled dough while you roll and cut the remaining batch. Repeat with the second batch of dough—you'll now have eight squares.

Mix together the egg yolk and water in a small bowl. Put one apple in the center of each pastry square. Spoon 1 tablespoon of the sugar-and-spice mixture into the cored-out section of each apple, and sprinkle a little brandy into each. Put 1 piece of butter on top of each apple. Brush the edges of each pastry square lightly with the egg yolk and water. Carefully lift the pastry up around each apple, and press the edges of the pastry together to seal each apple completely in pastry. Transfer the apples to a baking sheet lined with parchment or a Silpat. Brush the pastries with the heavy cream, giving two coats per apple, and sprinkle 1 tablespoon of the crushed sugar cubes on top of each. Bake in a preheated 425°F oven for 10 minutes, then reduce the oven temperature to 375°F and bake for 25–30 minutes longer, until the pastry is golden brown. Serve warm with Nutmeg-Brandy Sauce and clabber cream.

NOTE Once the pastry-covered apples have finished cooking, spoon off any juices released while baking and add them to the nutmeg sauce.

Warm Apple Crisp

MAKES ENOUGH TO SERVE 8

- 9 large cooking apples, such as Winesap or Granny Smith
- 2 tablespoons granulated sugar
- 1/4 teaspoon kosher salt
- Juice of 1/2 lemon
- 4 tablespoons unsalted butter

THE TOPPING

- 1 cup granulated sugar
- 2 tablespoons dark-brown sugar
- 1 cup unbleached all-purpose flour
- 1/2 teaspoon kosher salt
- 1/2 teaspoon ground Ceylon cinnamon
- 8 tablespoons (1 stick) unsalted butter, cold, cut into 1/2-inch pieces

I made this recently when a friend returned from a drive to North Georgia with a big basket of Winesap apples—the ones that Miss Lewis loves. In the past, I have tended to put either oatmeal or chopped nuts in the toppings to make them extra crispy. But these apples were so nice that it seemed anything more than a touch of brown sugar for flavor and a bit of cinnamon for spice would have been gilding the lily. When Miss Lewis tasted the crisp, she said it was "the best dessert I've eaten in ten years."

Preheat the oven to 350°F.

Peel and core the apples, then cut them into slices 1/3 inch thick. Put them into a mixing bowl, and sprinkle the sugar, salt, and lemon juice over. Toss well so the apple slices are evenly sugared, and set aside.

Using 1 tablespoon of the butter, grease a 9-by-9-inch baking dish. Turn the reserved, sugared apple slices into the dish—it will be rather full, but the apples cook down during baking. Cut the remaining 3 tablespoons of butter into small pieces, and scatter over the top of the apples.

Make the topping: Put the sugars, flour, salt, and cinnamon into a mixing bowl, and stir with a wire whisk to blend. Add the butter pieces and, using your fingers, quickly work the butter into the dry ingredients until the mixture resembles coarse oatmeal. Sprinkle the topping over the apples, and bake in the center of the oven for about 45 minutes, until the apples bubble in the corners of the baking dish and the topping is crisp.

Serve warm with a pitcher of Rich Custard Sauce (page 249) to pour over. Any leftovers are delicious warmed the next day or enjoyed at room temperature in a school or office lunch.

CANDIED MINT LEAVES AND VIOLETS

Fresh mint leaves
Fresh, unsprayed violets or other edible flowers
1 egg white, preferably organic
1–2 teaspoons water
Extra-fine sugar

Wash the mint leaves, and pat them dry between layers of paper towel. They must be perfectly dry: inspect the flowers for any debris or insect damage, and use an artist's brush to brush them clean. Beat the egg white lightly, adding just enough water to thin it down to a viscosity that you can apply in a thin layer to the leaves and petals.

Spread a thick layer of extra-fine sugar on a platter or in a shallow dish such as a pie plate. Using the paintbrush, apply as thin a layer of egg white as possible to the mint and violet leaves or flower petals, and lay them on the bed of sugar (take care not to brush on too much egg-white mixture or you will end up with unattractive, wet clumps of sugar when dry). Sprinkle additional sugar over the leaves and petals so that they are completely covered. Carefully remove them individually from the sugar bath, gently tapping or brushing away any clumps or excess sugar so that each piece appears frosted, and place them on a cooling rack or wax paper to dry. You may store them in an airtight container between layers of paper towel or wax paper and refrigerate overnight.

Mixed Berry Shortcake

MAKES ENOUGH TO SERVE 6

- 1 cup fresh blackberries
- 1 cup fresh raspberries
- 1 cup fresh blueberries
- 2 cups fresh strawberries
- 1/4–1/2 cup granulated sugar
- Small pinch of kosher salt
- 1 tablespoon bourbon (optional)
- 1 recipe Warm Tender Cakes (pages 252–253), baked and cooled
- Soft whipped cream (page 257), made with 1 1/2 cups whipping cream, 1 tablespoon plus 2 teaspoons granulated sugar, 1 teaspoon vanilla extract

If you're lucky enough to have fresh ripe strawberries, blueberries, raspberries, and blackberries available at the same time, tumble them all together—with a bit of sugar and bourbon—for this wonderful shortcake dessert. Of course, it will be equally delicious if you have only one or a couple of excellent berry varieties. Our favorite shortcake base is the cream biscuit that, when hot from the oven, we call Warm Tender Cakes and serve with guava syrup and cream (pages 252–253). Prepare them exactly as in that recipe, but let them cool before serving as shortcakes.

Gently rinse the blackberries, raspberries, and blueberries in a colander under cool running water, and drain well. Remove any stems or leaves, and put the berries into a large mixing bowl. Rinse the strawberries, remove their caps, and slice them lengthwise before adding them to the mixing bowl. Sprinkle 1/4 cup of the sugar and the salt over the berries, and toss gently. Taste carefully for sweetness, and add more sugar if desired. Remember that the whipped cream will be sweetened too. Sprinkle over berries the optional bourbon, and again toss gently. Cover the berries and let them sit for 10 minutes or so, until the sugar is dissolved and they have exuded some of their juices but still retain their berriness.

To serve, split the cream biscuits and spoon the berries over the bottom half of each. Spoon the whipped cream generously over the berries, and cover with the top halves of the biscuits. Serve immediately.

Menus

Nowhere is the Southern spirit and attitude more evident than in the hospitality of the Southern table. We celebrate everything related to food. It can be a seasonal occasion, such as the running of the shad or the harvesting of the very first blackberries or butter beans of summer. Or it can be a festive occasion, where we serve turtle soup in antique teacups with little dumpling clouds floating on top. The meal can be as simple as (though certainly no less worthy than) a dish of sliced, perfectly ripe tomatoes in high summer, followed by juicy peaches sprinkled with sugar and bathed in milk; or it might center around the first opening and tasting in fall or winter of a jar of preserves put up in summer, or a pot of greens from a friend's garden. All of these food moments become events around the Southern table.

A non-Southern friend of ours observed to us that she thought it as much the way we put things together as the way we prepared them that made them uniquely Southern: the relishes and condiments and preserves, the wealth of vegetable dishes on the table all at once in the summer, picnics of fried chicken with pimento cheese sandwiches and deviled eggs, and the small details of nibbles like beni wafers spread with shrimp paste, or cornmeal crisps and cheese straws, or tiny biscuits stuffed with bits of country ham.

These are the elements that, along with the pure and intense flavors of food carefully prepared, make a distinctively Southern table.

The following is a selection of highly personal, seasonal menus that we hope will illustrate the Southern style and help you to mix and match the recipes in this book to create your own Southern menus.

SPRING

Country Breakfast for a Late Sunday Morning

Corn Griddle Cakes

Trout Roe with Scrambled Eggs

Candied Bacon

Skillet Asparagus

Warm cane syrup

Hot Crusty Buttermilk Biscuits with a dish of soft butter

Old-Fashioned Fig Preserves

Fresh Apple Cake with Caramel Glaze

pitcher of milk

strong hot coffee

LATE SPRING

Celebrating the Running of the Shad

Shad with Shad Roe Stuffing

Cornmeal Soufflé

Wilted Salad

Skillet Scallions

Country-Style Rhubarb Tart with Rich Custard Sauce

SPRING

Late Spring Supper

Asparagus with Cucumber Dressing

Catfish Stew

Beni Wafers

Lemon Chess Pie with Soft Whipped Cream and Berries

LATE SPRING

Delights of Late Spring—A Satisfying Supper

Minted Soup of English Peas

Fried Soft-Shell Crab with Brown Butter and Capers

Creamed Scallions

or

Simmered Yellow Squash

Lemon-Glazed Sweet Potatoes

Cornmeal Muffins

Tangerine Ice with Candied Mint Leaves and Violets

Cats' Tongues

or

Spritz Cookies

LATE SPRING

A Gathering of Delicate Flavors

Purée of Yellow Crookneck Squash Soup

Chicken Baked with Delicate Herbs and Bread Crumbs

Hot Buttered Roasted Beets

Braised Vidalia Onions

Warm Tender Cakes with Guava Syrup and Cream

SUMMER

A Summer Dinner of Big Flavors

Caveach

Slow-Cooked Oxtails over grits

Sauté of Heirloom Tomatoes and Okra with Bacon Garnish

freshly churned Strawberry Ice Cream with cookies

SUMMER

Summer Crab Cake Dinner

Chilled Tomato-Basil Soup

Honestly Good Crab Cakes with Spicy Dipping Sauce

Lady Peas Cooked in Pork Stock

Red Onion, Cucumber, and Tomato Salad

Three-Layer Carrot Cake

SUMMER

A Simple Supper in High Summer

Chanterelles on Toast

large dish of perfect tomatoes

Fresh Corn Fritters

Sliced Peaches in Milk

SUMMER

The Vegetable Plate of Summer

Macaroni and Cheese
Fried Eggplant
scalloped or fresh tomatoes
Pole Beans Simmered in Pork Stock
or
Fresh Crowder peas
Roasted Beets in Ginger Syrup
Okra Pancakes
Chowchow
Blackberry Cobbler

SUMMER

An Outdoor Fish Fry for Porgy

A Fish Fry for Porgy
Hot Pepper Vinegar
Red Pepper Catsup
Cucumber Pickles
thick slices of raw red and white onion
sliced fresh tomatoes
Coleslaw
Homemade Lemonade
Iced Tea
Watermelon Ice and/or Homemade Vanilla Ice Cream

FALL

A Seafood Supper for Fall

Fried Oysters with Spicy Dipping Sauce

Whole Roasted Snapper

Whipped Rutabagas

Spicy Collards in Tomato-Onion Sauce

Warm Apple Crisp

An Early Fall Dinner of Veal and Green Tomatoes

Shrimp Paste on toast

Lamb or Veal Shanks Braised with Green Tomatoes

Yellow Rice

Apples Baked in Pastry

FALL

A Rich Harvest Dinner

Silken Turnip Soup

Baked Pork Chops with Cranberries

Braised Cabbage

Cardamom-Scented Whipped Sweet Potatoes

simple leaf salad of fall greens

Pineapple Upside-Down Cake

FALL

An Alabama Thanksgiving

Purée of Pumpkin Soup

Roast Turkey with Giblet Gravy and Cornbread-Pecan Stuffing

Sweet Potato Casserole

Butter Beans in Cream with Country Ham and Chives

Scalloped Green Tomatoes

cranberry sauce

relish tray

Cloverleaf Rolls

Lane Cake

strong hot coffee

FALL

Saturday Night Supper After Thanksgiving

Turkey Hash with Chestnuts

salad greens with Old-Fashioned Dressing

warm Chocolate Fritters with Soft Whipped Cream

WINTER

A Winter Meal of Earthy Flavors

Chestnut Soup

Roast Duckling Stuffed with Oysters and Red Rice

Roasted Parsnips

Pear Relish

Cornmeal Crisps

salad of bitter greens, cucumber, and radishes

Bourbon-Pecan Pie

Blackberry Cordial

WINTER

Hearty Dinner for a Cold Winter Night

Braised Beef Short Ribs

whipped potatoes

Angel Biscuits

Dark Molasses Gingerbread Cake with Soft Whipped Cream

WINTER

A Winter Breakfast for Supper

Country Ham Steak with Red-Eye Gravy

a skillet of eggs cooked sunny-side up

Old-Fashioned Creamy Grits

Hot Crusty Buttermilk Biscuits

soft butter

Strawberry Preserves

fresh-squeezed orange juice

pitcher of whole milk

strong hot coffee

WINTER

Winter Supper of "Grandmaw's" Chicken and Rice

Grandmaw Peacock's Chicken and Rice

a big green salad

Hot Crusty Buttermilk Biscuits

Old-Fashioned Fig Preserves

Very Good Chocolate Cake

WINTER

A Grilled Trout Dinner

She-Crab Soup

Grilled Bacon-Wrapped Mountain Trout with Green Onion Sauce

Garlic Green Beans

Dorothy Peacock's Skillet Cornbread

Pound Cake with Lemon-Butter Glaze, sugared berries,
and soft whipped cream

A Dinner of Wild Bounty

Miss Lewis's Very Rich Chicken Broth with wild mushrooms and cresses

Sautéed Frogs' Legs with Brown Butter and Capers

an assembly of Southern greens cooked in Pork Stock

salad of tender lettuces

First Strawberries of Spring with Cream

Curry Dinner from Georgia

Country Captain

Coconut Rice and condiments

tossed green salad

Banana Pudding

Mail-Order Sources

The Baker's Catalogue
1-800-827-6836
Ceylon cinnamon, Silpats, and many other wonderful tools and ingredients for baking

Basses Choice
www.smithfieldham.com
1-800-222-2110
Smithfield country hams and shoulders by Gwaltney and Luter

Bridge Kitchenware
www.bridgekitchenware.com
212-838-1901
Silpats and Lodge cast-iron cookware

J. Martinez & Company, Coffee Merchants
3934 Green Industrial Way
Atlanta, Georgia 30341
1-800-642-5282
in our opinion, the very best coffees available

J. T. Pollard Milling Company
334-588-3391
our favorite cornmeal supplier

Logan Turnpike Mills
706-745-5735
1-800-84-GRITS
producers of our favorite stone-ground grits

Northern Brewer
www.northernbrewer.com
1-800-681-2739
tartaric acid

Palmetto Pigeon Plant
P. O. Box 3060
Sumter, South Carolina
1-803-775-1204

Priester's Pecans
www.priesters.com
1-800-277-3226
excellent quality pecans

White Lily Flour
www.whitelily.com
1-800-264-5459

Acknowledgments

from Scott

Heartfelt gratitude and appreciation goes to the following:

Alice Ericson and Bob Wagner, for their hospitality and friendship, and the use of their New York City home and kitchen during the writing of this book.

My mother, Dorothy Walls, who generously shared her food memories, recipes, and kitchen.

My father, Franklin Peacock, for his stories of food and farm life, his deliveries of fresh seasonal produce, his general support, and his emergency FedExes of cornmeal.

Madeline Kamman, an early influence and friend whose impact remains lasting and profound.

Chris Brooks, director of the Tullie Smith Farm at the Atlanta History Center, for his generosity and the use of the Tullie Smith Farm as a learning center and backdrop for some of the photographs in this book.

Margaret Simmons, who demonstrated unflagging belief, friendship, and support.

Janet Peacock, Liz Lorber, Jim Laber, Emily, Leslie, Ross, Sue, and the Watershed team, Lois Swords, Libby Cates-Robinson, David and Page Crossland, Judith Alexander, The Hambidge Center, Xenia Zed, and Jonathan Williams—who each contributed in unique and important ways.

from Edna

I am grateful to my late sister, Mrs. Virginia Ellis, who was an excellent cook, and to the memory of the people of Freetown, Virginia.

from both of us

David Nussbaum, for his tremendous enthusiasm, tenacity, and understanding.

Christopher Hirsheimer, for her beautiful and insightful photographs.

Ken Schneider, who as editor's assistant on this project demonstrated talents, aside from publishing, that would serve him well on the comedic stage as well as in the field of diplomacy.

And finally, our editor, Judith Jones, without whose patience and persistence there would be no book. Part schoolteacher, part therapist—we will forever be grateful to her for her brilliance, deep understanding, and especially, her friendship.

INDEX

A NOTE ABOUT THE AUTHORS

EDNA LEWIS is the recipient of numerous awards, including the Grande Dame of Les Dames d'Escoffier International (1999). She is the author of *In Pursuit of Flavor, The Taste of Country Cooking,* and *The Edna Lewis Cookbook.* She lives in Decatur, Georgia.

SCOTT PEACOCK was born and raised in Alabama. He has served as chef to two governors of Georgia and at two restaurants, Atlanta's Horseradish Grill and, most recently, the highly regarded Watershed in Decatur, where he lives.

A NOTE ON THE TYPE

This book was set in Adobe Garamond. Designed for the Adobe Corporation by Robert Slimbach, the fonts are based on types first cut by Claude Garamond (c. 1480–1561). Garamond was a pupil of Geoffroy Tory and is believed to have followed the Venetian models, although he introduced a number of important differences, and it is to him that we owe the letter we now know as "old style." He gave to his letters a certain elegance and feeling of movement that won their creator an immediate reputation and the patronage of Francis I of France.

Composed by North Market Street Graphics,
Lancaster, Pennsylvania

Printed and bound by Butler and Tanner Ltd.,
Frome, England

Designed by Cassandra J. Pappas

FALL

A Rich Harvest Dinner

Silken Turnip Soup

Baked Pork Chops with Cranberries

Braised Cabbage

Cardamom-Scented Whipped Sweet Potatoes

simple leaf salad of fall greens

Pineapple Upside-Down Cake